Extinction Rebellion Sorcery

Black & White Photography
with Daily Meditations

Lucas Klesch
MSc.

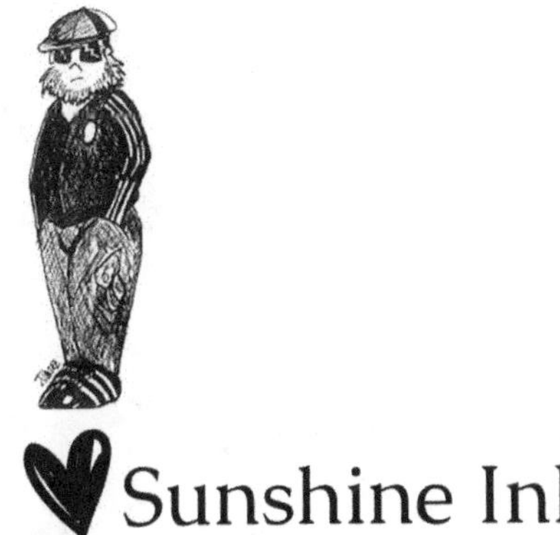

Sunshine Ink

This book is dedicated to the idea we are connected to each other on a quantum level, and water is the means by which we communicate across spacetime.

Prologue

The darkness of climate grief has come to stay for those who understand the science, mathematics, and solutions to our shared climate reality. At least this is the reality I see in my eyes, my child's eyes, and those aware enough to sense the existential threat closing in on all sides. This is the angst of the elephant in the room. It is welling up in the rest of earth's populace as we hurtle through space on the only habitable planet in our solar system. Yet we humans can barely act like this is even occurring, and as we scurry through our daily lives perpetuating all of the amplification factors that are driving our extinction. We are complicit in the refusal to come together fast enough to transform the earth's trajectory.

As a climate scientist who has spent his entire adult life fighting for humanity's ability to exist in the future, I do not see the critical amassing of willpower that must come before the massive transition needed to solve our climate issues. It is a shame, because given all of mankind's enginuity and perseverance, it looks like we are going to crumble in the final days.

I get it, I struggle myself with the fact I know what we are up against, from the science to the mathematics (which works against us), and the dark depression that comes from living in the golden age of greed and consumption. I get ill watching people caught up in the trappings of consumerism, and their gleeful embrace of the capitalistic society currently committing planet genocide.

I get it, it is hard to know what to do when we do not have idols voicing solutions, or glowing examples of humans walking the walk. We do not have leaders transforming policy, and there is no collective culture painting of how we change our fate. It is an extinction level event currently being parading in the open, the elephant in the room. Sad, and disturbing because we currently have all the technology needed to solve our issues before it is too late; before it is super costly; before all humanity suffers, and life is extinguished. We could solve it all right now, and find ourselves at the beginning of a wonderful future, but we are all a collective are currently stuck without the will to change. Paralized by the fear, angst, and indecisions of change which come when you consciously or unconsciously see the elephant in the room, but take no action to address it.

Unfortunately, we must change, and fast or there will be catastrophic effects, and yes, extinction. The science is quite clear, but worse yet are the mathematics working against us this late in the game, and as of right now in 2019, we have the means and capability to address things right now and limit the impact. It is too late to reverse it, and though I fear that without a shift in thinking, and a cleansing of the old ways. We are just going to fold under the weight of our shame for actively participating in our own extincion. We stand right now at the critical moment where we must act, we must! Or humanity will find itself with a history that is irrelevant and a future which is nonexistent.

First though, we have to orchestrate a massive upheaval of our values. We have to shed the artificial lines drawn on maps that divide us. We must embrace the simple truth is that we are all inhabitants of earth, and earth is being cooked of its ability to sustain life by our actions. The task of change is actually significantly harder than the tasks of fixing the problem.

In that, my ultimate hope is to change the world rapidly through a convergence of quantum science, water mysticism, and the intent of fellow humans projecting the same ethos into the world. This hopeful intersection of willful dynamics brings me to these pages of photographs of water, coupled to meditative writings. We need to sustain life on earth, and to start, we must change rapidly. This type of change can only start from within, and I propose a simple daily mysticism we can take into our life to share with the universe, using quantum science.

My friends and I have put this into practice over the last couple of years as we attempt to give hope to our grief. It is a last ditch effort to give humanity a chance to exist in the future, and is rooted in mindful thinking, being present in your decisions, accepting consequences, and seeking within yourself, the love and strength to change. It means we must put all actions and decisions in the context of changing our climate based realities. It is not easy given the darkening times on earth, but

t is highly possible to change. We must first face the
elephant in the room, and its effect on our grief. This
is the angst of feeling the moral implications of our
collective apathy and inaction. We must meet this
head on if we are to move into a future of balance
in the world. It is the only way forward, collective
change, but first you must take direct action in your
life, and second you must project those actions into
the world using quantum metaphysical principles.

You have likely heard people say, "put it out into
the world" or "manifest it." This is an idea rooted
in our ability to affect the reality around us through
the projection of thoughts, hopes, and dreams. It
is a sound principle of quantum science rooted in
two major understandings. First, humans are made
up mostly of water, and the atmosphere on earth is
also composed of water vapor. Second, water aligns
is electrons and crystalline structure according to
positive and negative sentiments. So, given these two
things together with some very focused and direct
projections, a small group of people can transform
themselves, those around them, and ultimately the
earth.

This book represents my daily meditations that I
have been projecting into the world mostly when it
rains or snows. I will also lay my hands in a creek,
river, or lake when I am out on an adventure. It
has changed my approach to my climate grief,
and has pushed me to continue my walk the walk
transformation. I hope you will help me take up this
mantle, so that our children can thrive on earth.

lucas

the tragedy of these dark days
can only be overcome by hope
and direct transformative action.

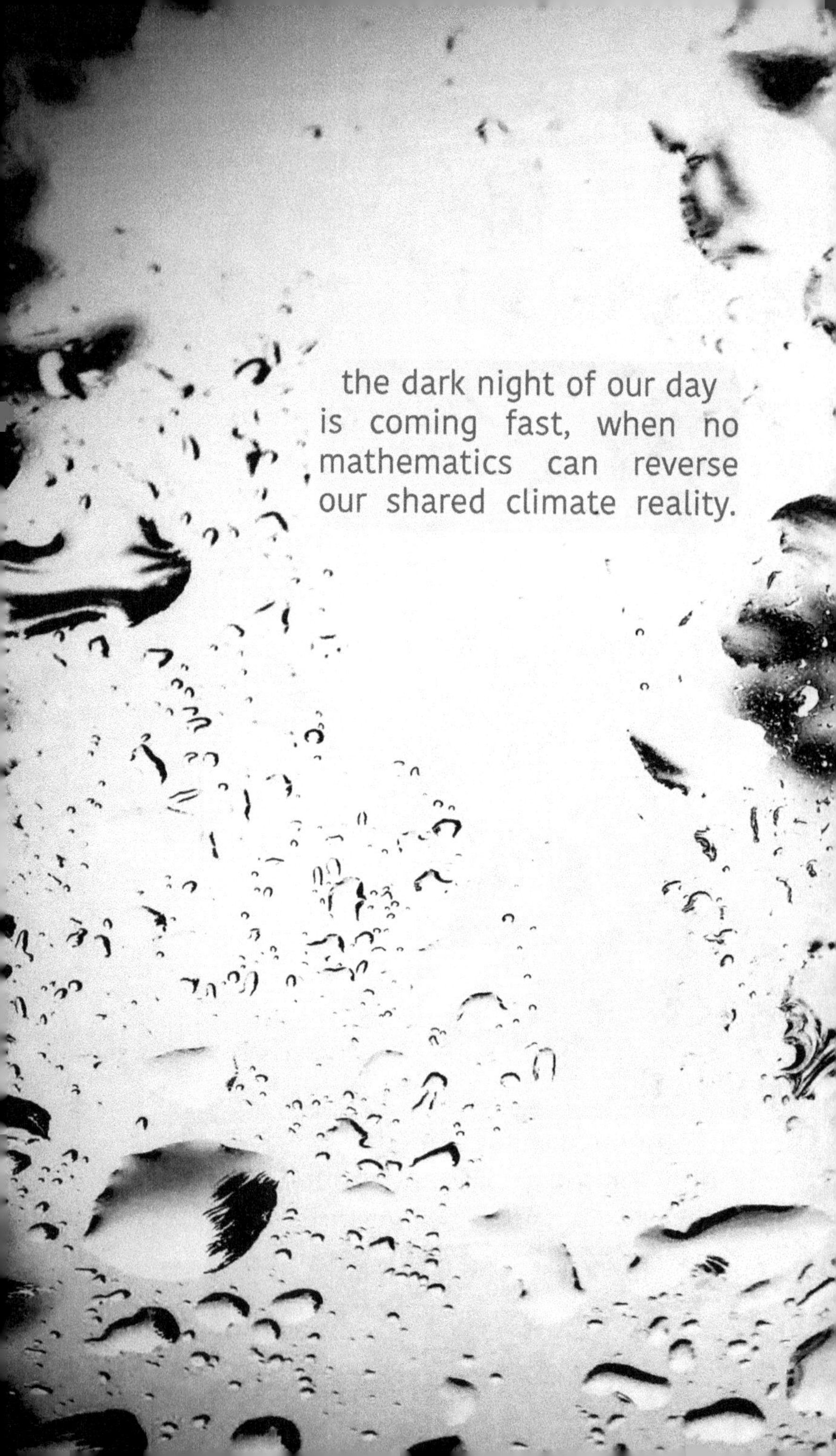
the dark night of our day
is coming fast, when no
mathematics can reverse
our shared climate reality.

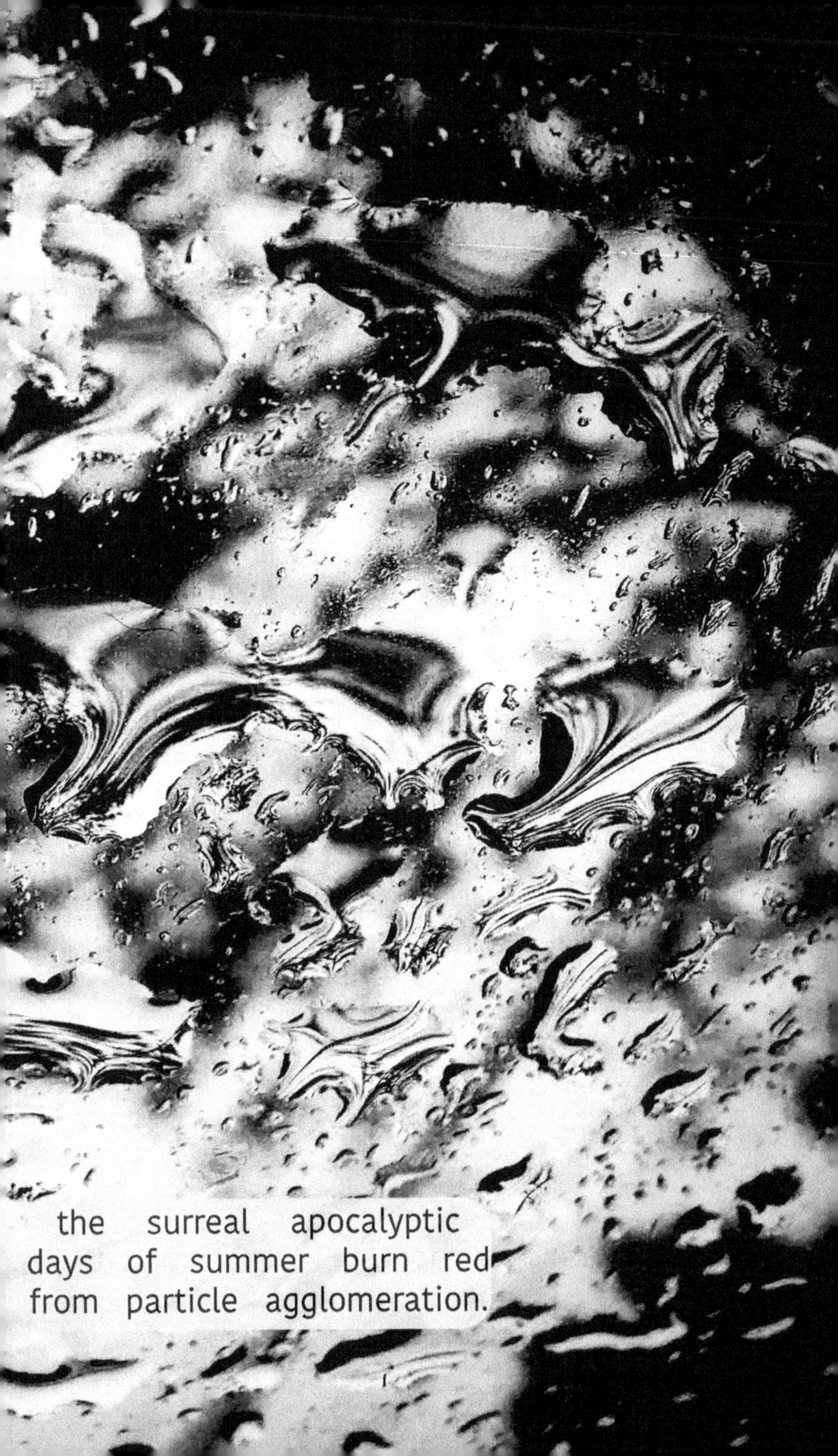
the surreal apocalyptic
days of summer burn red
from particle agglomeration.

the time of the sagging
sun is upon us, when liquid
sunshine replaces all the
apocalyptic summer days
of our climate catastrophe.

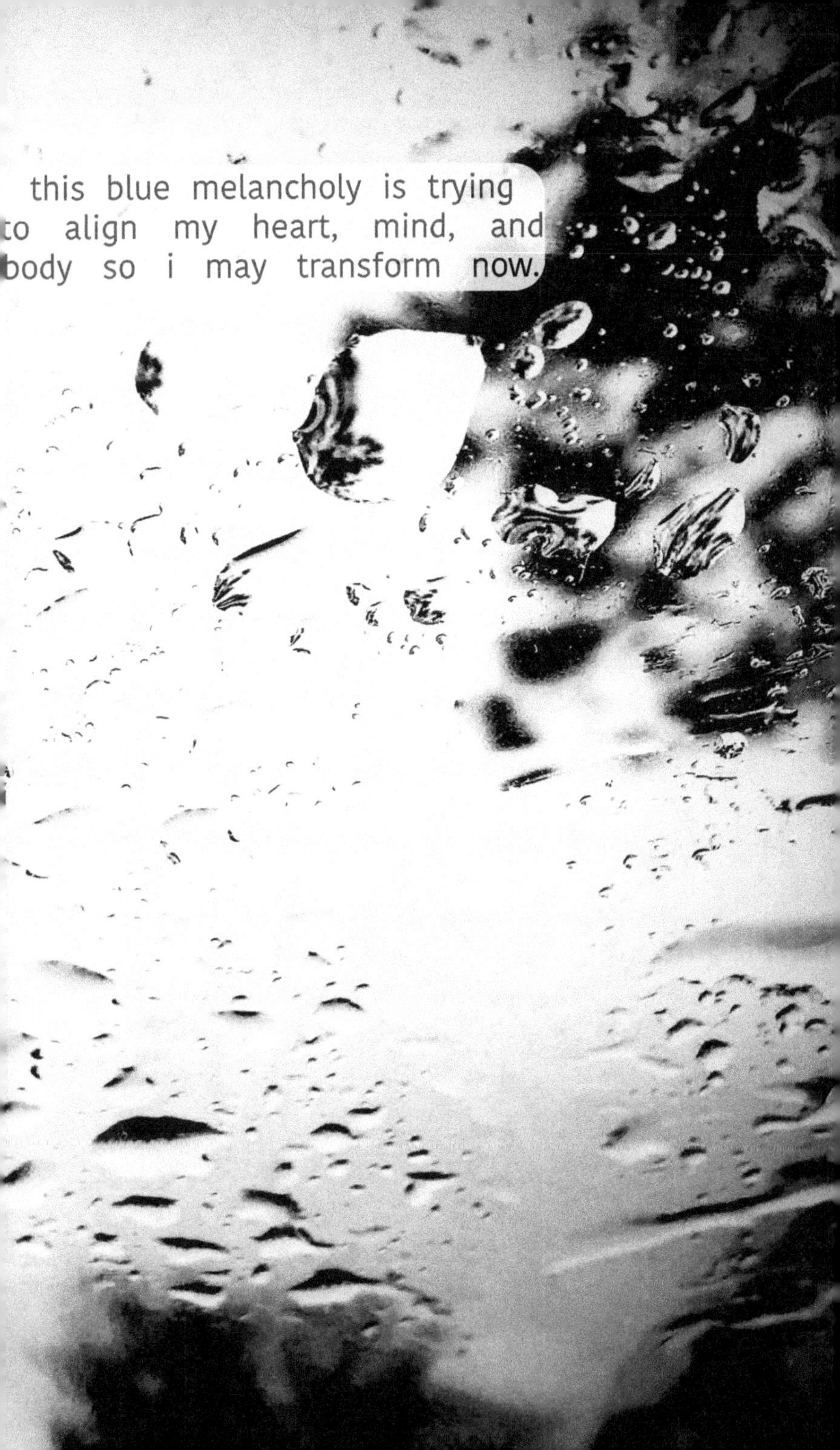
this blue melancholy is trying
to align my heart, mind, and
body so i may transform now.

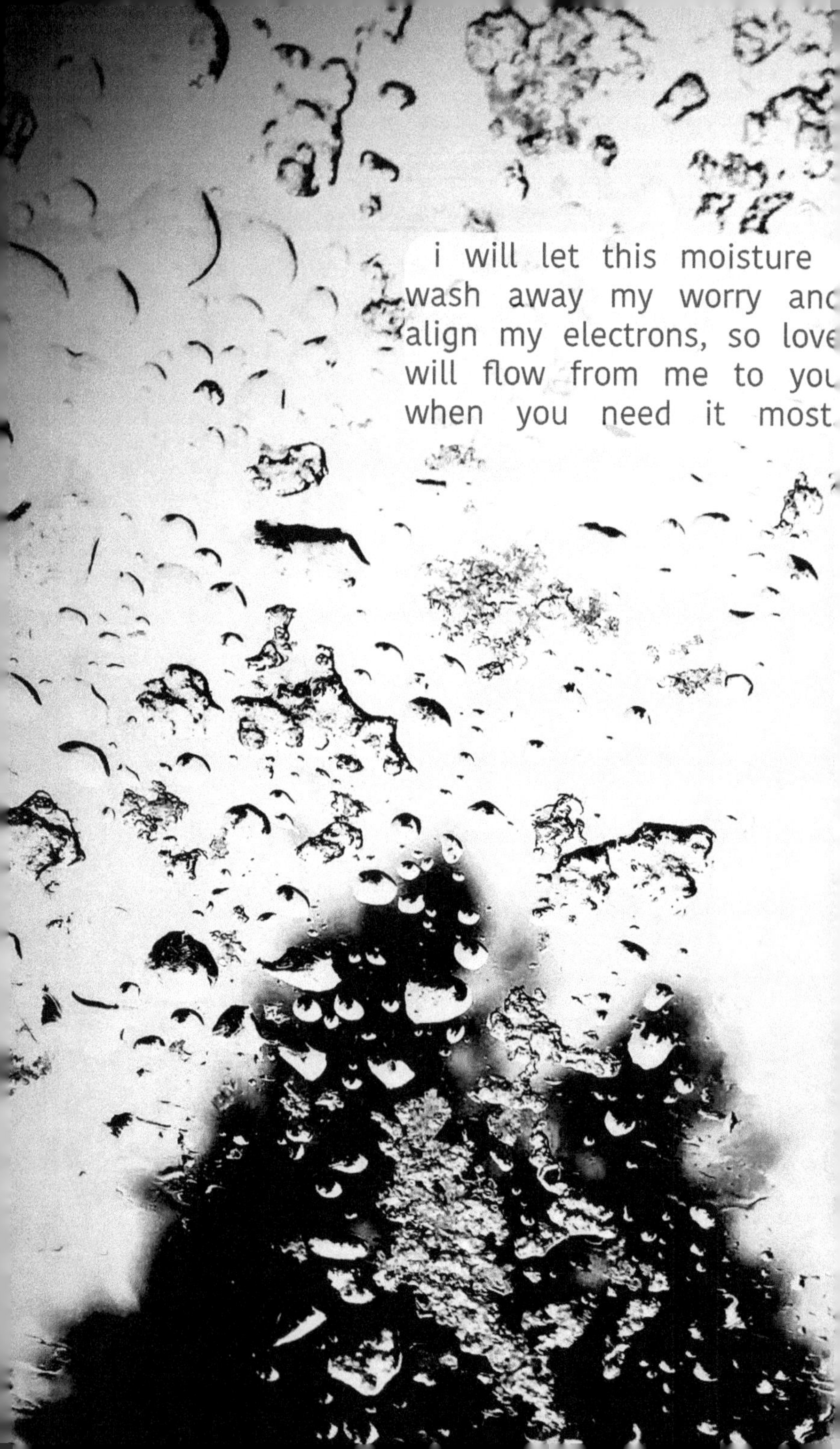
i will let this moisture
wash away my worry and
align my electrons, so love
will flow from me to you
when you need it most

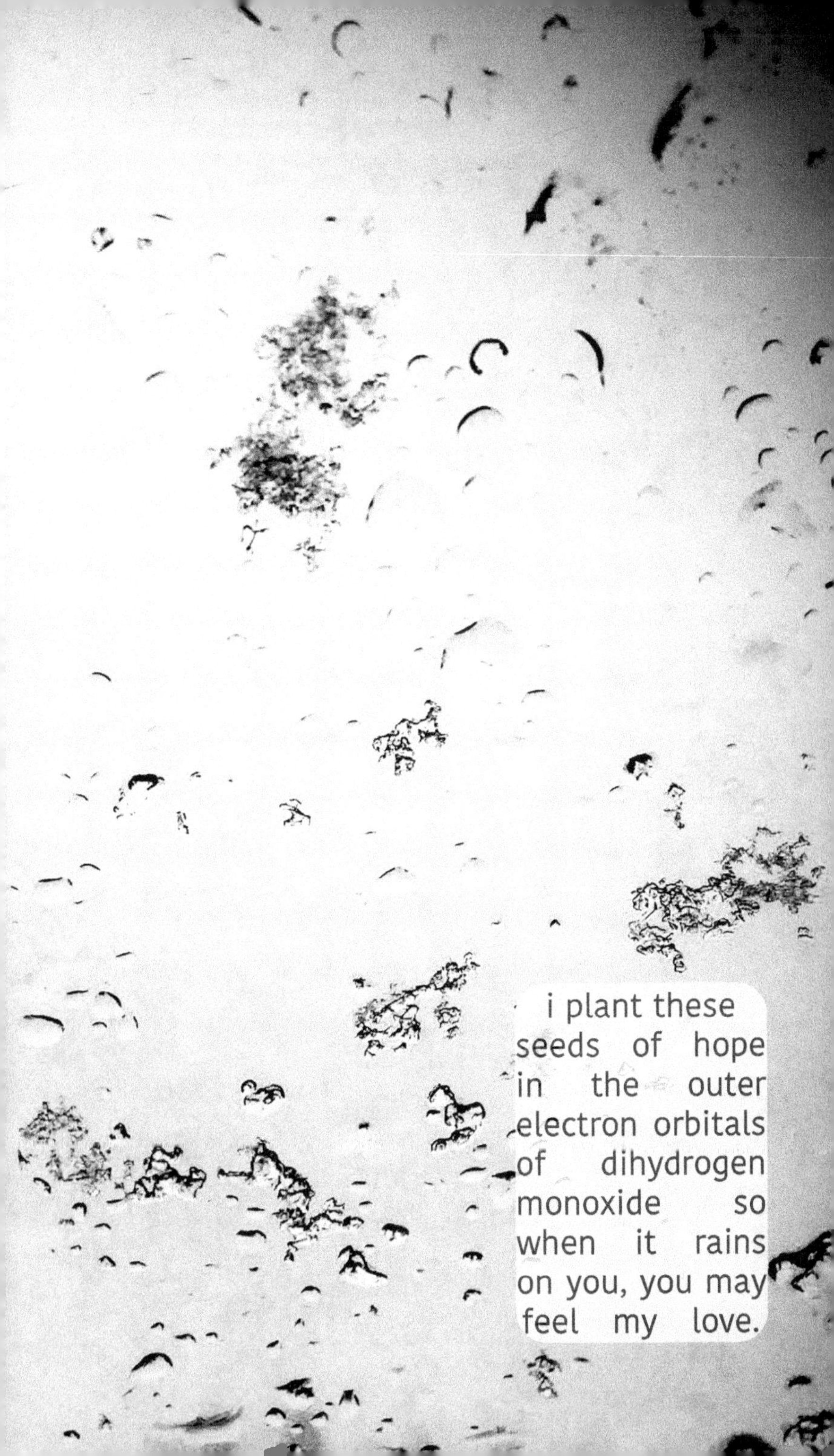

i plant these
seeds of hope
in the outer
electron orbitals
of dihydrogen
monoxide so
when it rains
on you, you may
feel my love.

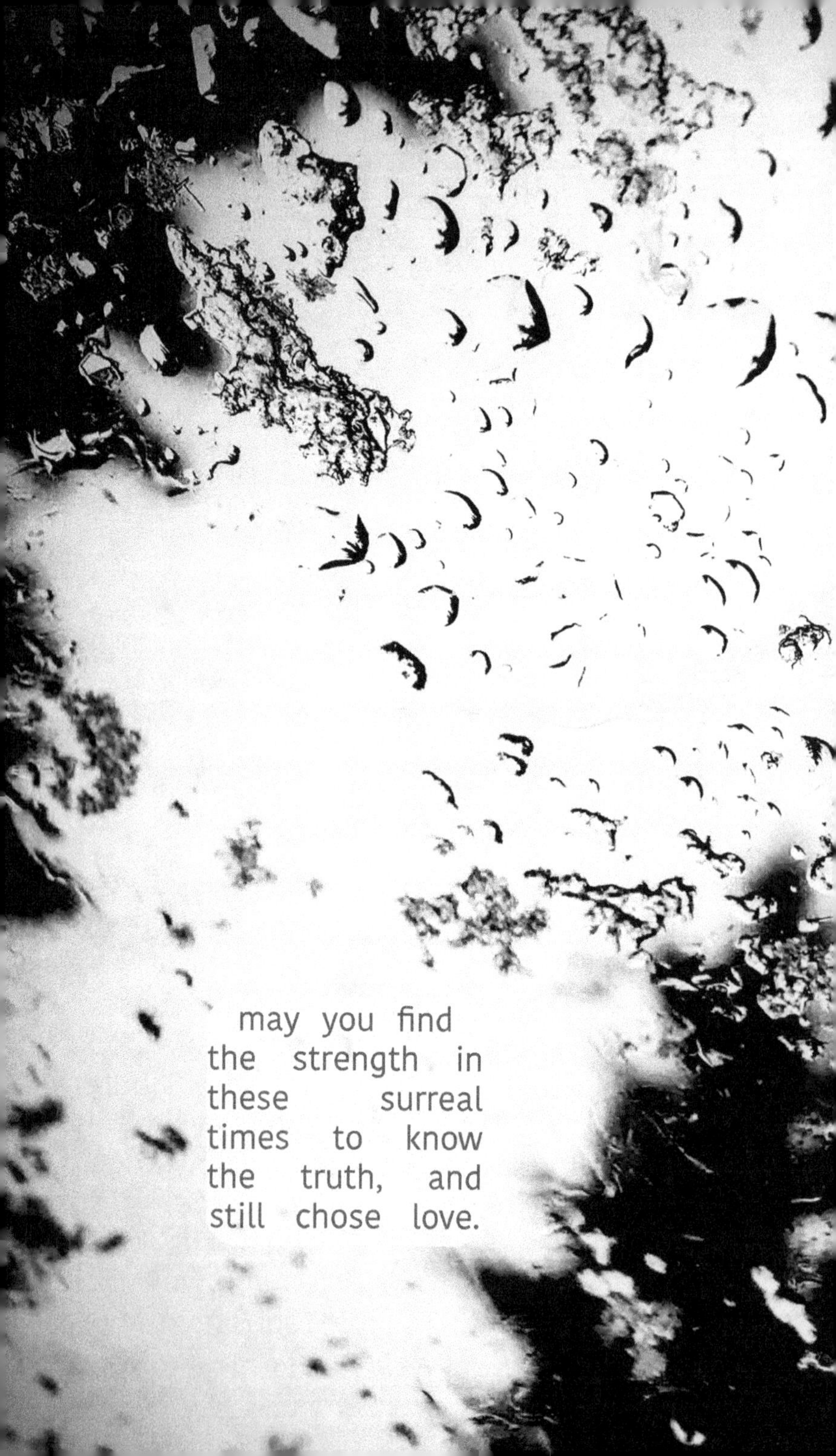

may you find
the strength in
these surreal
times to know
the truth, and
still chose love.

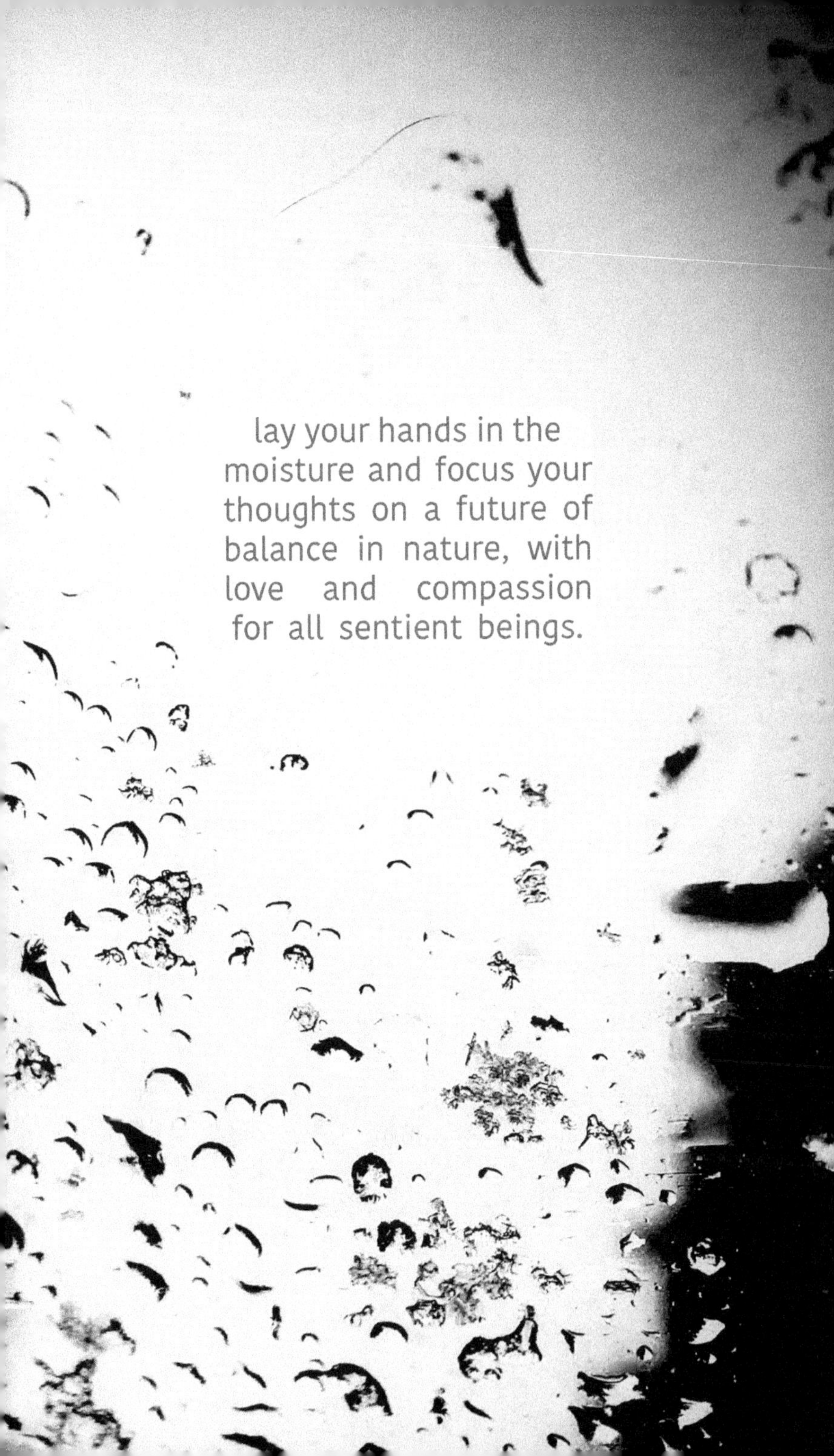

lay your hands in the moisture and focus your thoughts on a future of balance in nature, with love and compassion for all sentient beings.

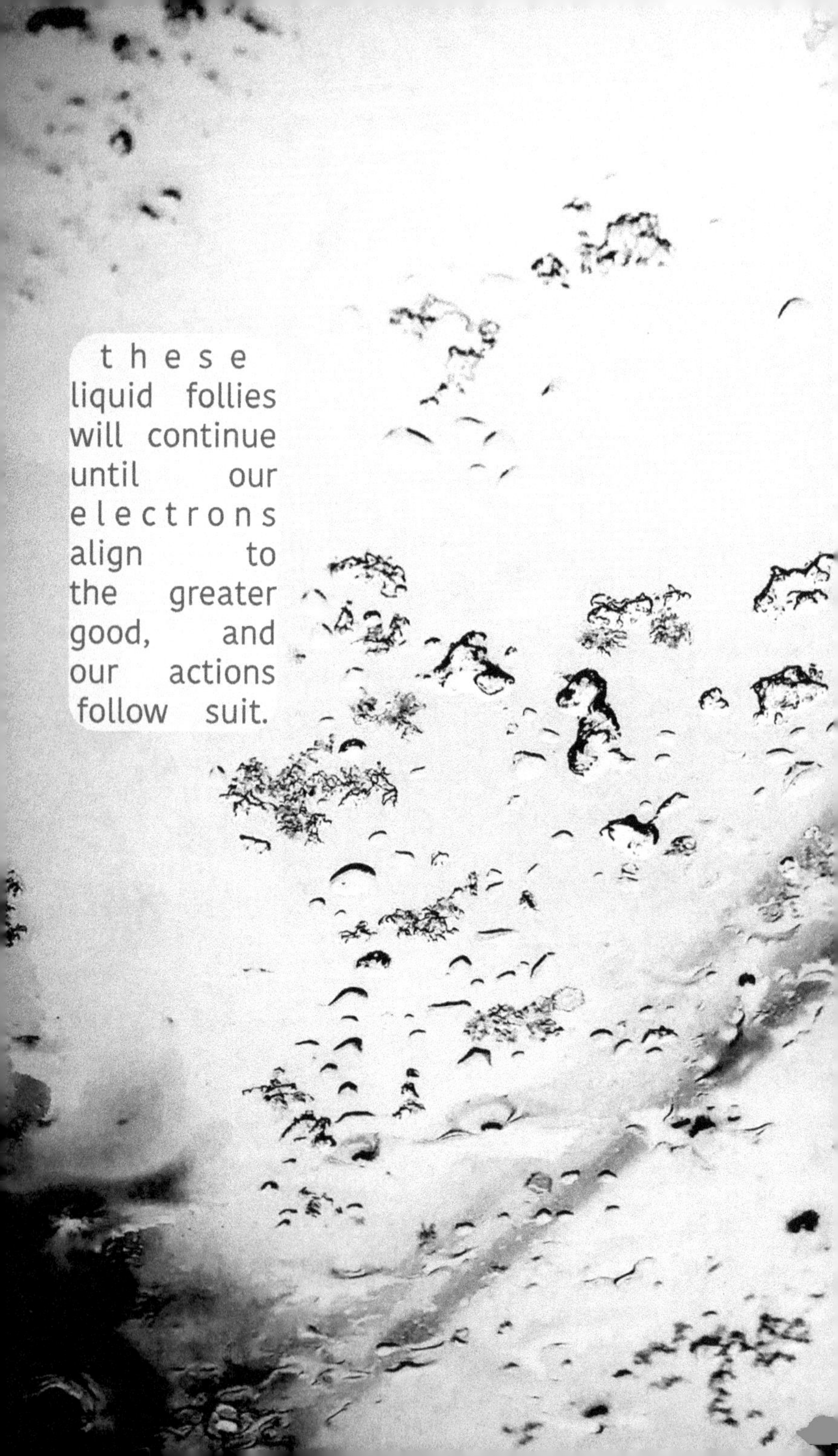

t h e s e
liquid follies
will continue
until our
e l e c t r o n s
align to
the greater
good, and
our actions
follow suit.

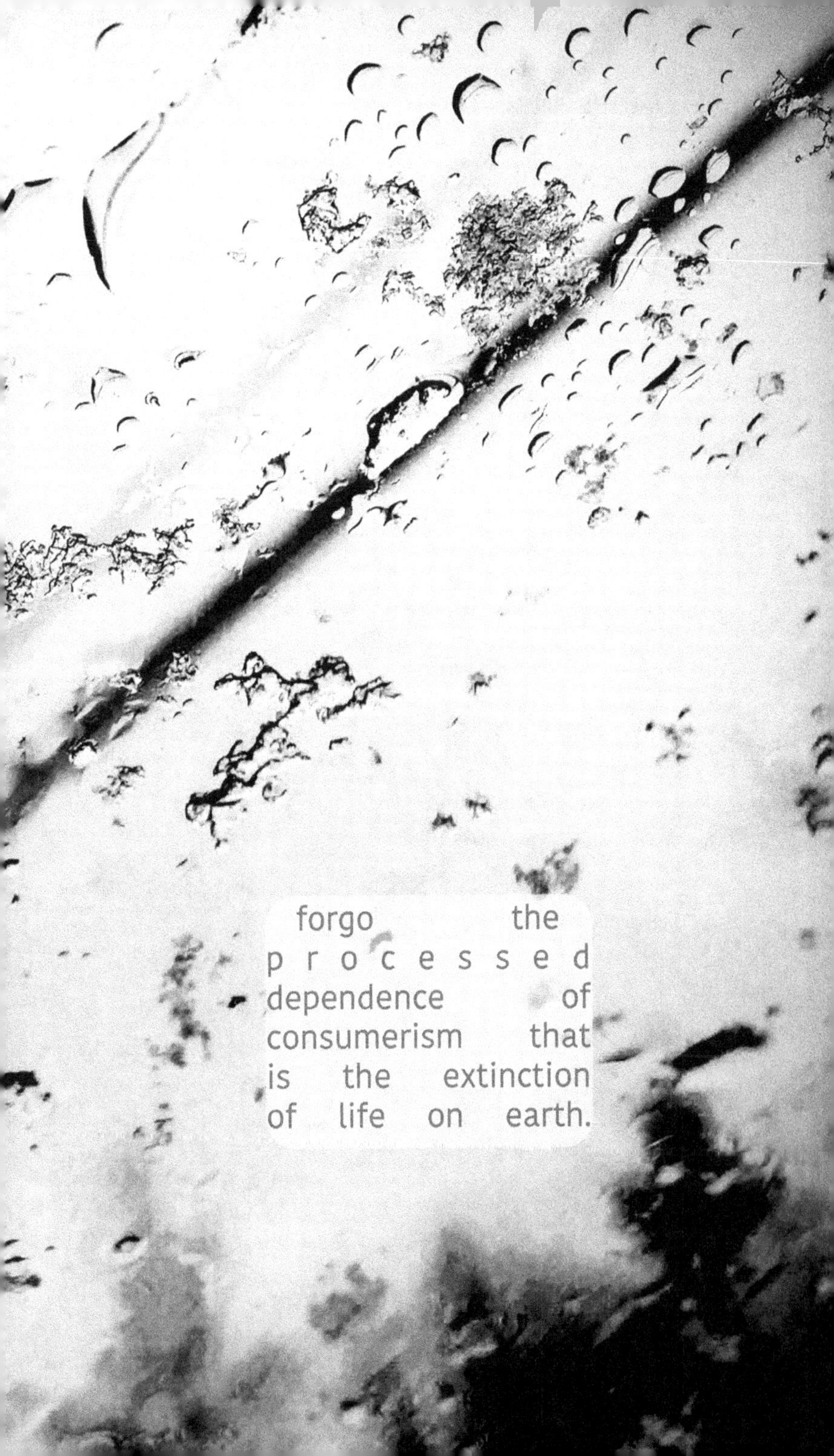
forgo the processed dependence of consumerism that is the extinction of life on earth.

these are the days
when everything twists
in the waning light
until all is revealed.

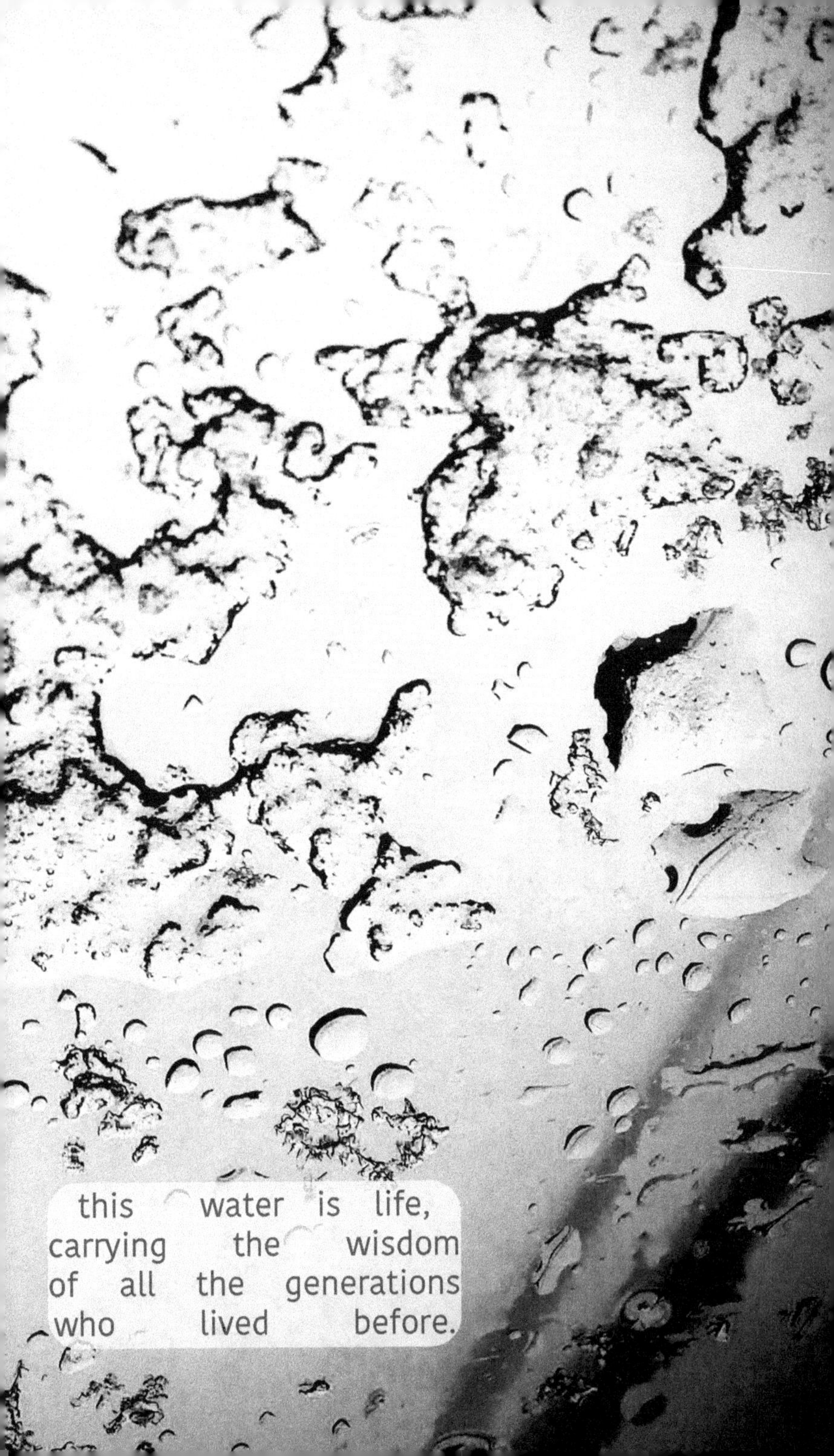

this water is life,
carrying the wisdom
of all the generations
who lived before.

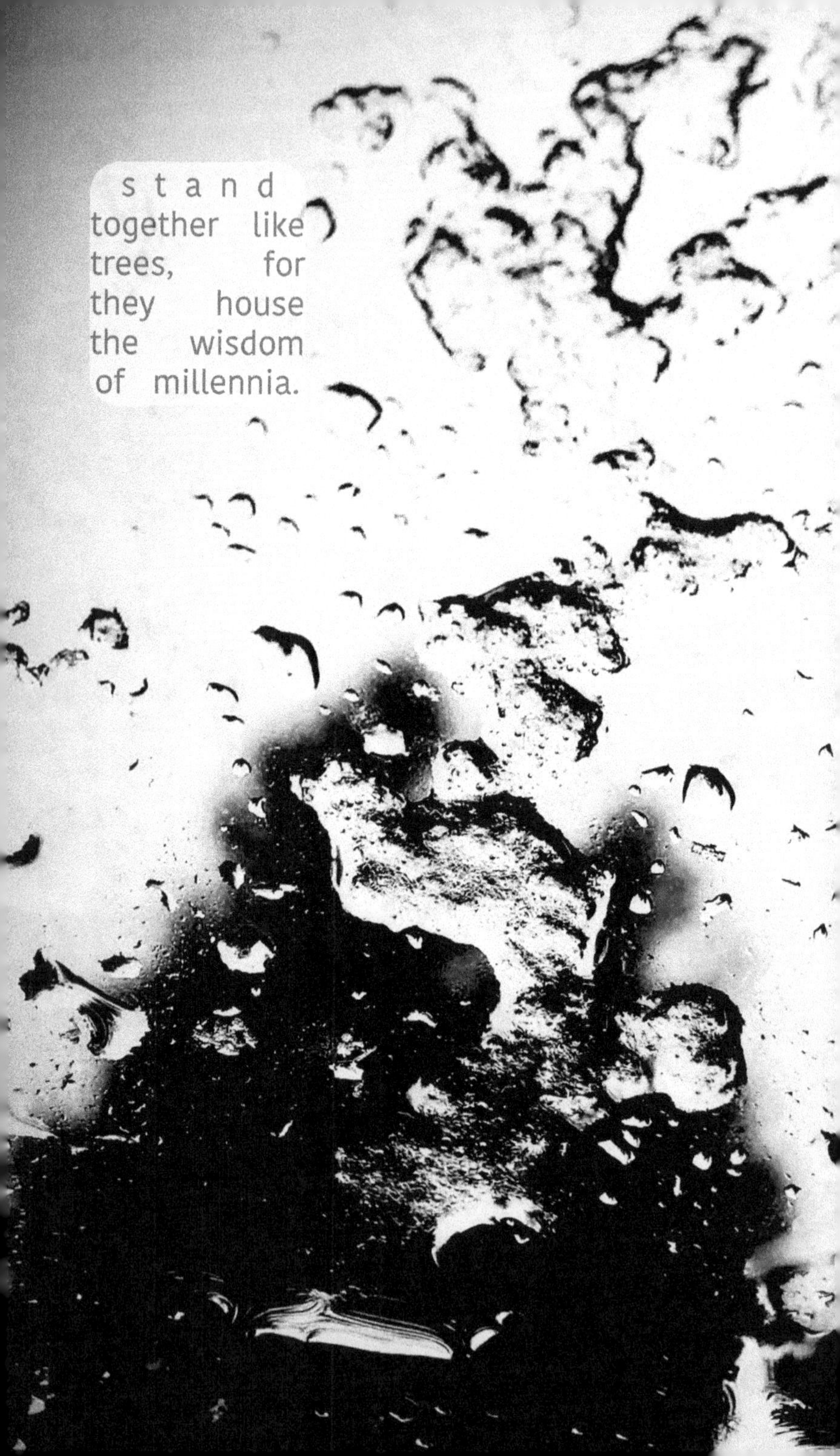
stand
together like
trees, for
they house
the wisdom
of millennia.

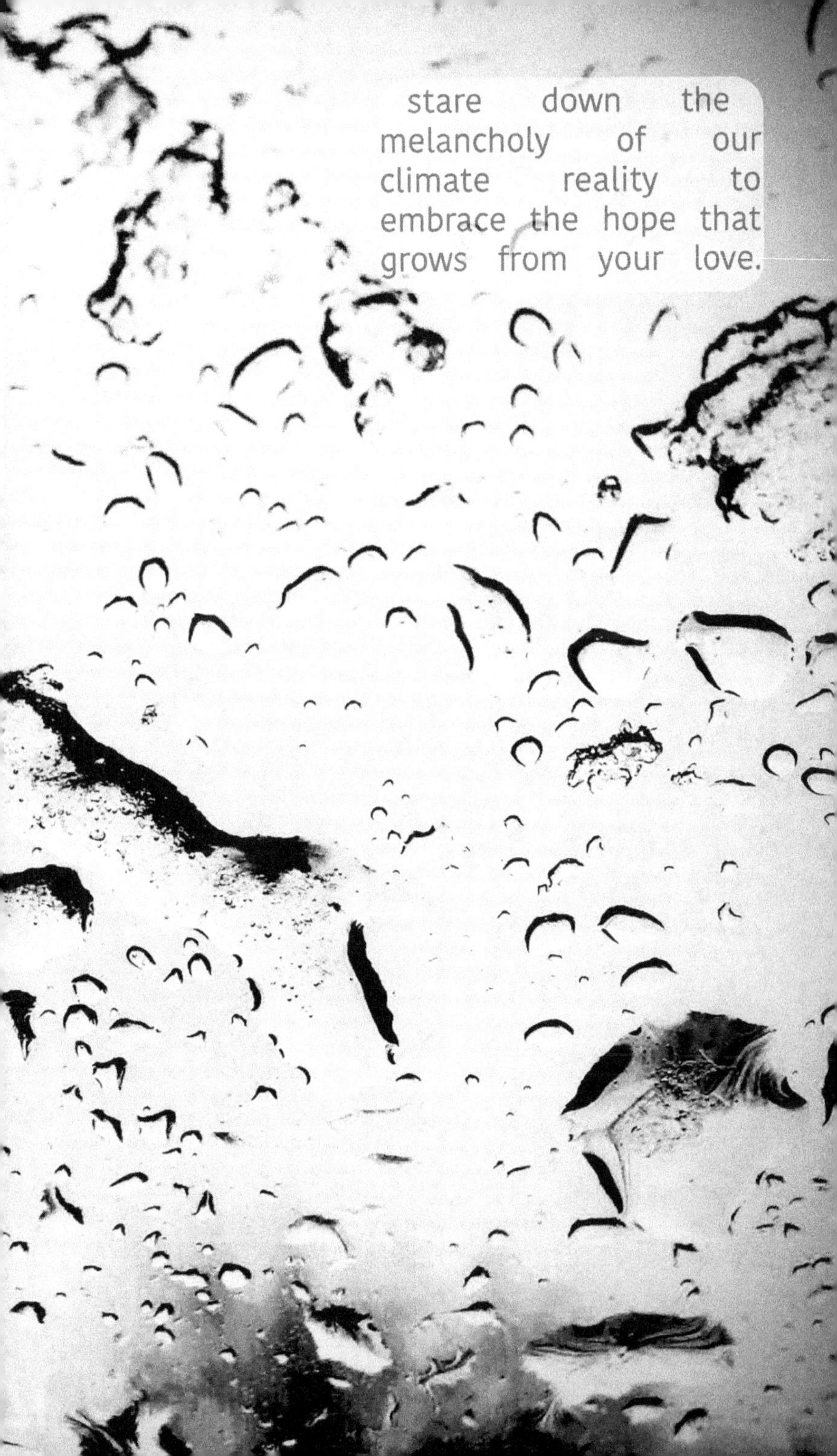
stare down the
melancholy of our
climate reality to
embrace the hope that
grows from your love.

the mystical of
today is the quantum
mathematics of
tomorrow we must
learn to embrace.

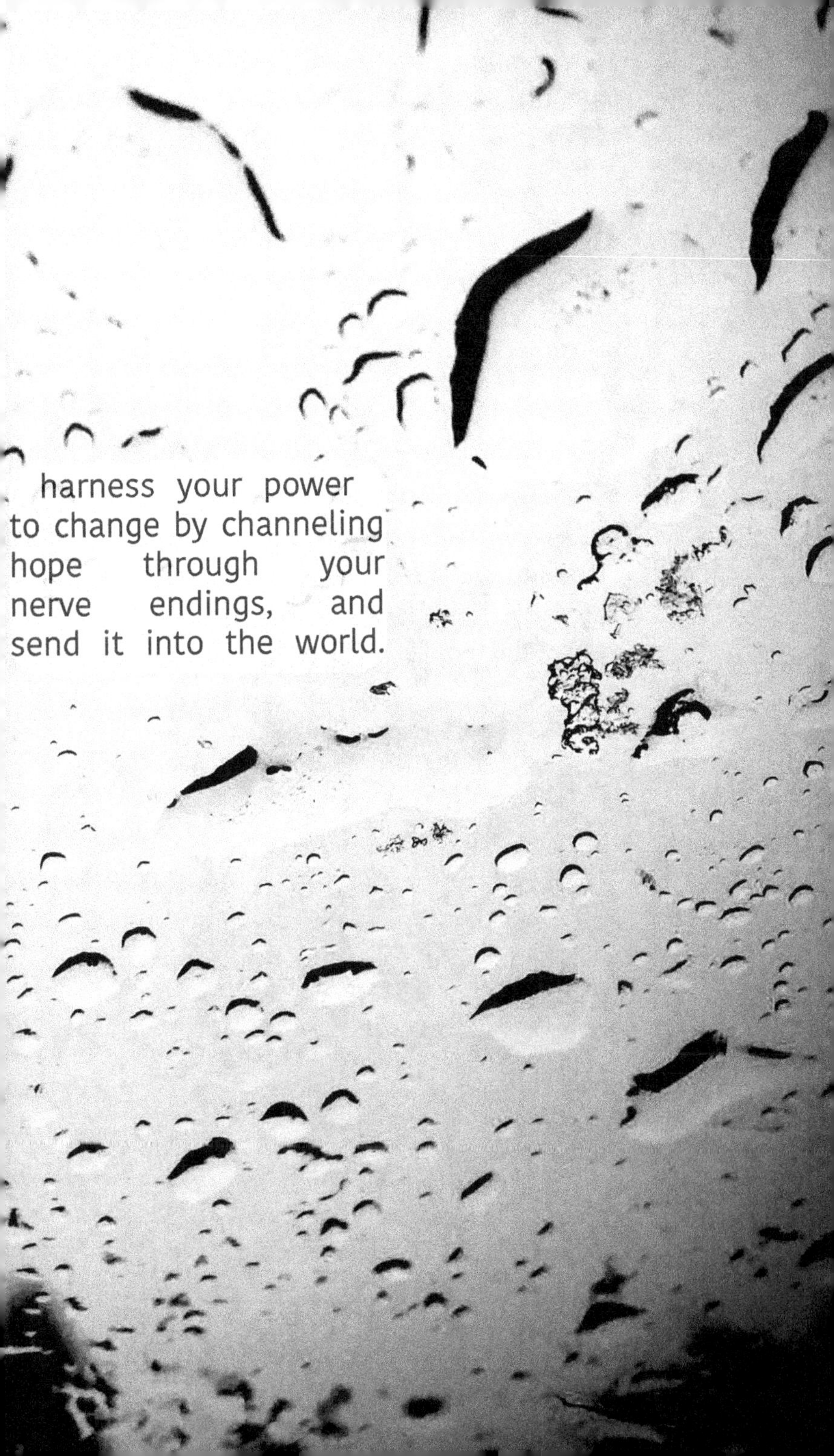
harness your power
to change by channeling
hope through your
nerve endings, and
send it into the world.

feel the moist
follies of ancient
wisdom as it reigns
down hope into
the hearts of all
earth's warriors.

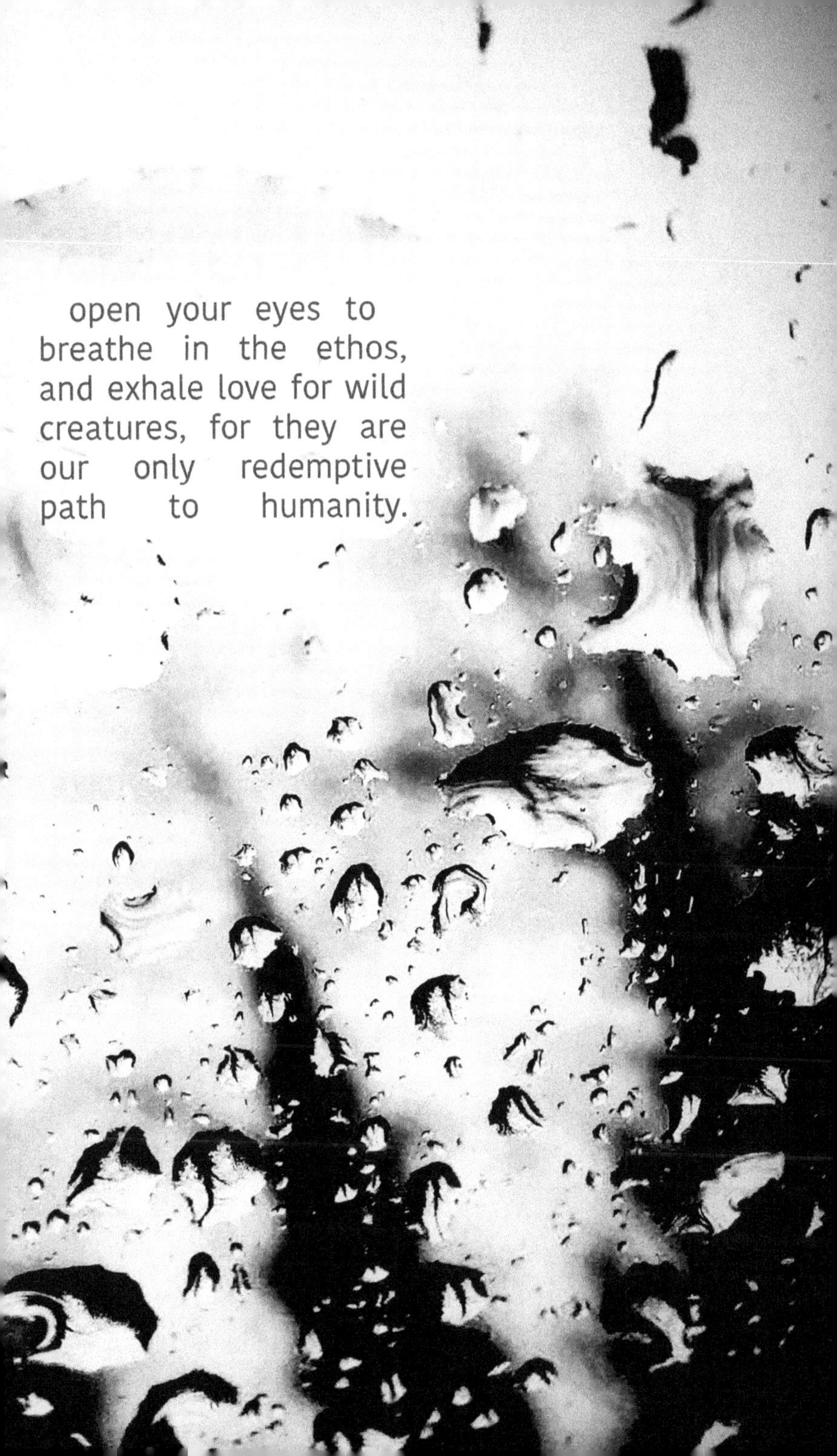

open your eyes to breathe in the ethos, and exhale love for wild creatures, for they are our only redemptive path to humanity.

this grey blanket clings to my
hope as i pray for the love to seep
into my pores so our intent aligns.

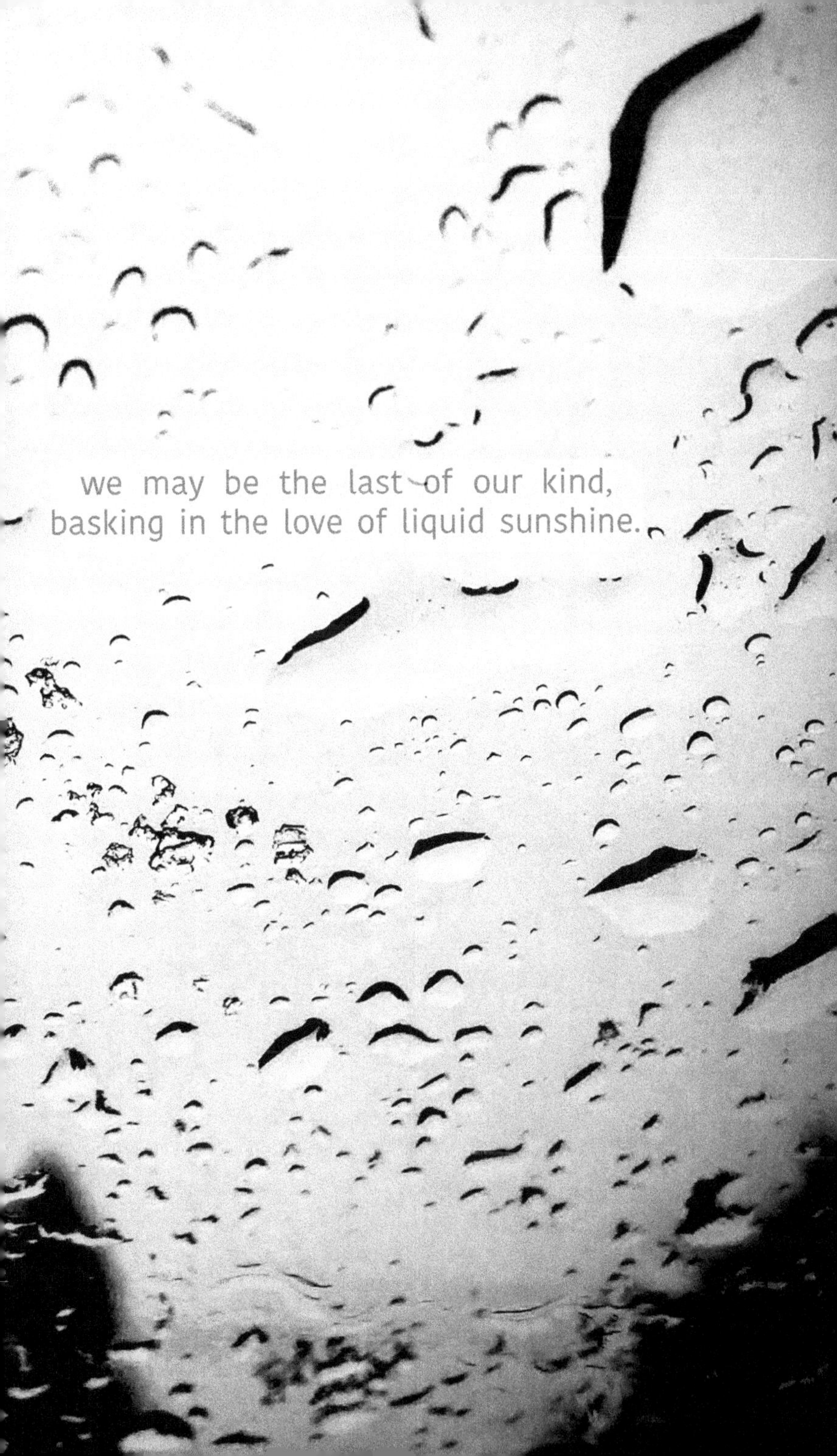
we may be the last of our kind,
basking in the love of liquid sunshine.

we grow together with our intent and
love, to transform earth before it is too late.

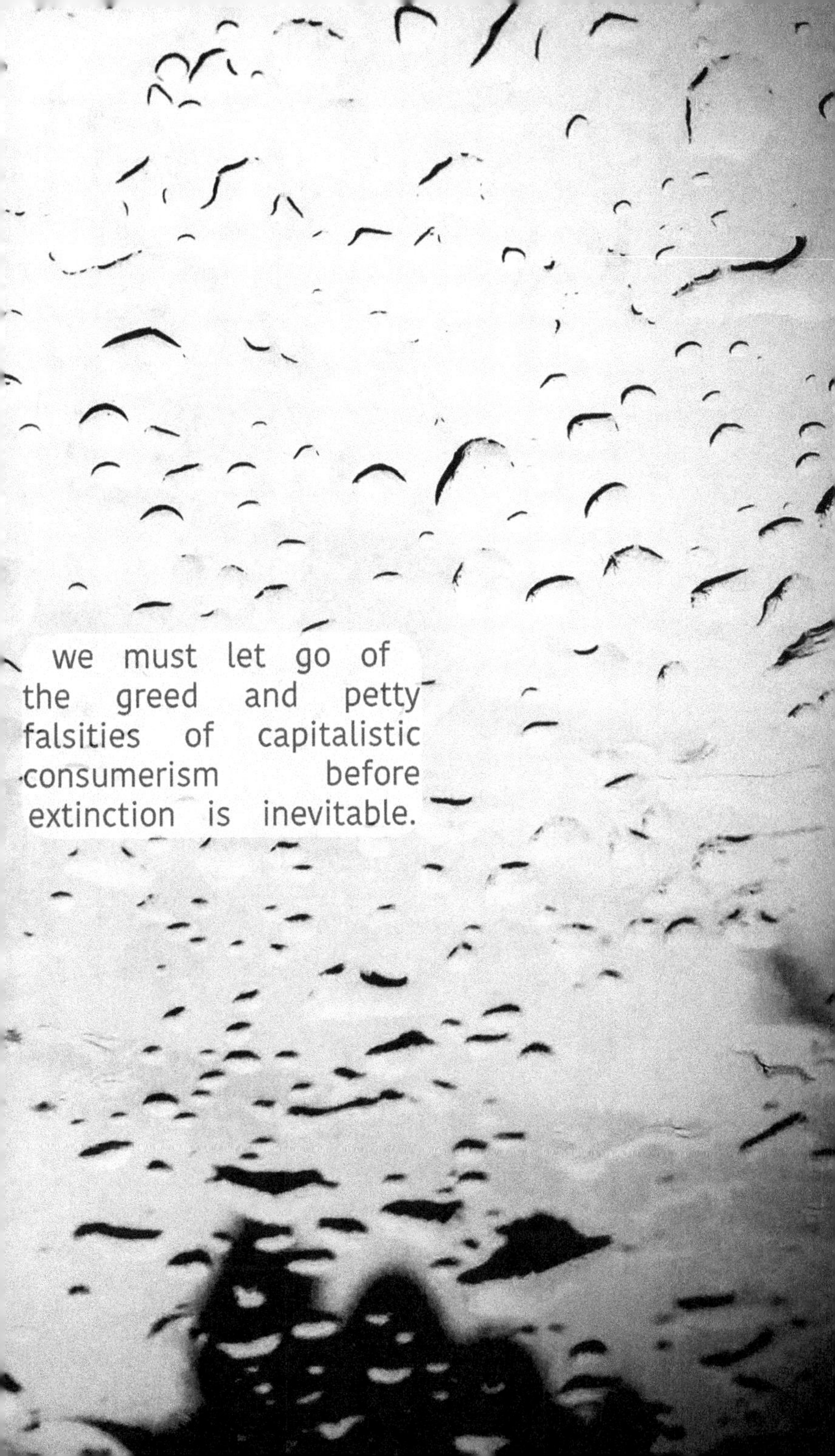

we must let go of the greed and petty falsities of capitalistic consumerism before extinction is inevitable.

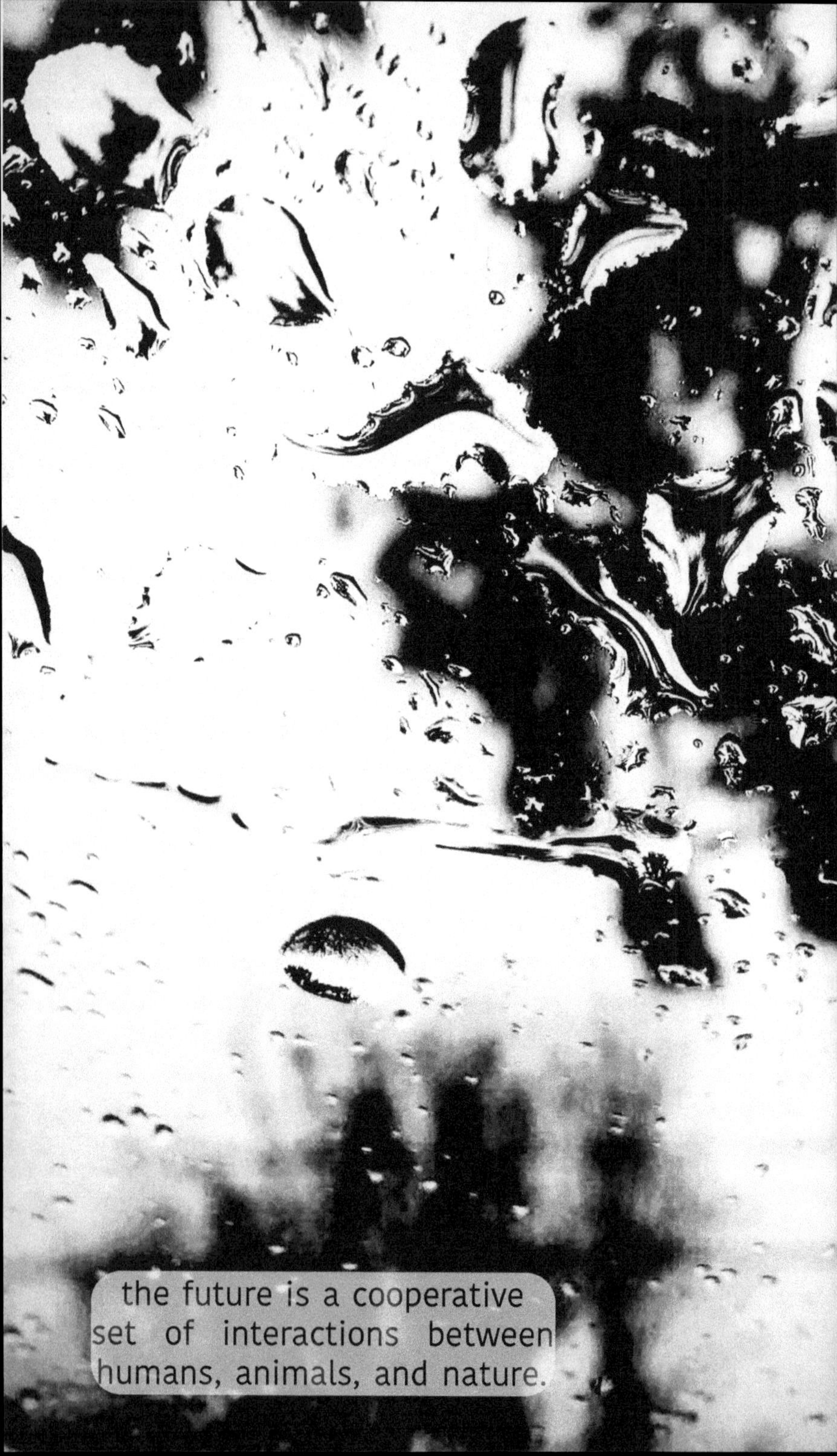

the future is a cooperative
set of interactions between
humans, animals, and nature.

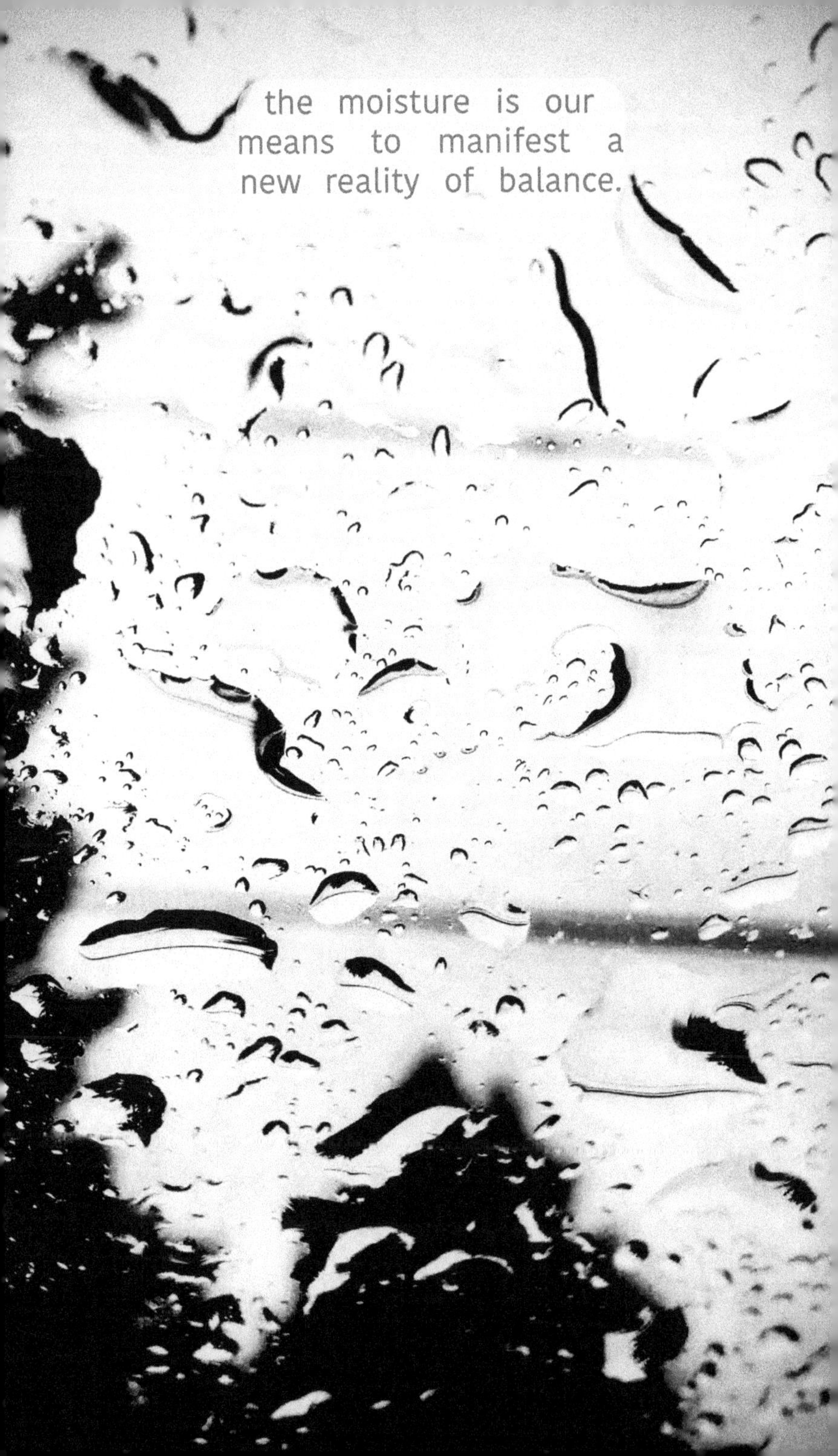
the moisture is our
means to manifest a
new reality of balance.

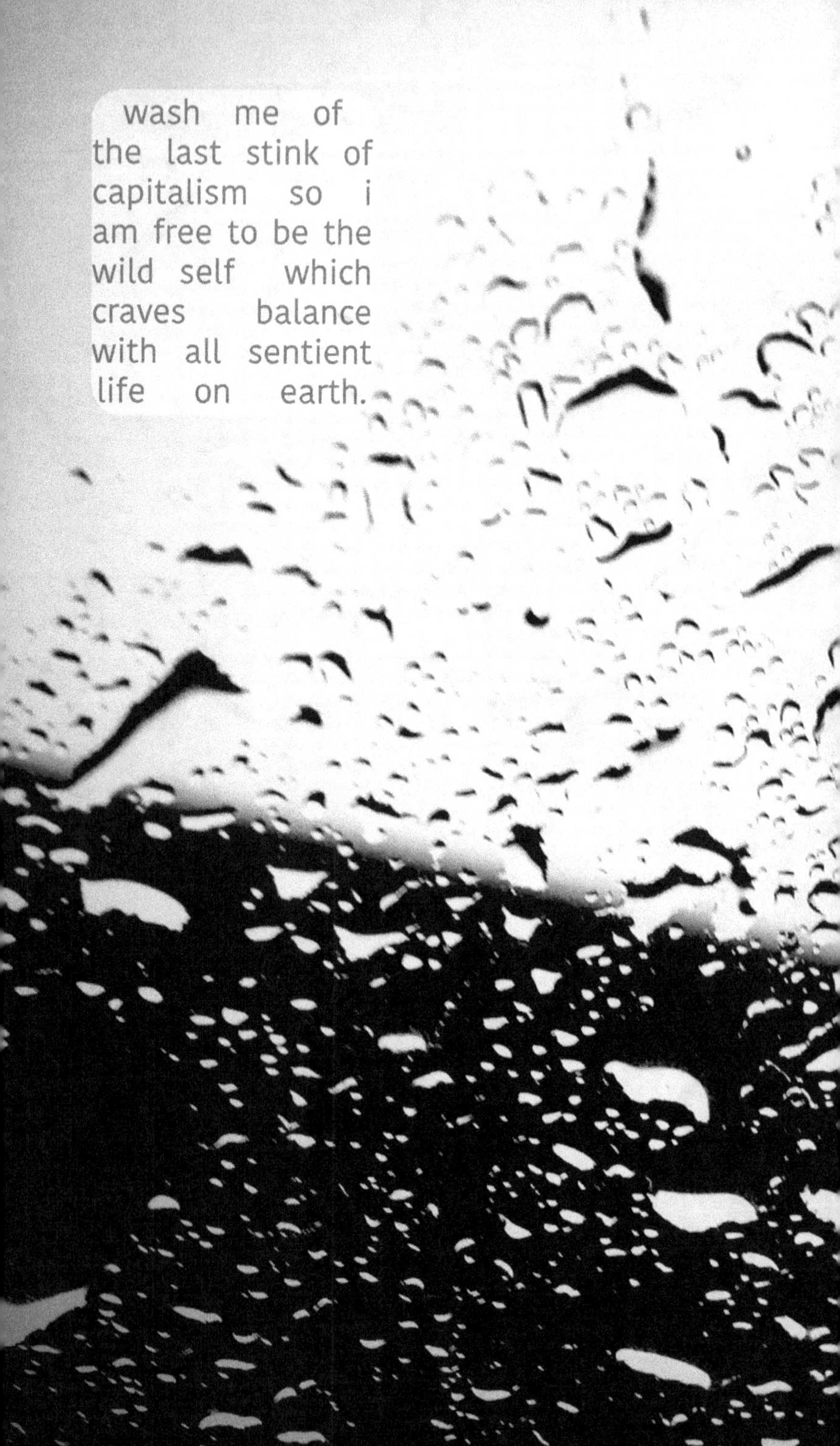

wash me of
the last stink of
capitalism so i
am free to be the
wild self which
craves balance
with all sentient
life on earth.

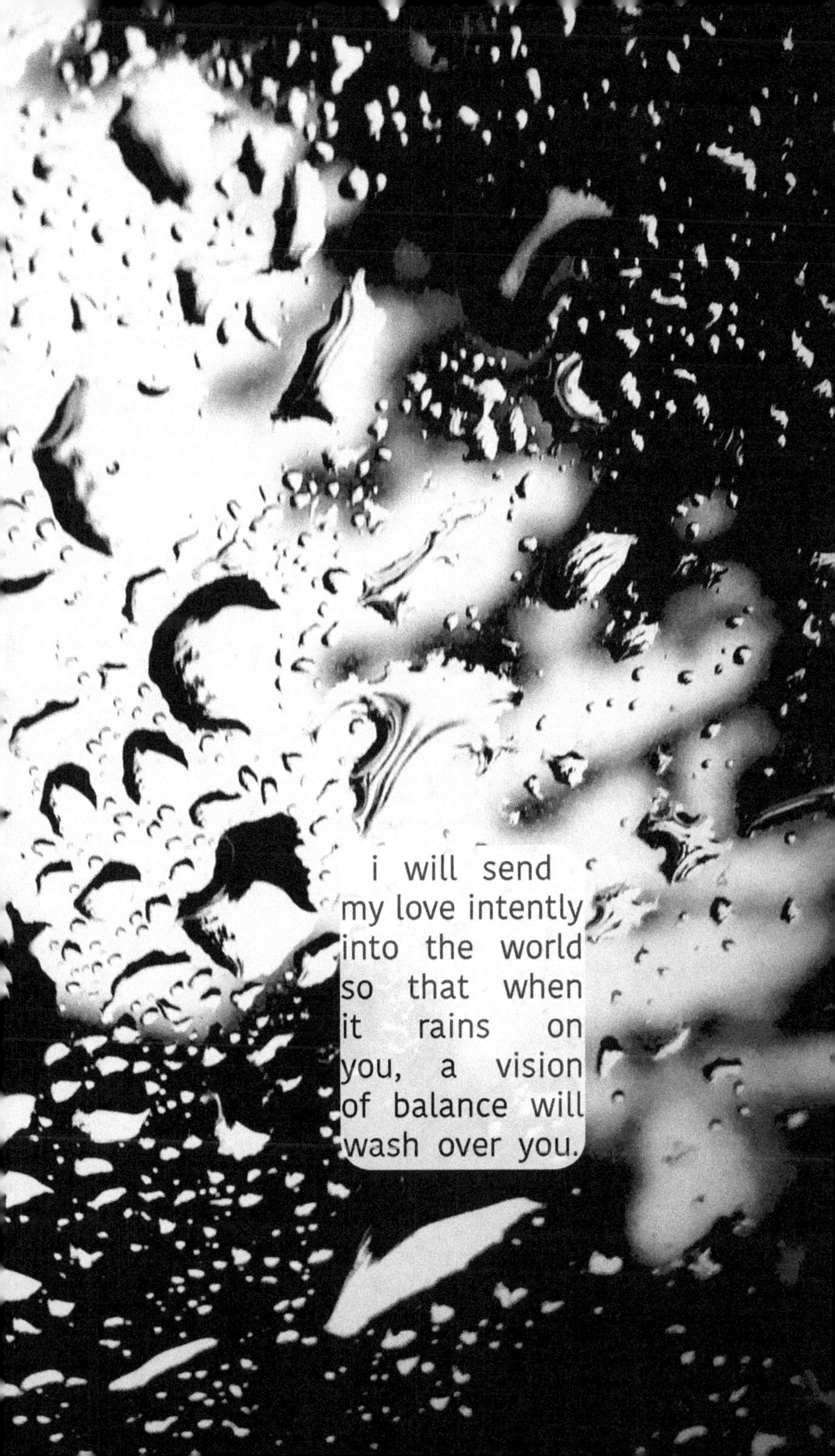
i will send
my love intently
into the world
so that when
it rains on
you, a vision
of balance will
wash over you.

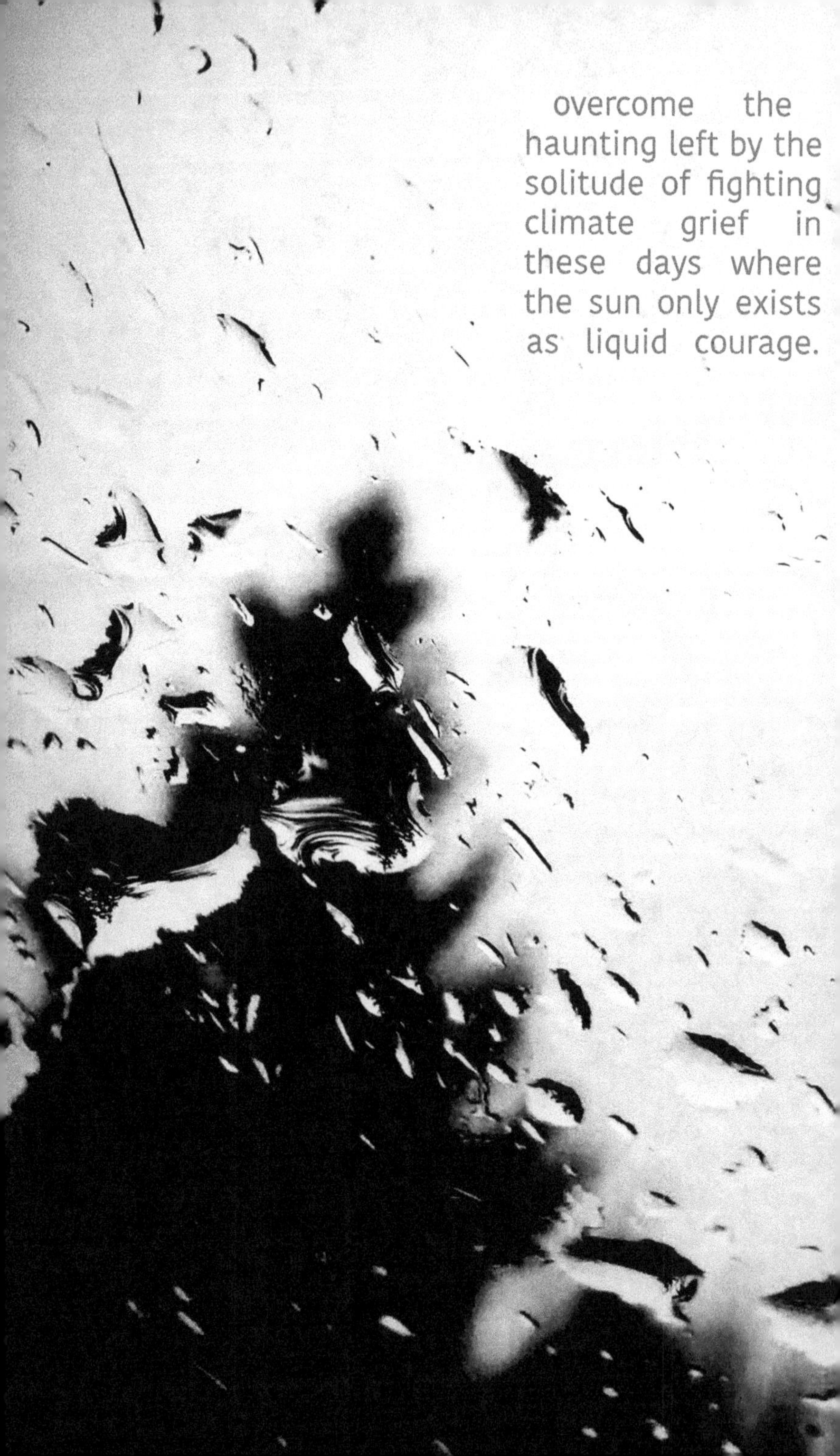
overcome the
haunting left by the
solitude of fighting
climate grief in
these days where
the sun only exists
as liquid courage.

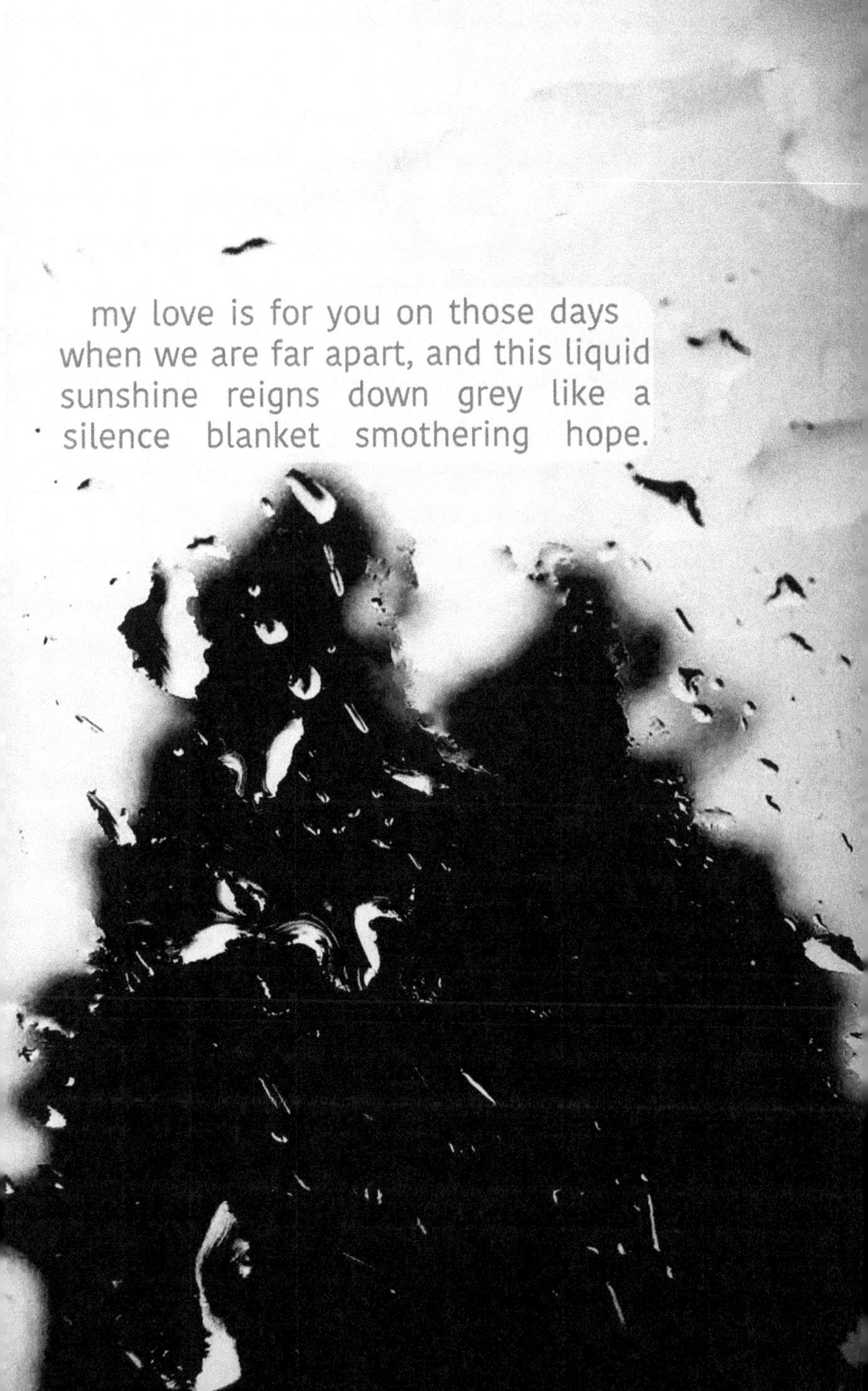

my love is for you on those days
when we are far apart, and this liquid
sunshine reigns down grey like a
silence blanket smothering hope.

you have the strength to stand up, and
the character to choose the earth today.

do not fear the
grey of apathy, instead
make choices that
move you to crave
a balance with all
sentient life on earth.

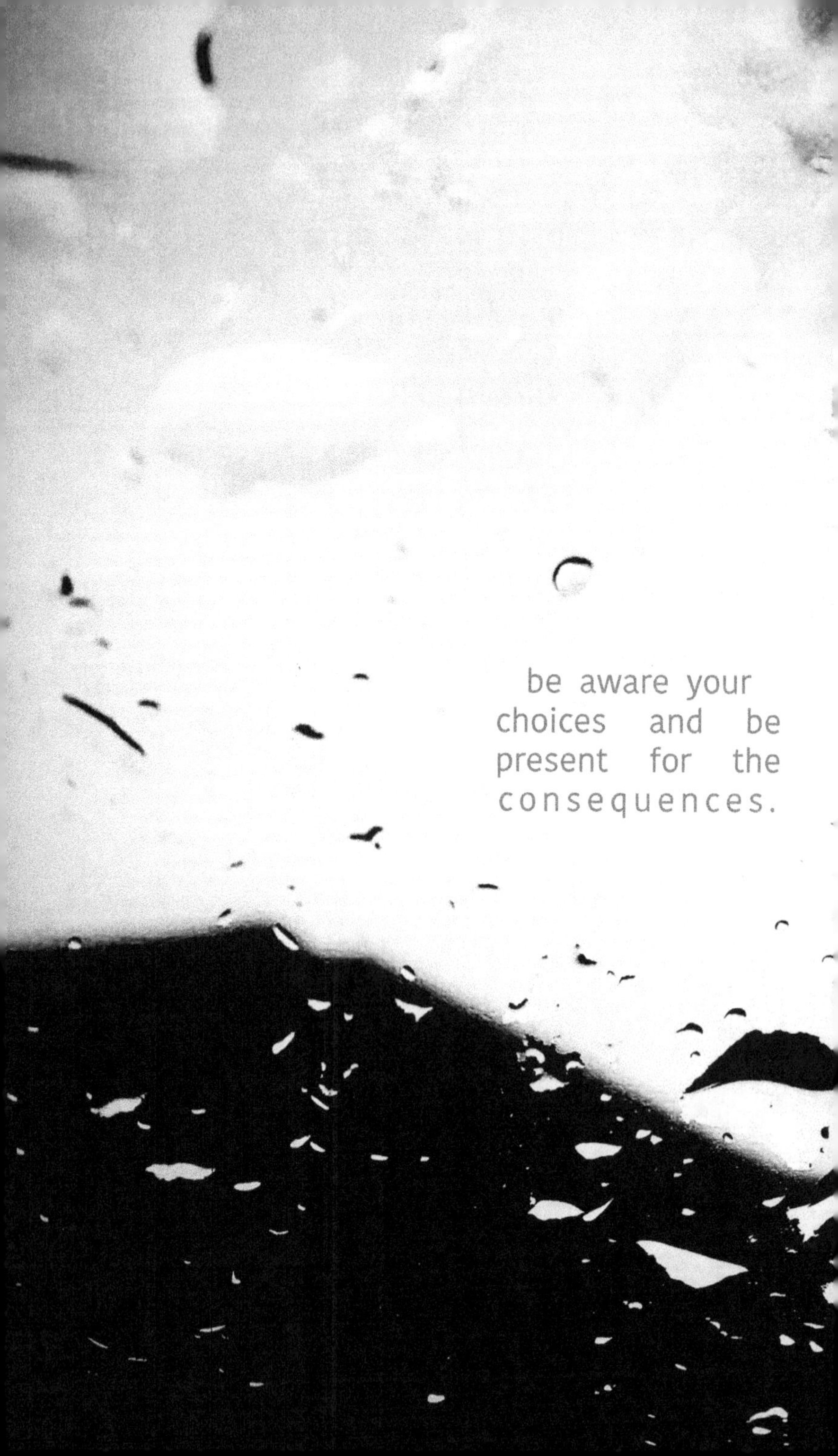
be aware your
choices   and   be
present   for   the
c o n s e q u e n c e s .

love yourself like the
tree loves the moisture.

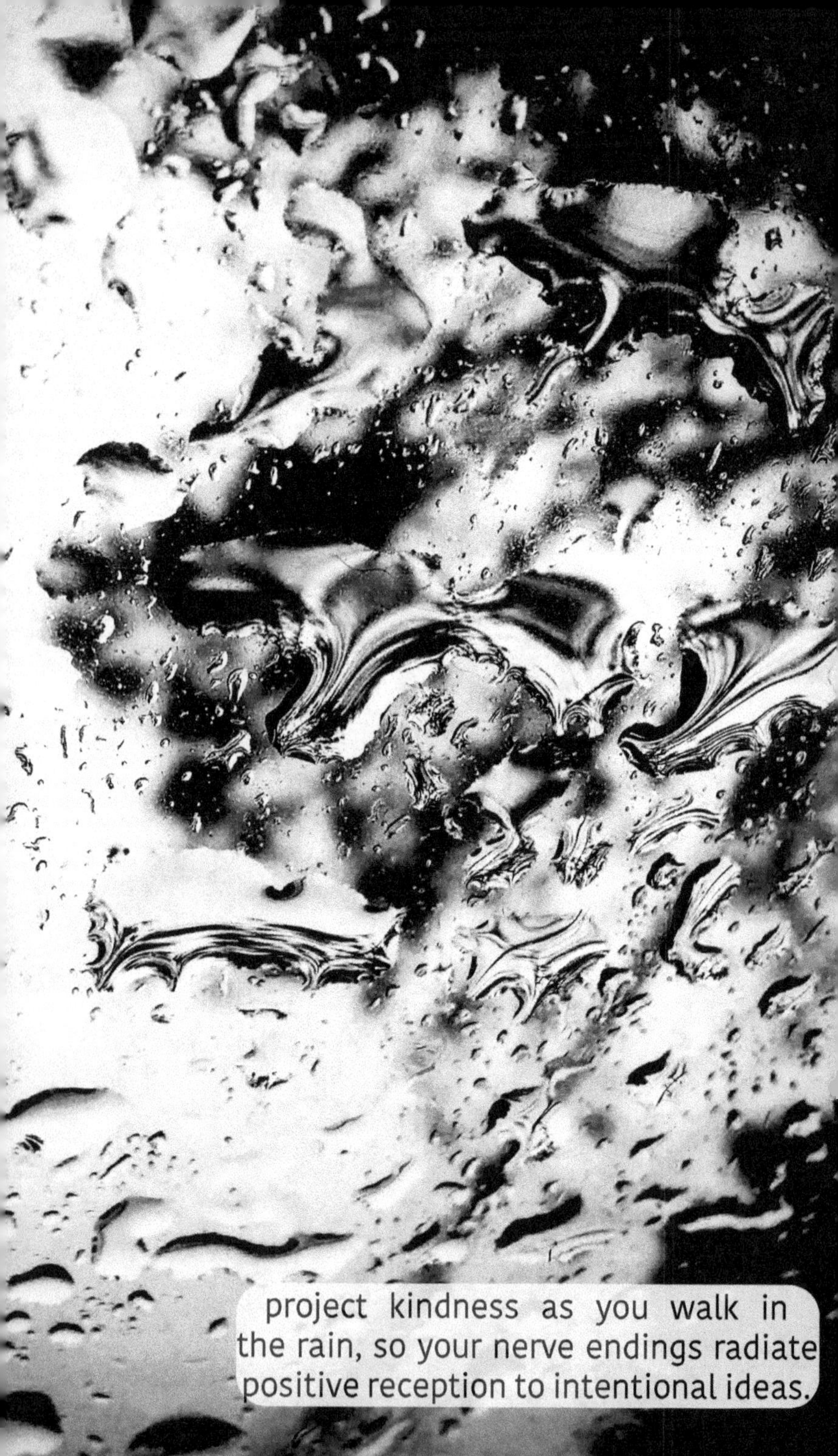
project kindness as you walk in the rain, so your nerve endings radiate positive reception to intentional ideas.

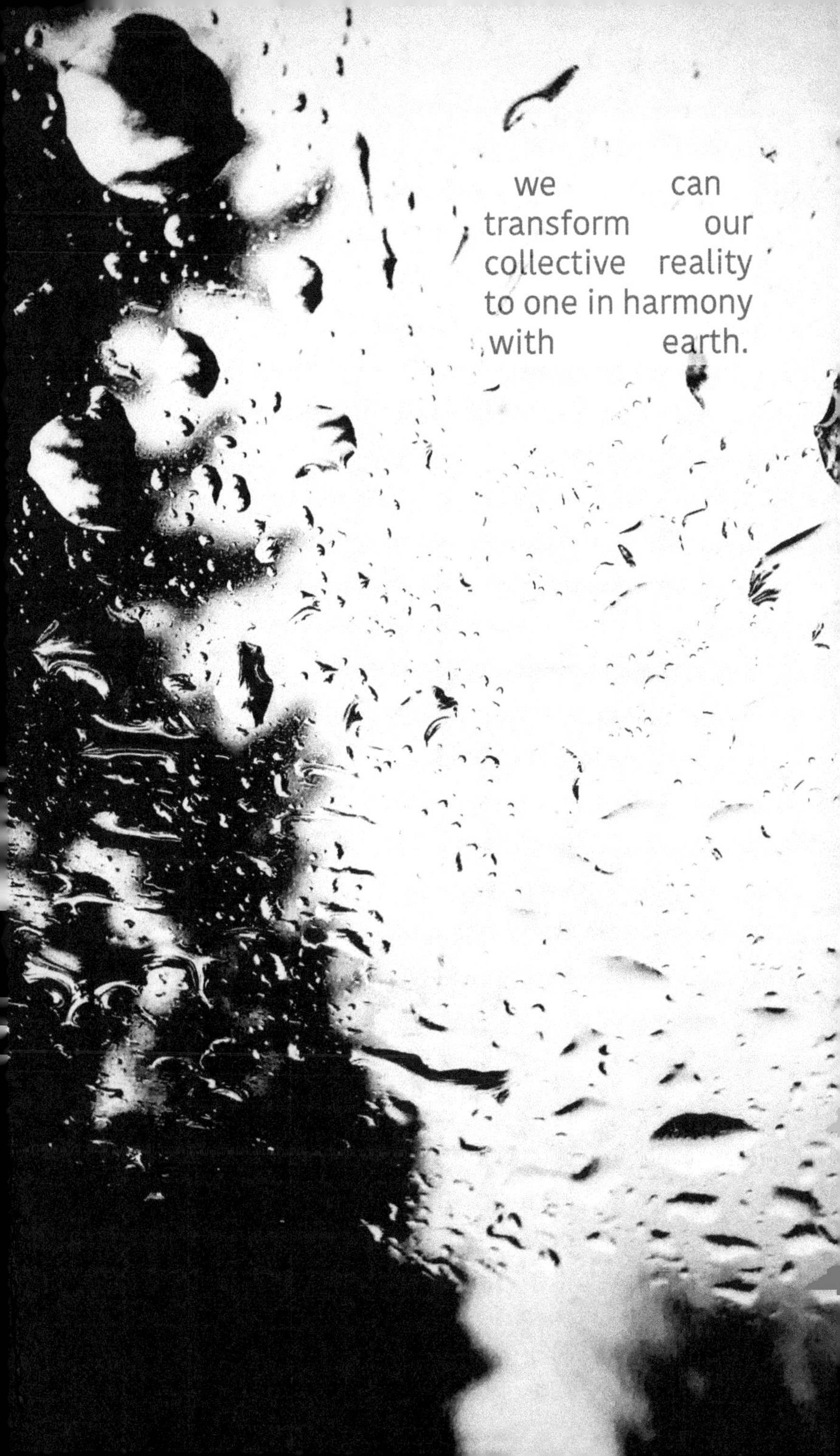
we   can
transform   our
collective   reality
to one in harmony
with   earth.

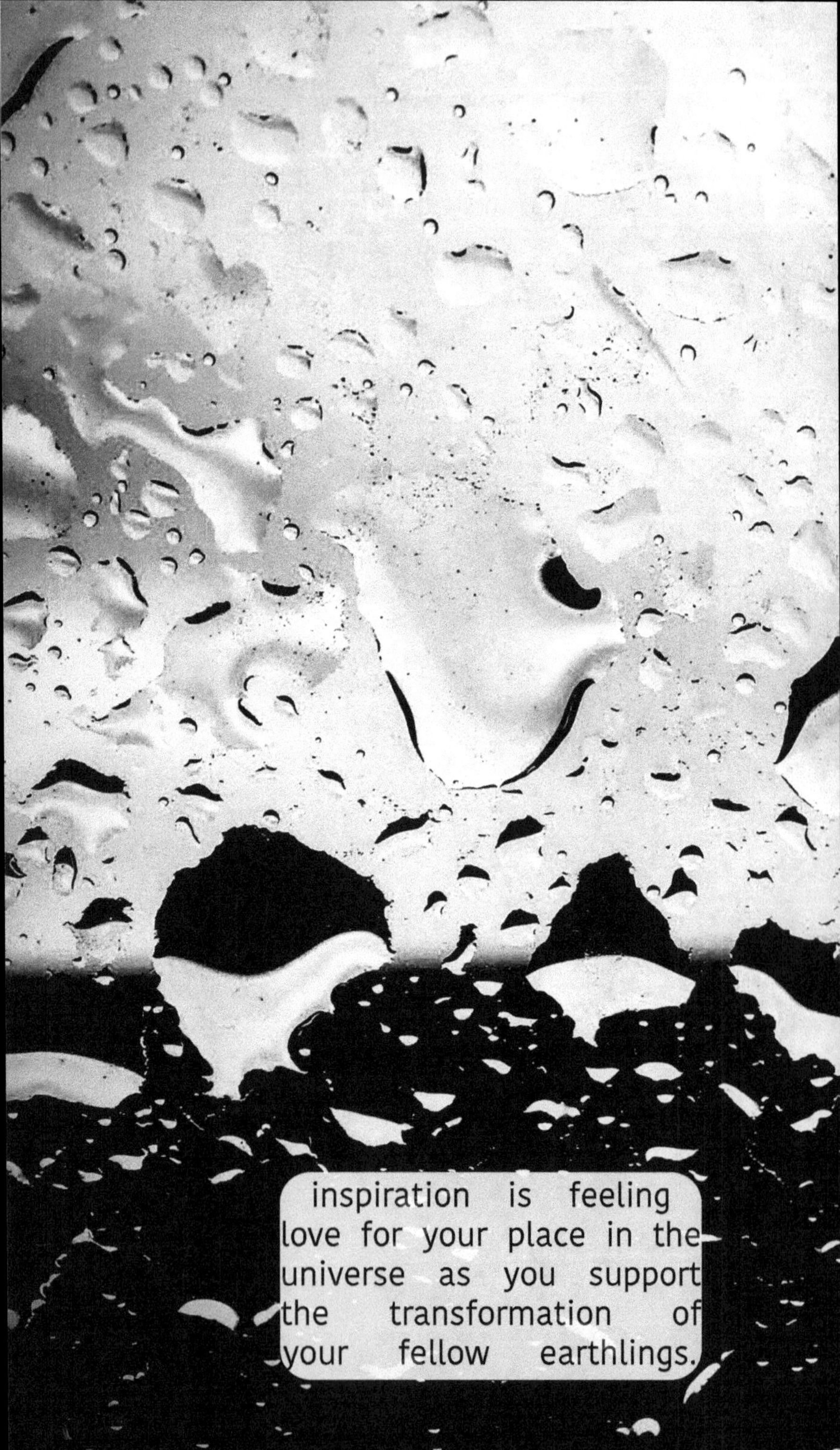

inspiration is feeling
love for your place in the
universe as you support
the transformation of
your fellow earthlings.

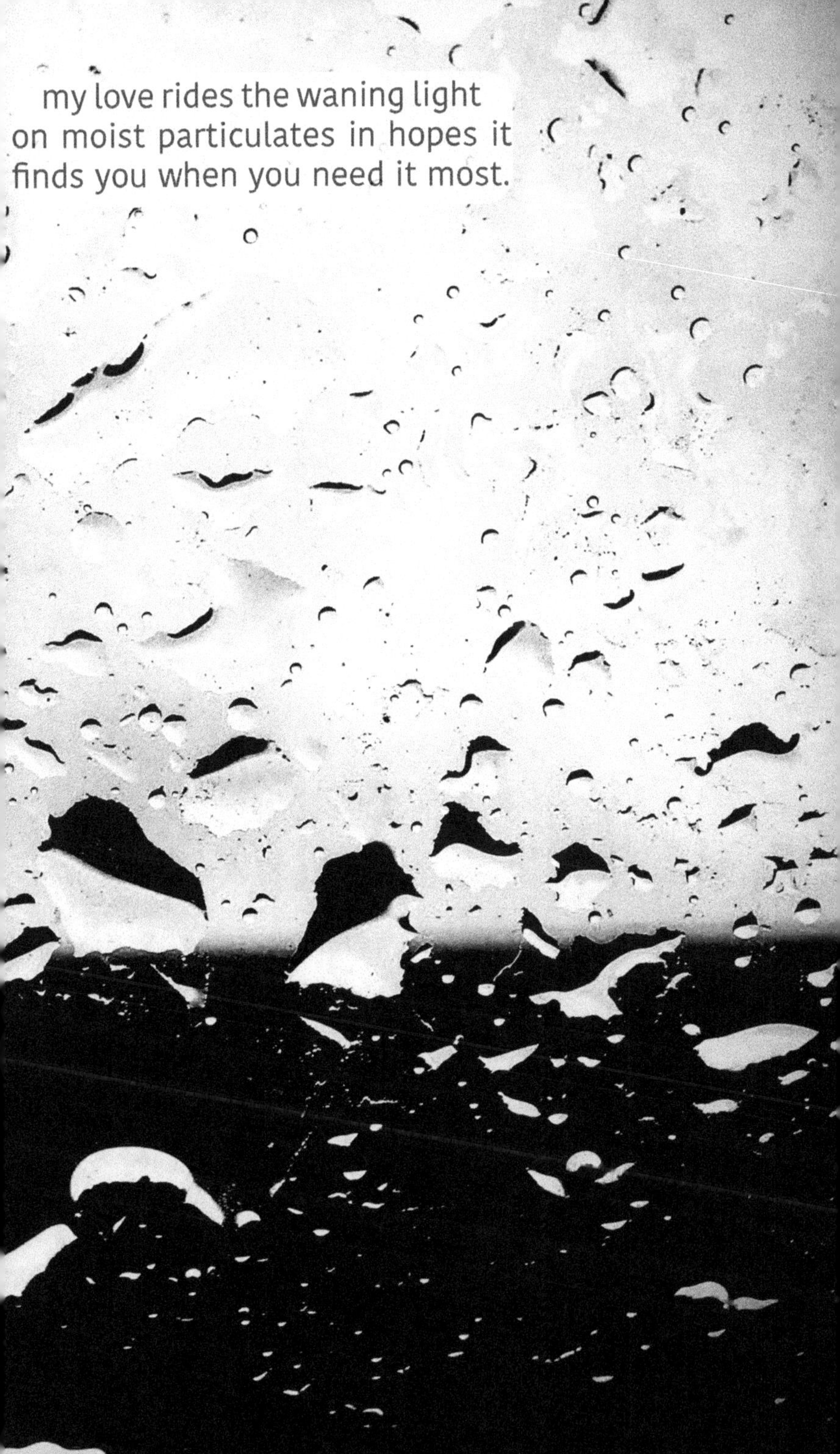

my love rides the waning light
on moist particulates in hopes it
finds you when you need it most.

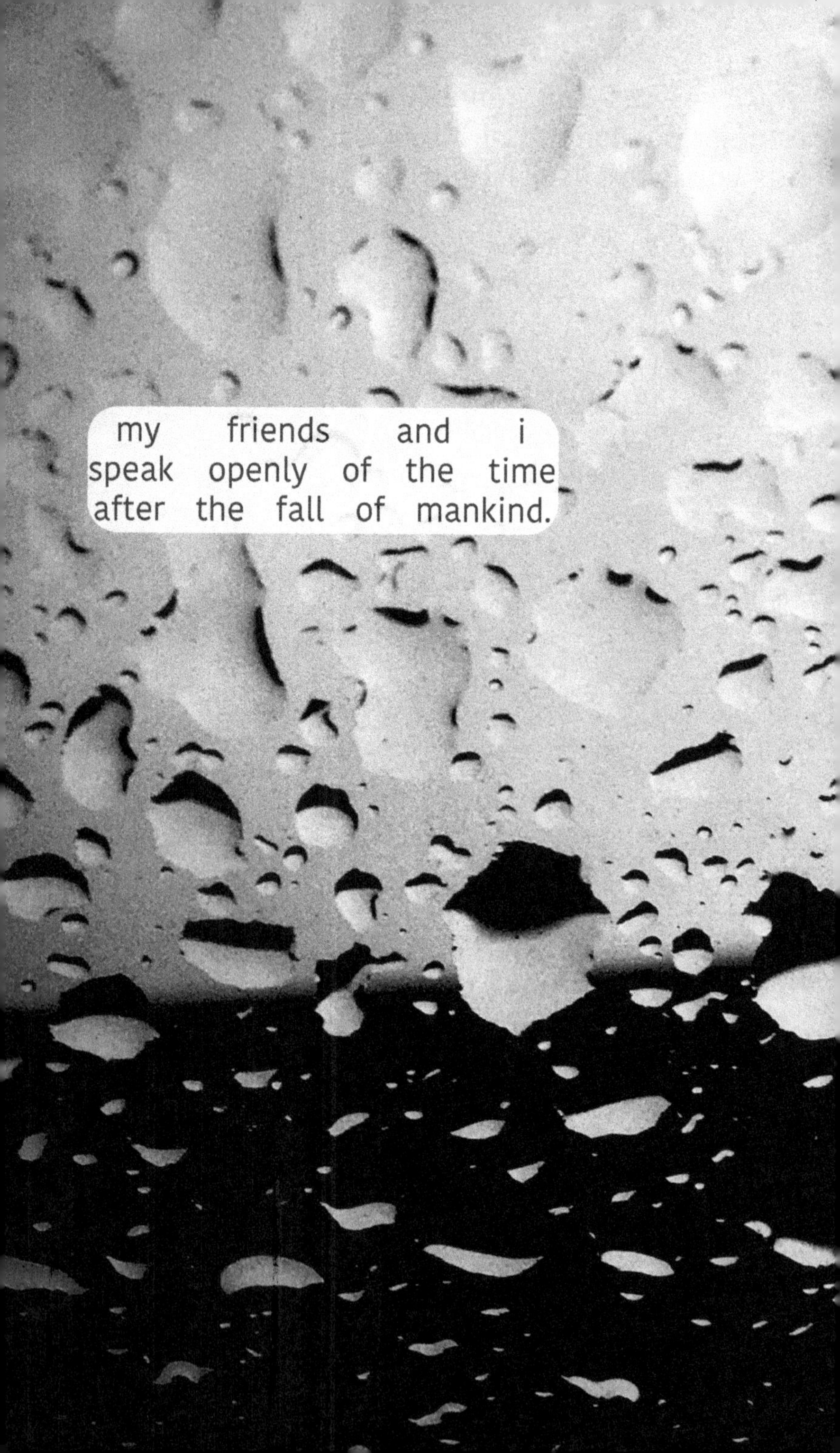

my friends and i speak openly of the time after the fall of mankind.

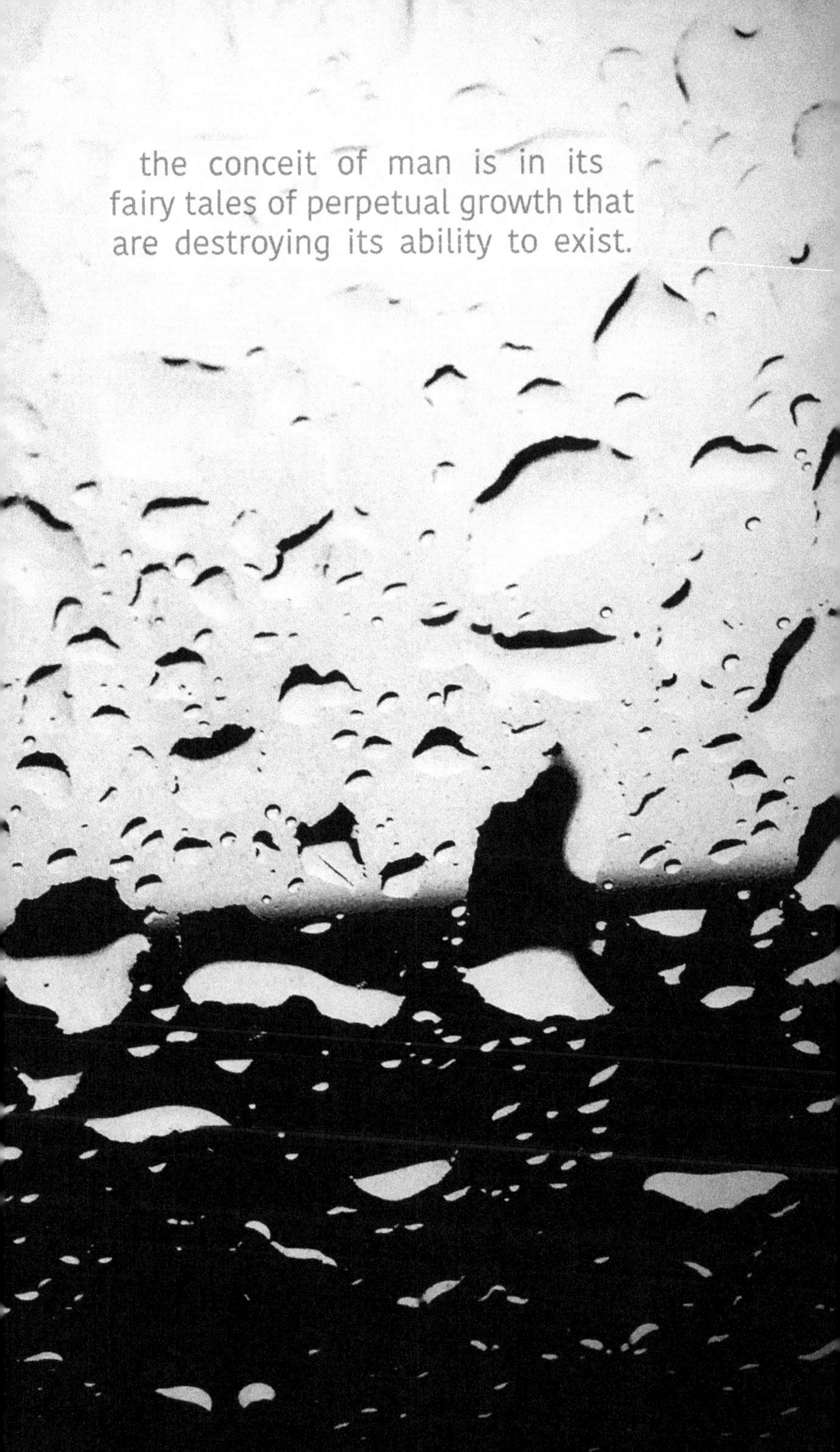
the conceit of man is in its
fairy tales of perpetual growth that
are destroying its ability to exist.

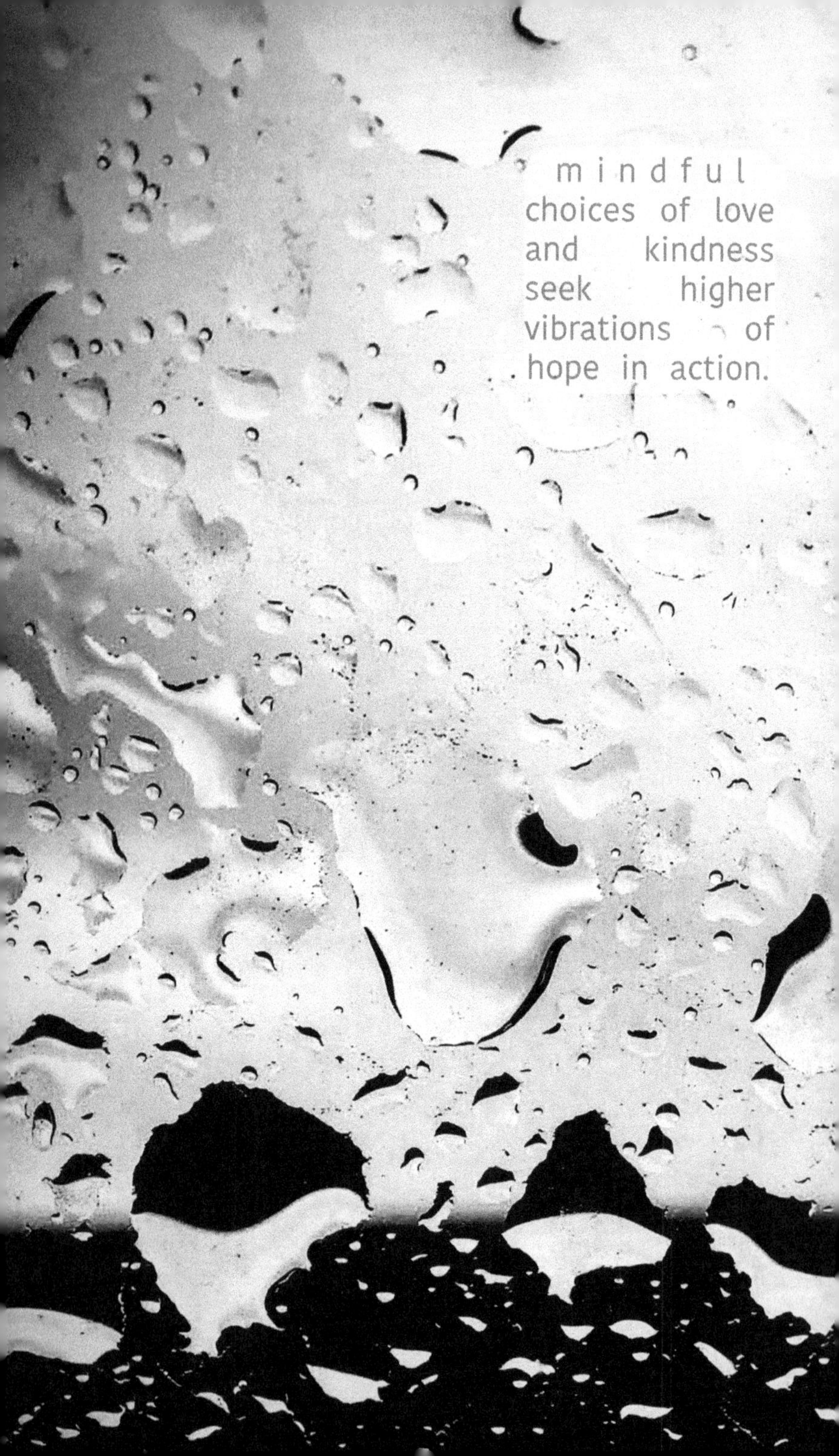

m i n d f u l
choices of love
and   kindness
seek   higher
vibrations   of
hope in action.

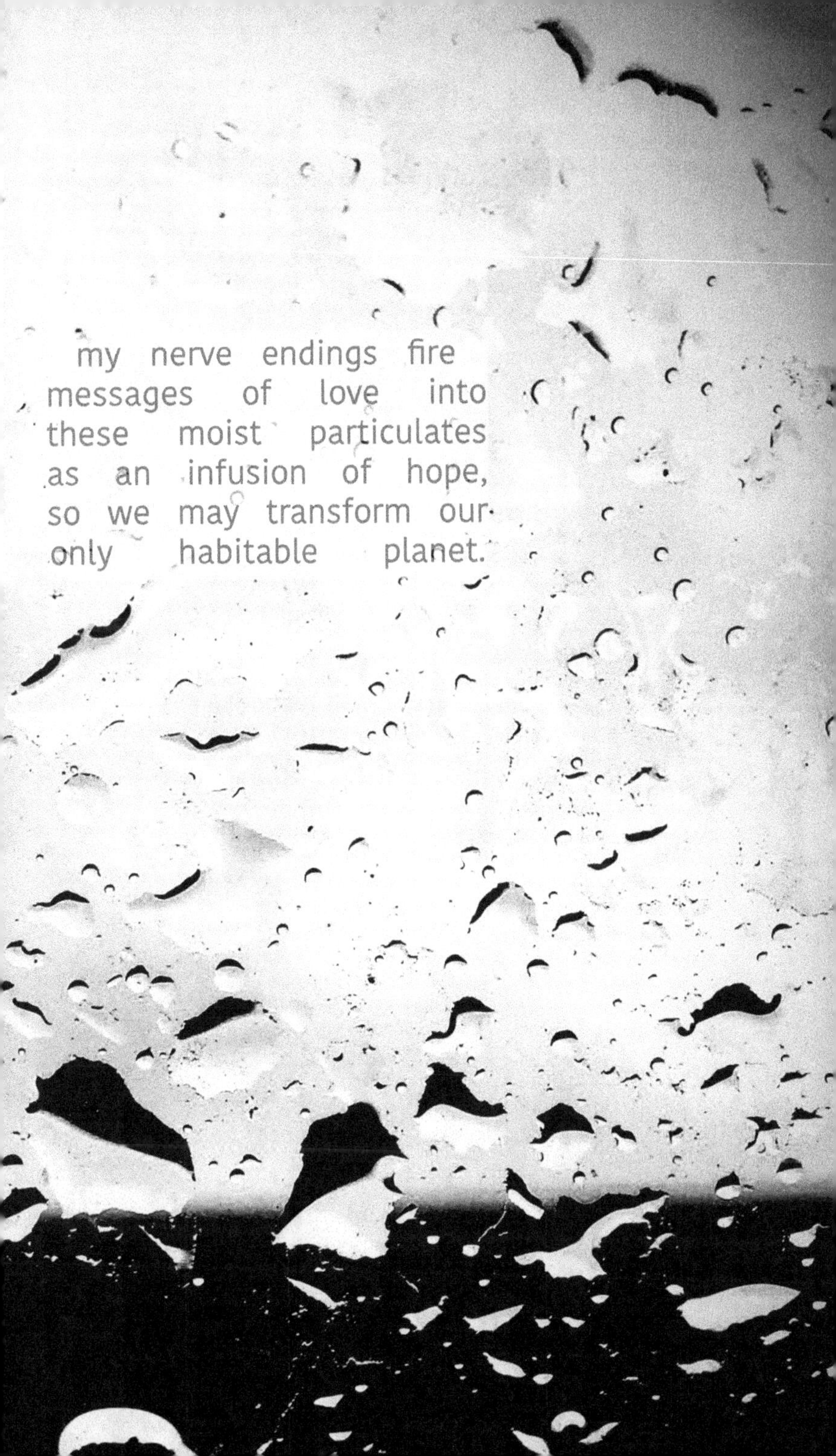
my nerve endings fire
messages of love into
these moist particulates
as an infusion of hope,
so we may transform our
only habitable planet.

your apathy is overcome with acceptance of the choices you must make to survive extinction.

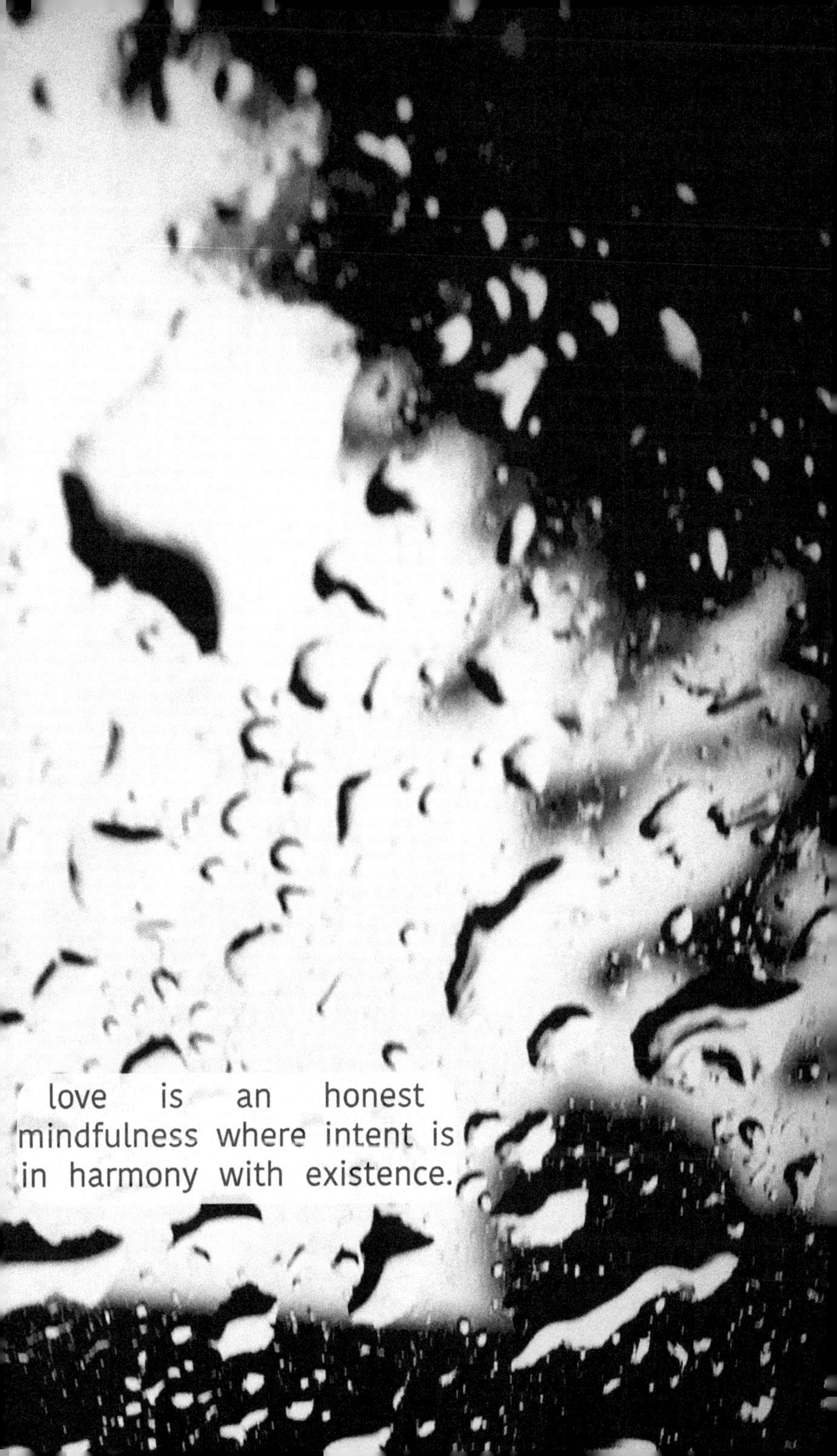

love   is   an   honest
mindfulness where intent is
in harmony with existence.

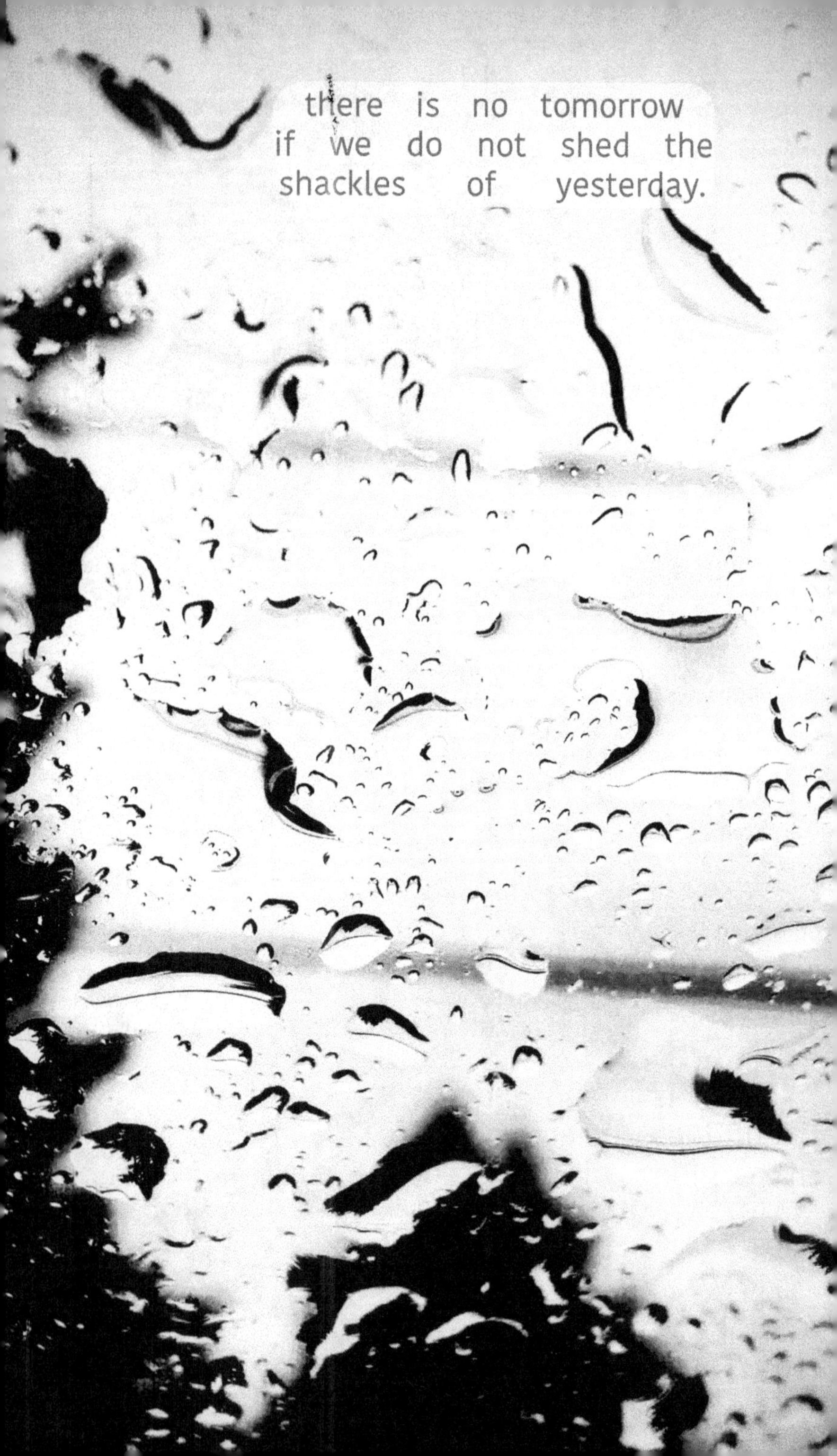

there is no tomorrow
if we do not shed the
shackles of yesterday.

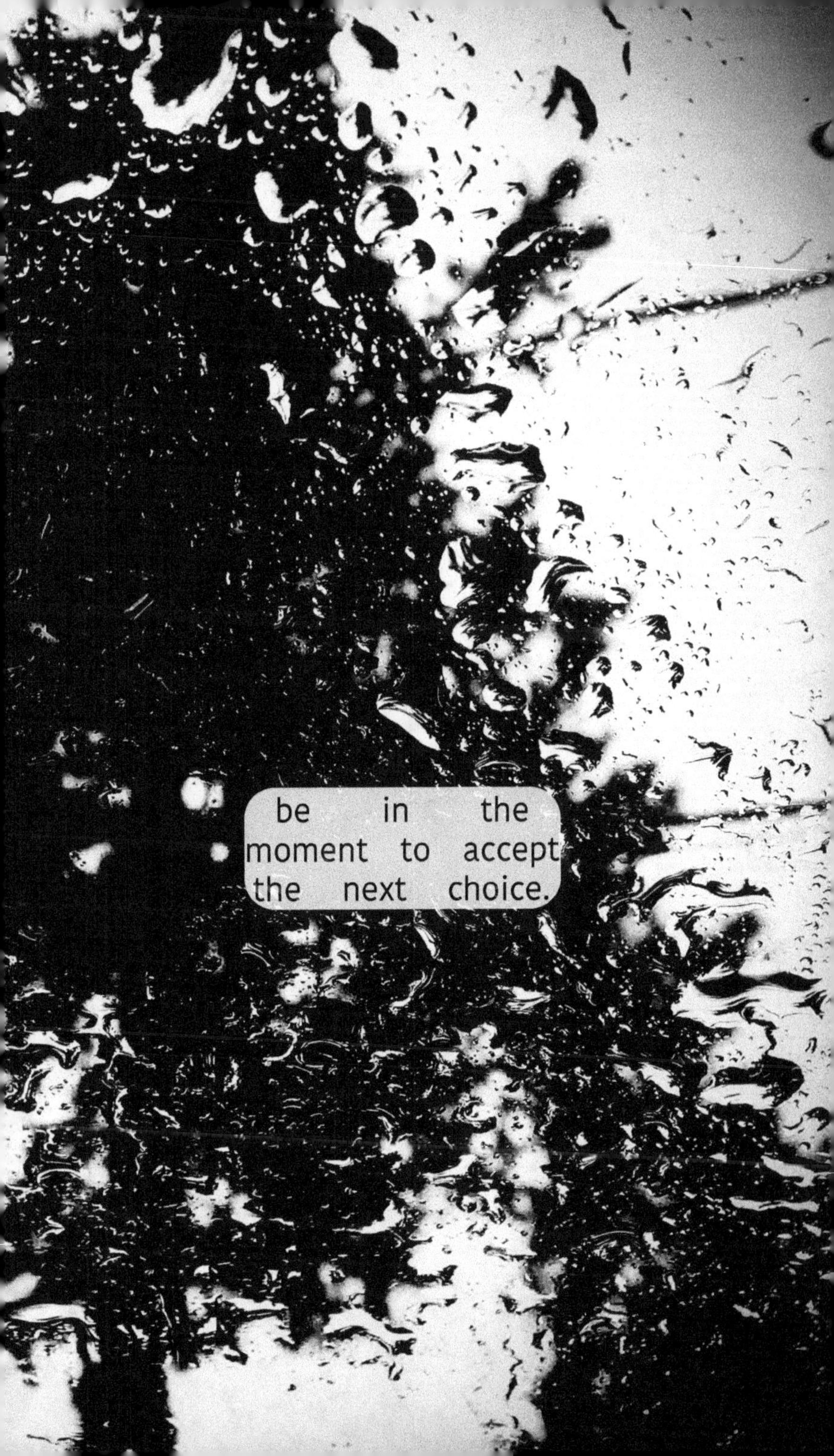
be in the
moment to accept
the next choice.

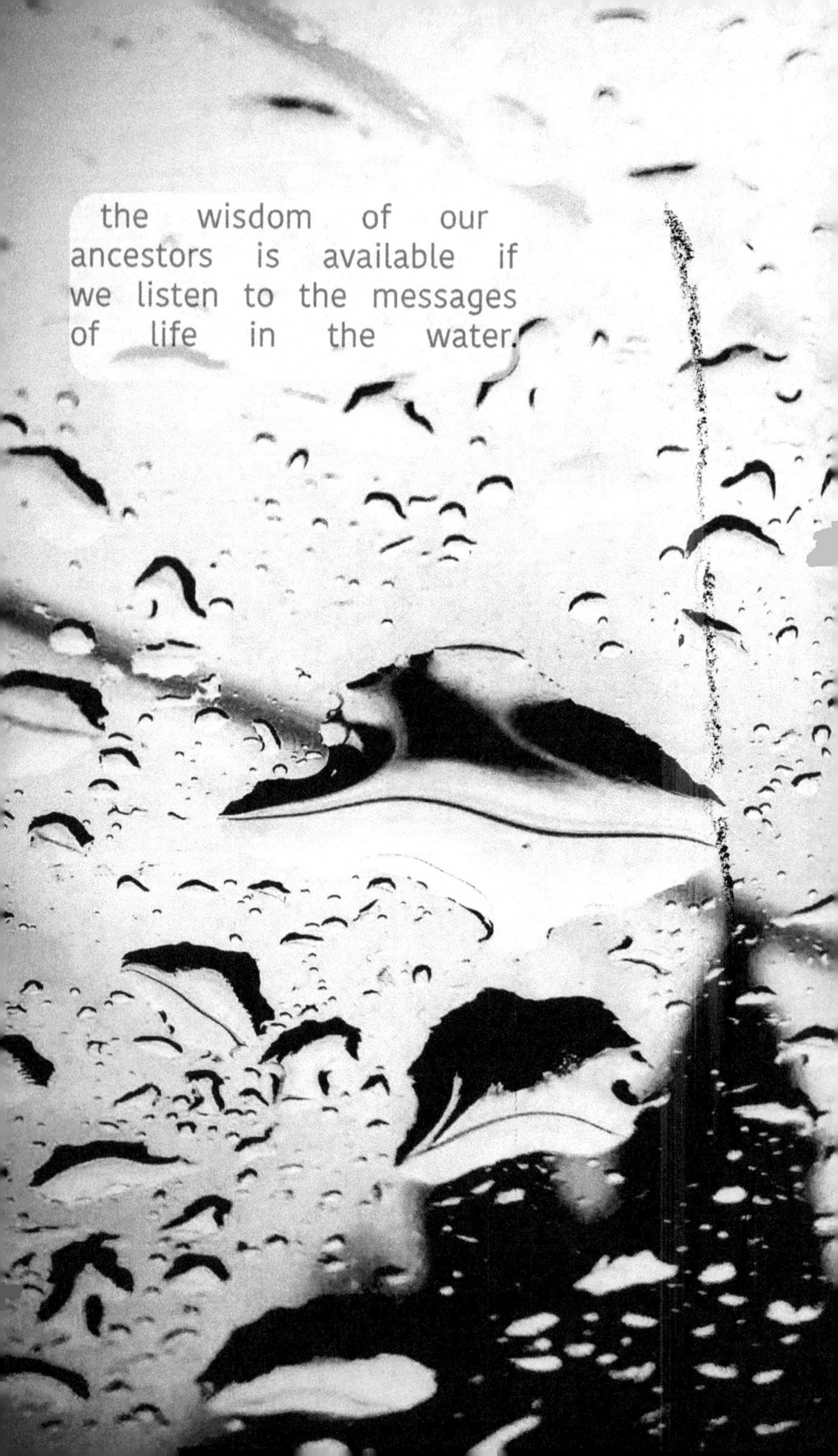
the   wisdom   of   our
ancestors   is   available   if
we listen to the messages
of   life   in   the   water.

listen for the harmony in mindful thoughts, and send that love out into the universe.

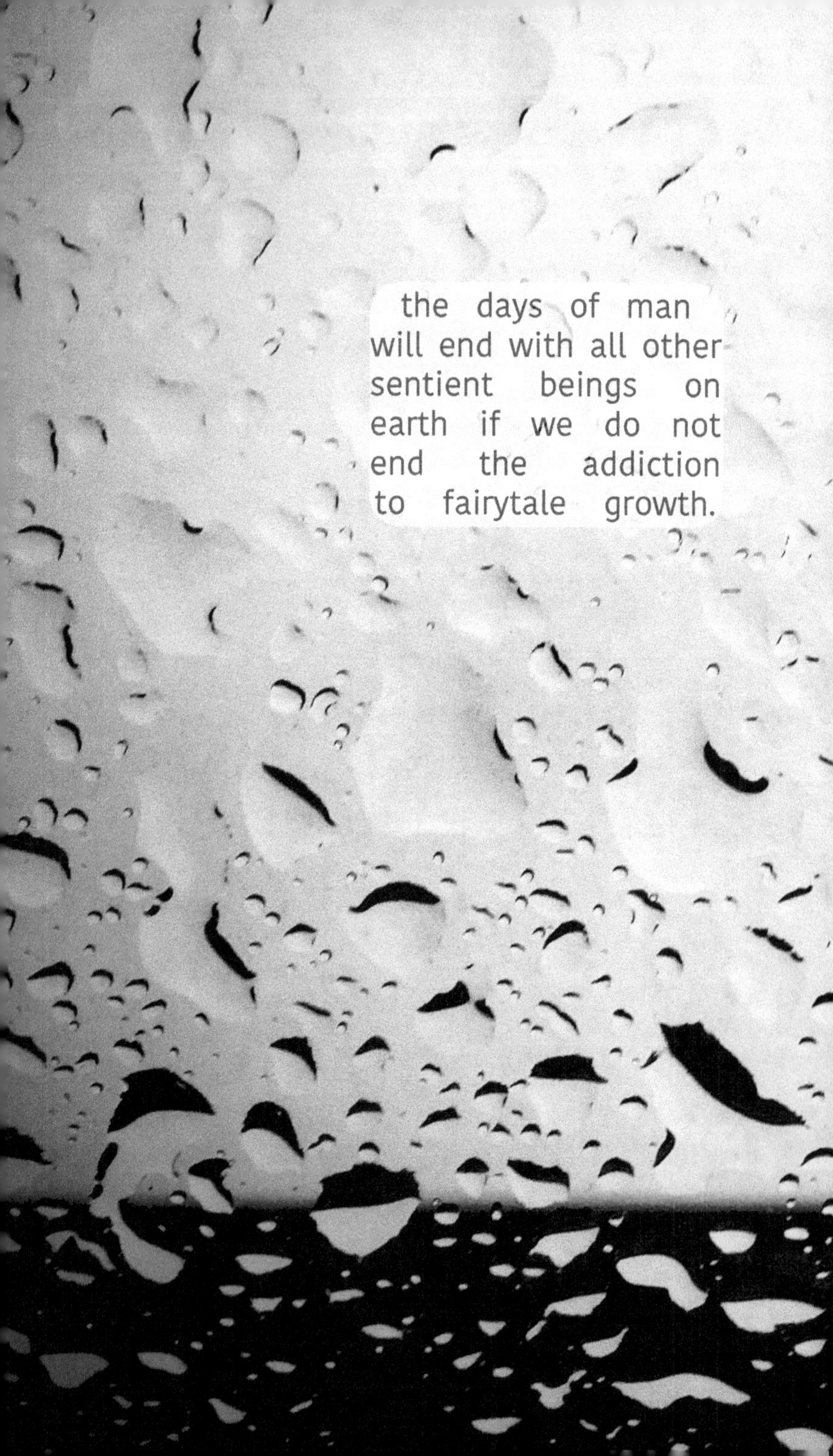

the days of man will end with all other sentient beings on earth if we do not end the addiction to fairytale growth.

the future is a utopia of mindful joy at being balanced with the universe, if we let go of consumption fairy tales of perpetual growth.

be kind to
all   sentient
b e i n g s .

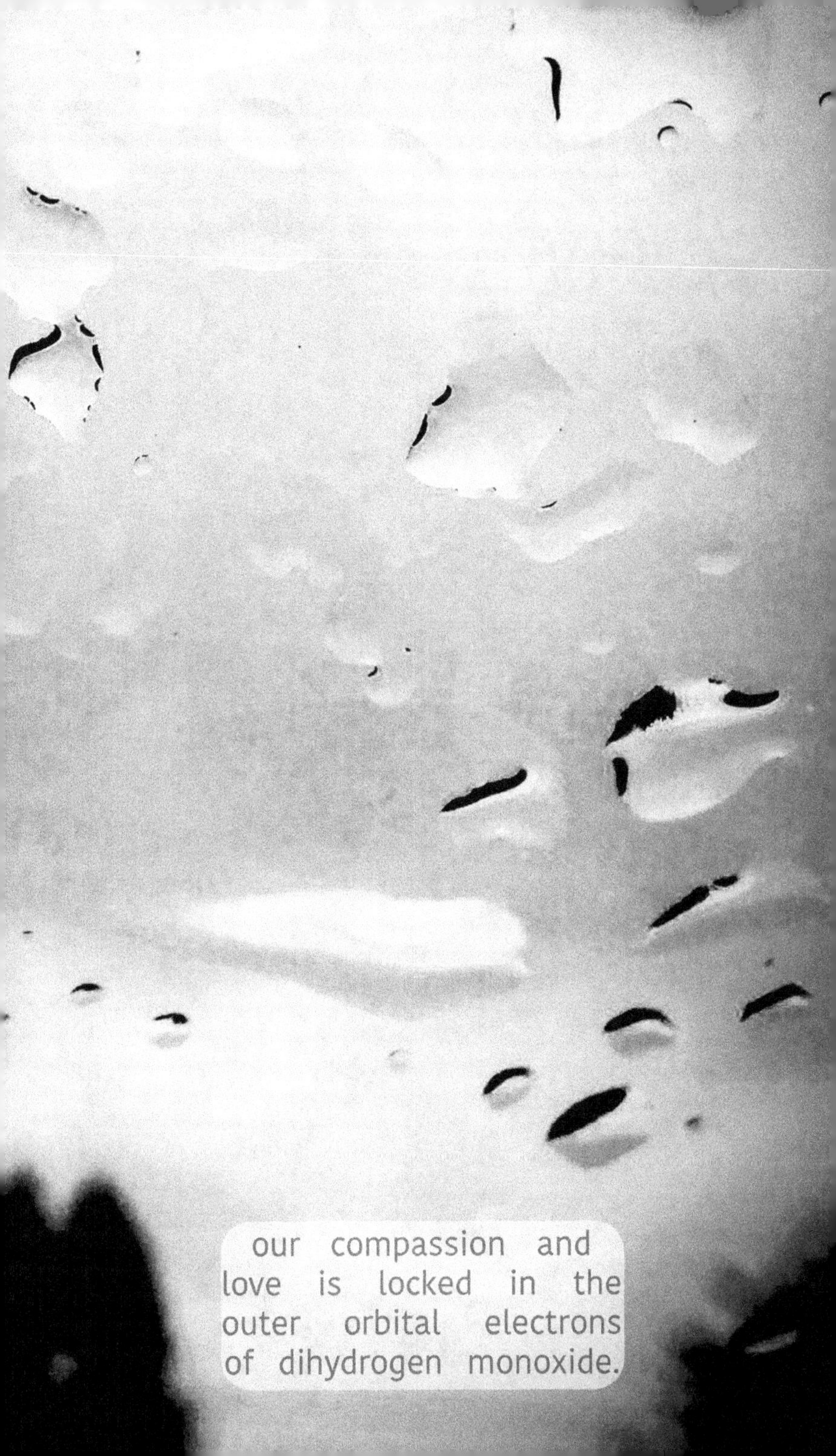

our compassion and
love is locked in the
outer orbital electrons
of dihydrogen monoxide.

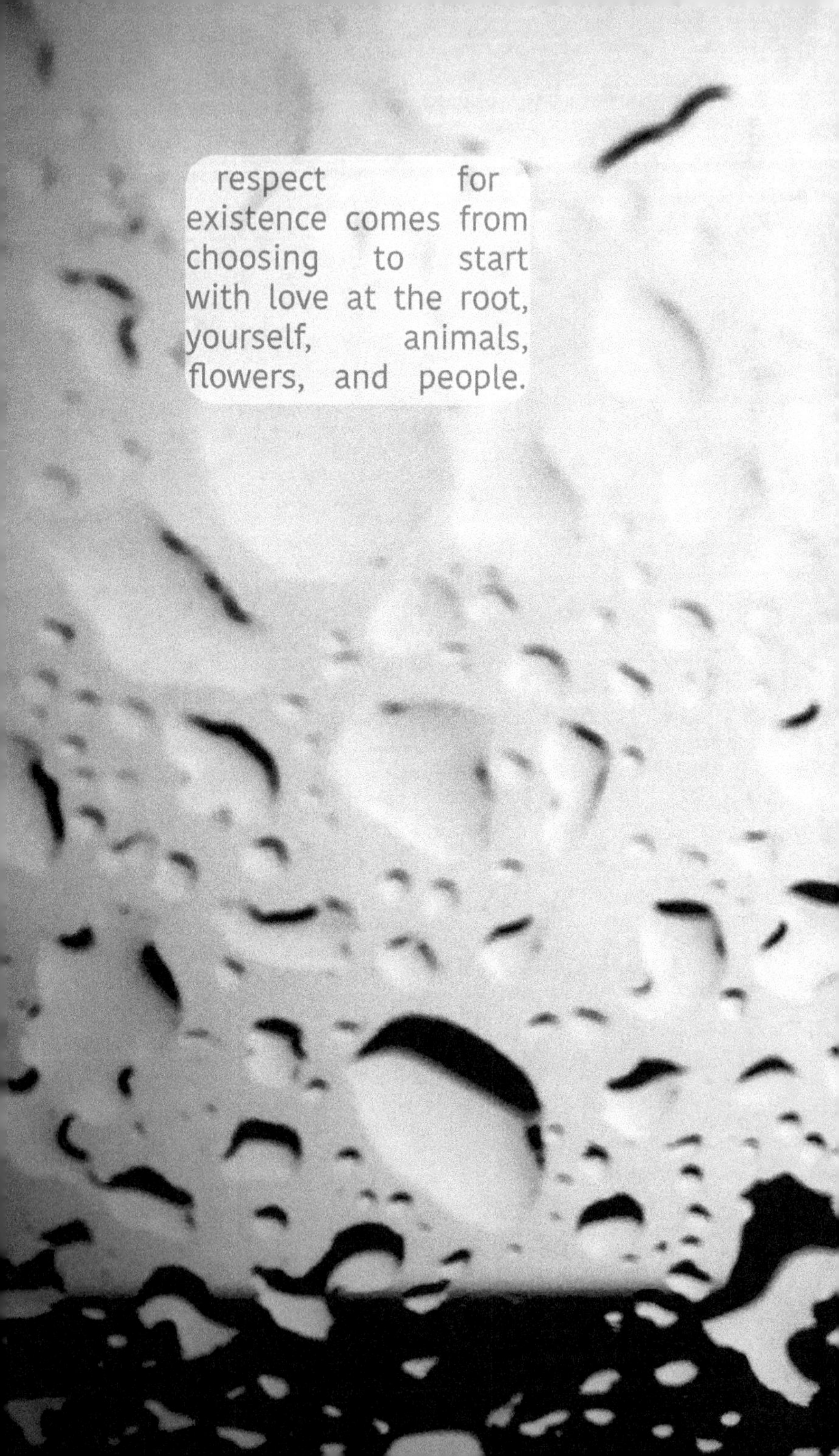
respect for existence comes from choosing to start with love at the root, yourself, animals, flowers, and people.

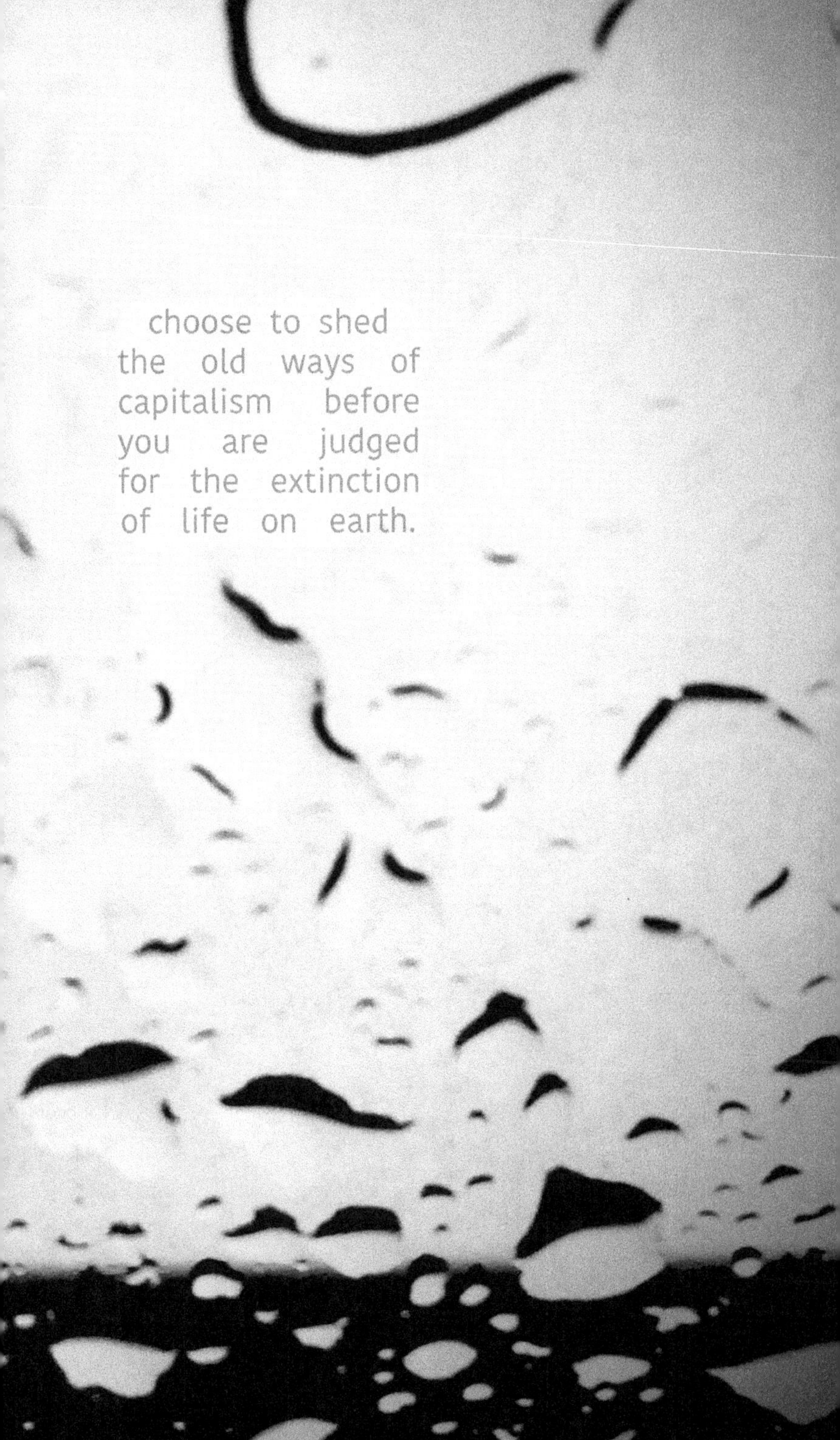
choose to shed
the old ways of
capitalism before
you are judged
for the extinction
of life on earth.

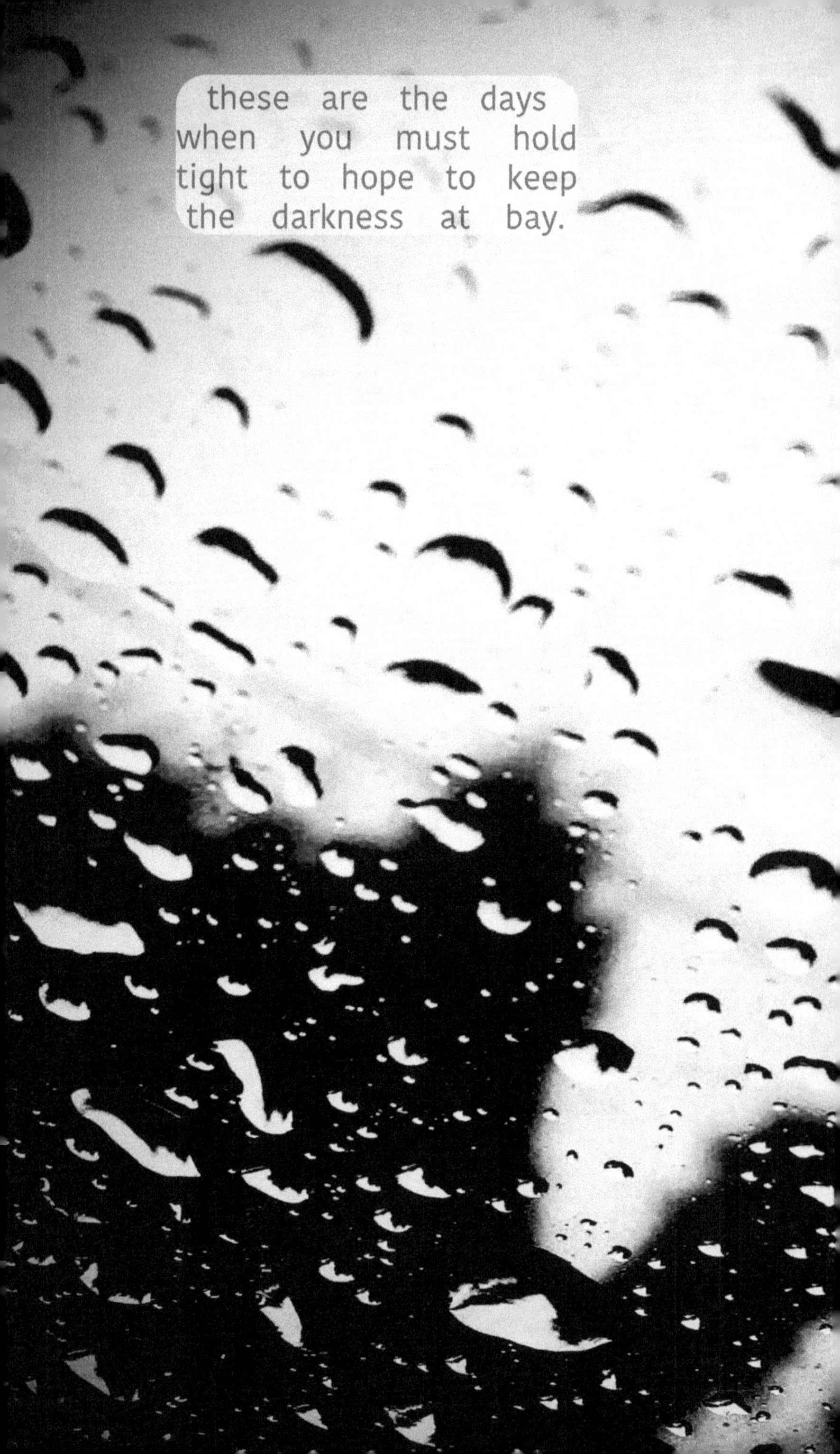

these are the days
when you must hold
tight to hope to keep
the darkness at bay.

these moist droplets carry all the love and hope required to change course if we reach deep inside for the strength to make selfless choices.

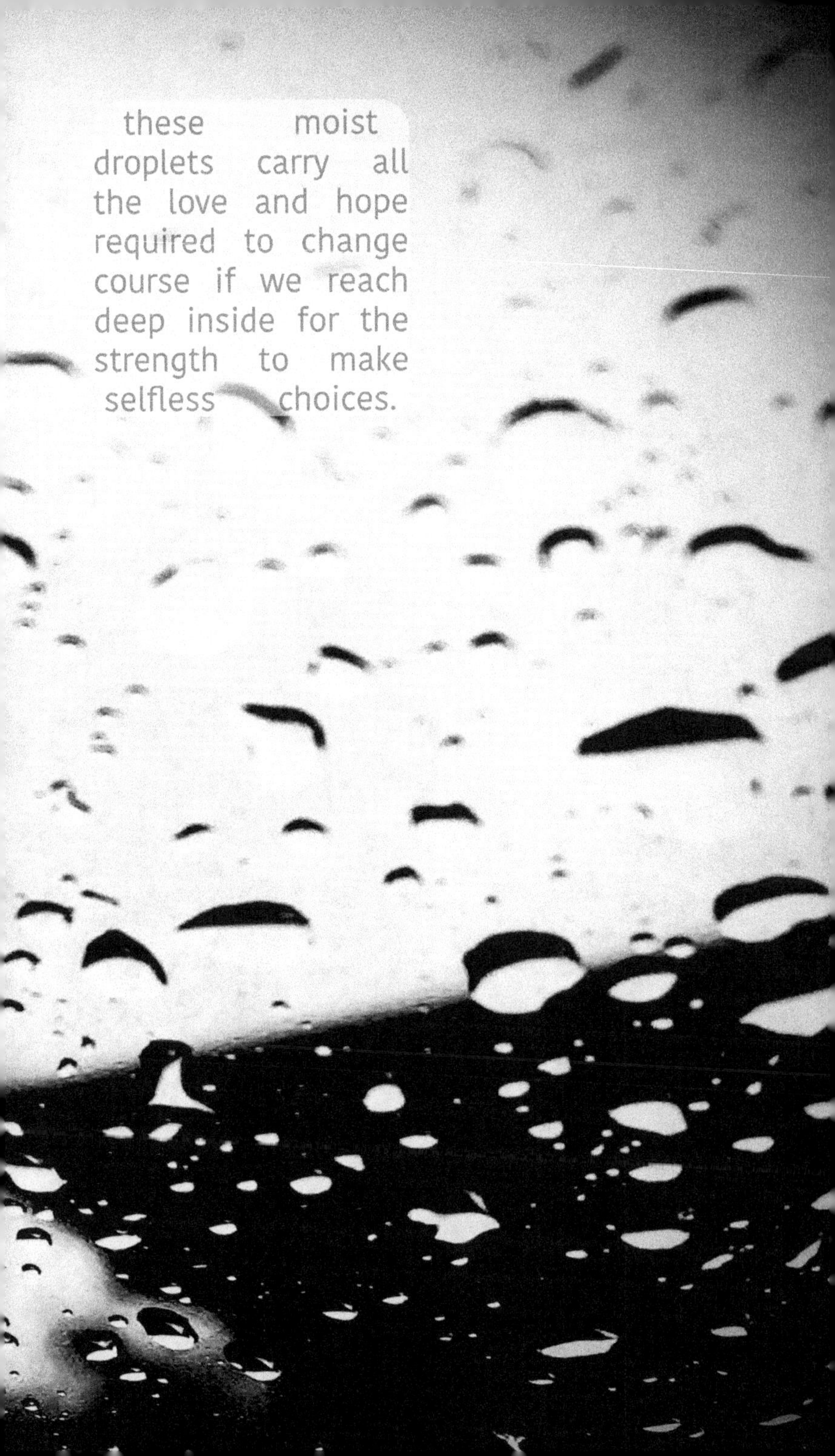

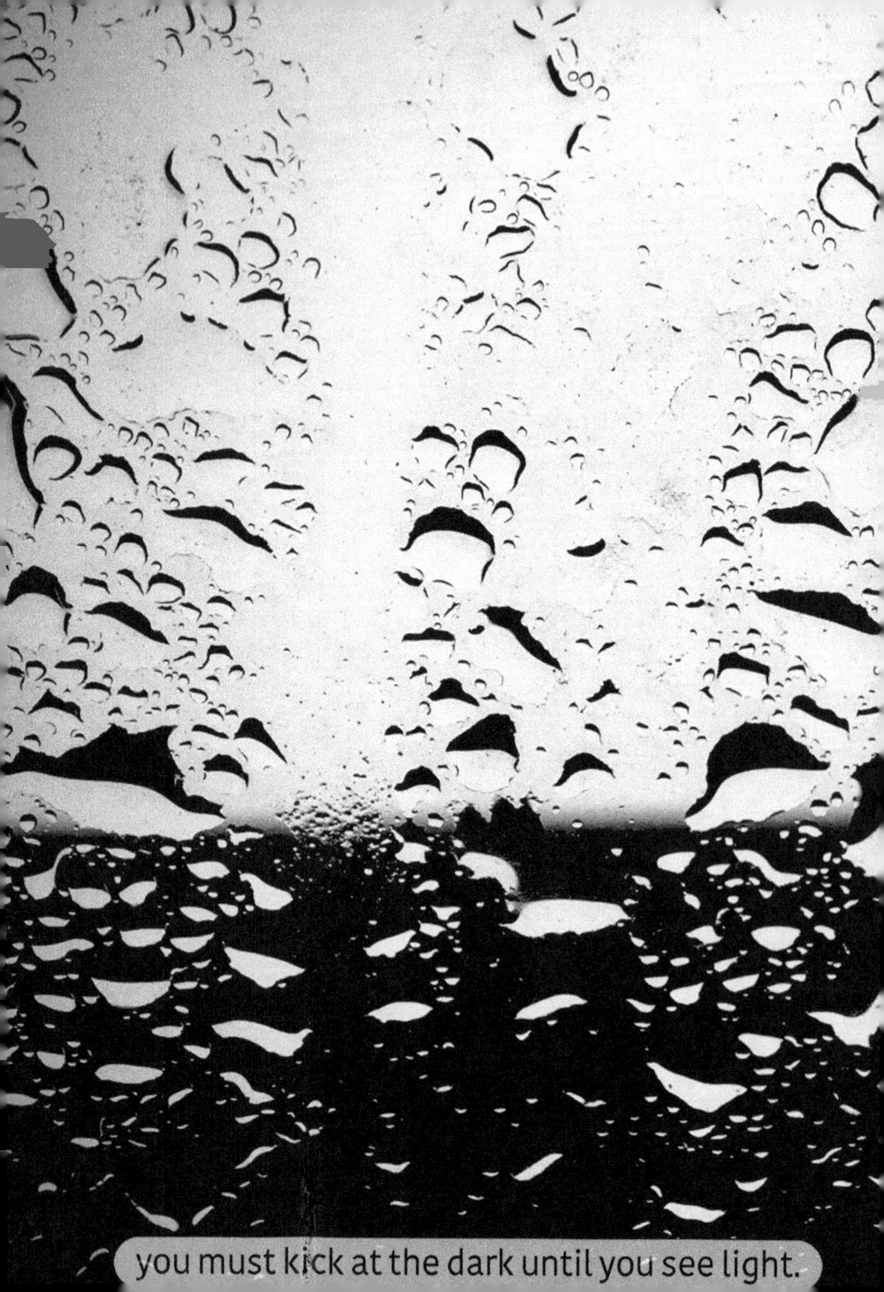
you must kick at the dark until you see light.

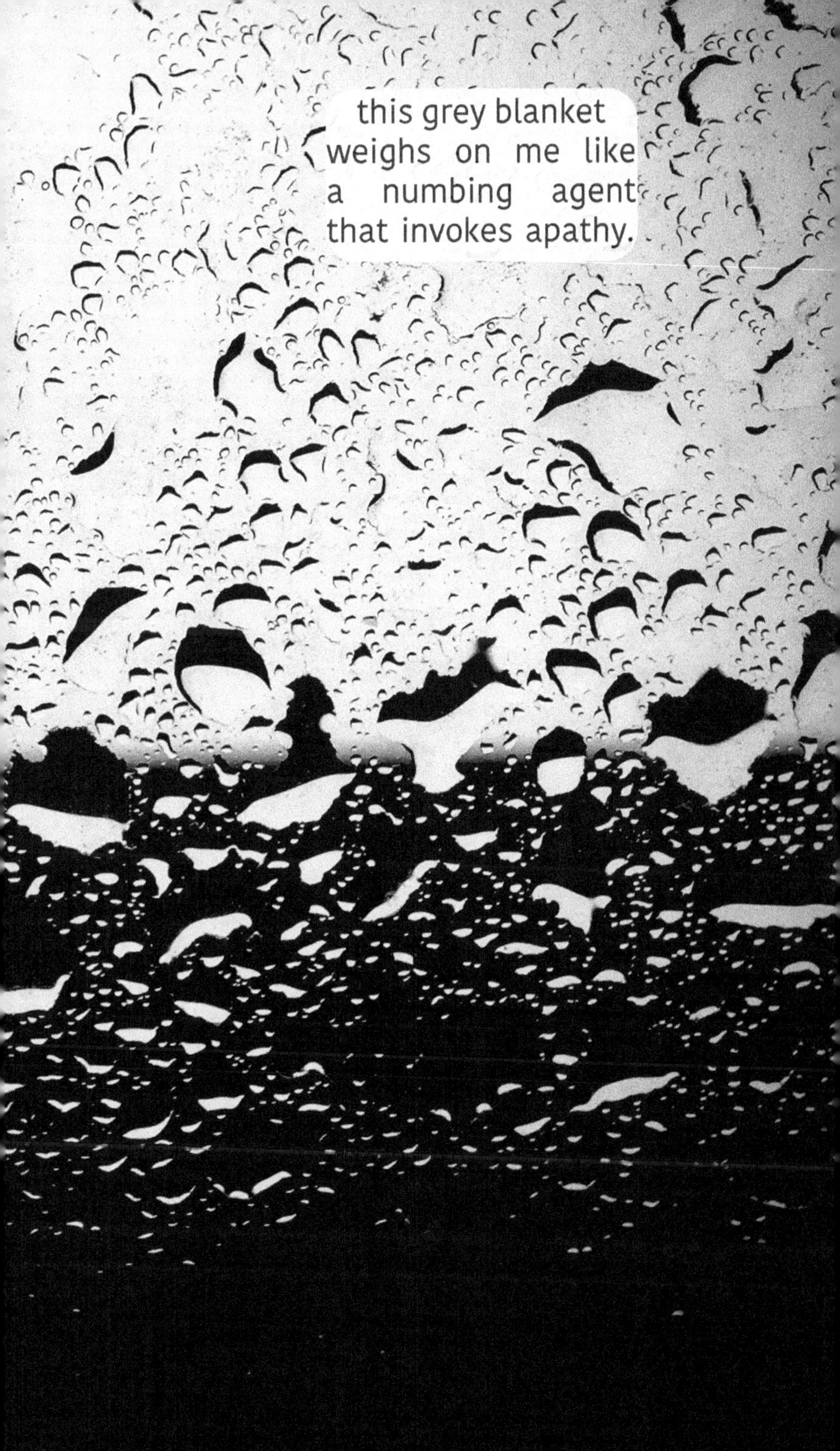

this grey blanket
weighs on me like
a numbing agent
that invokes apathy.

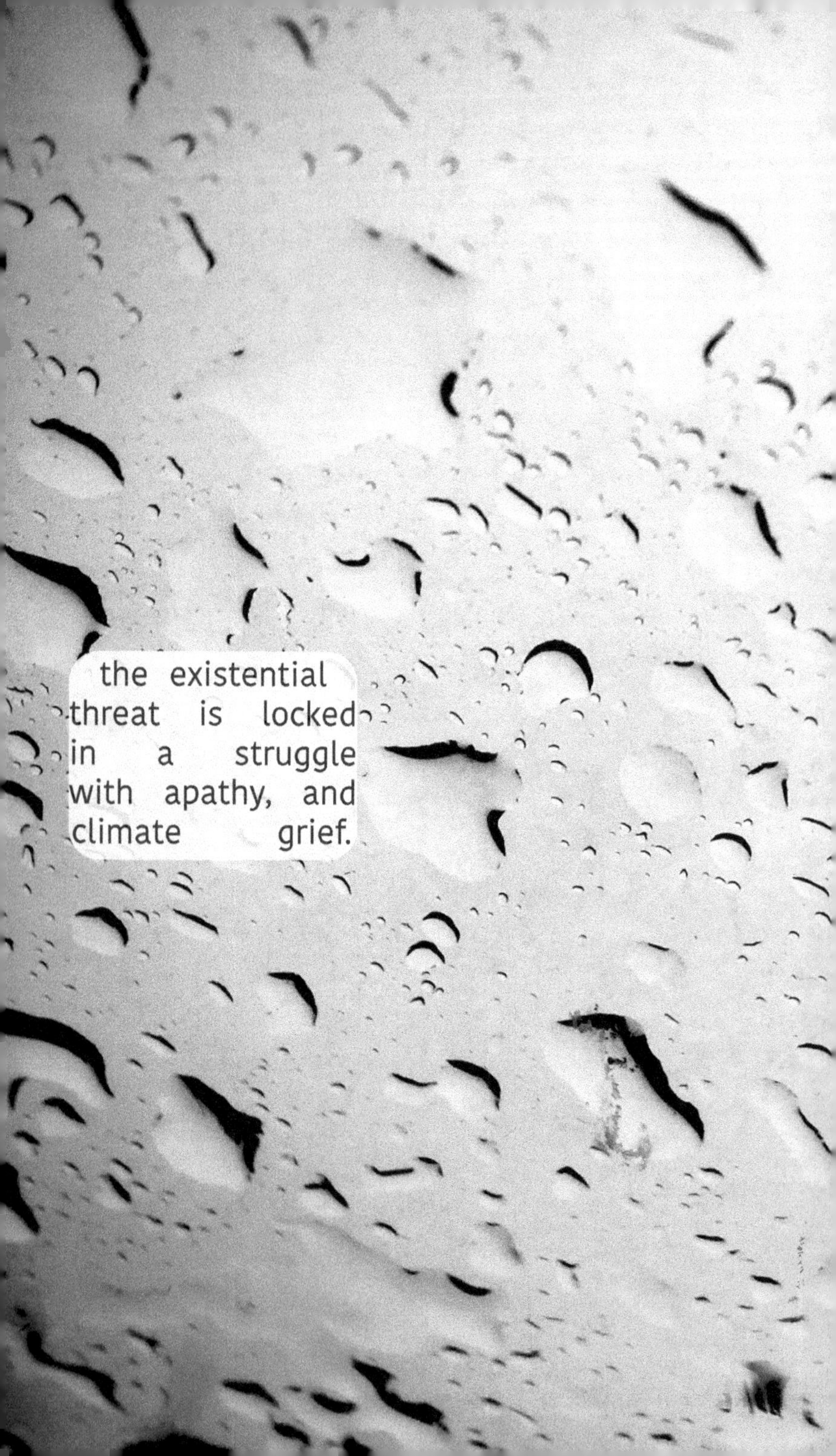

the existential threat is locked in a struggle with apathy, and climate grief.

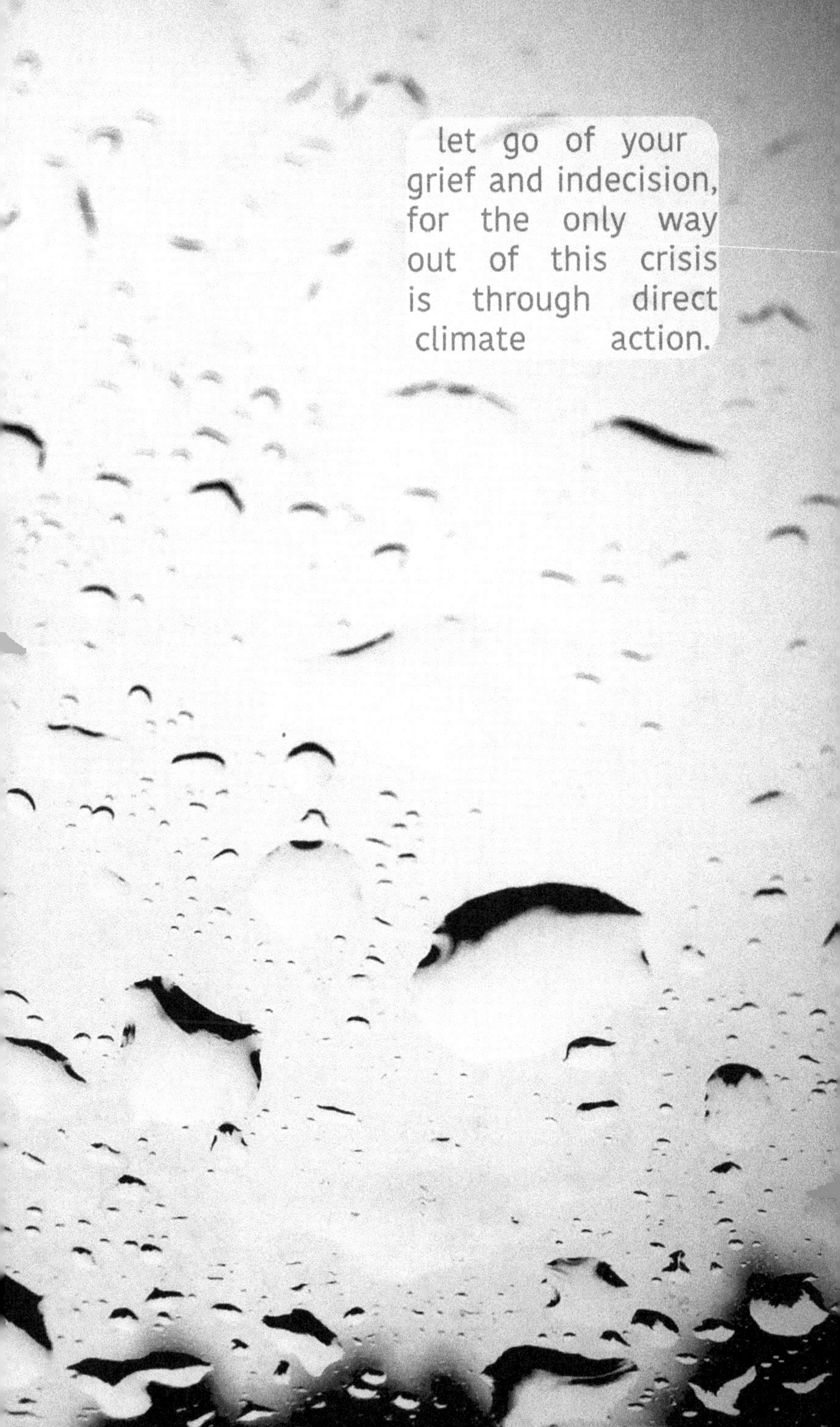
let go of your grief and indecision, for the only way out of this crisis is through direct climate action.

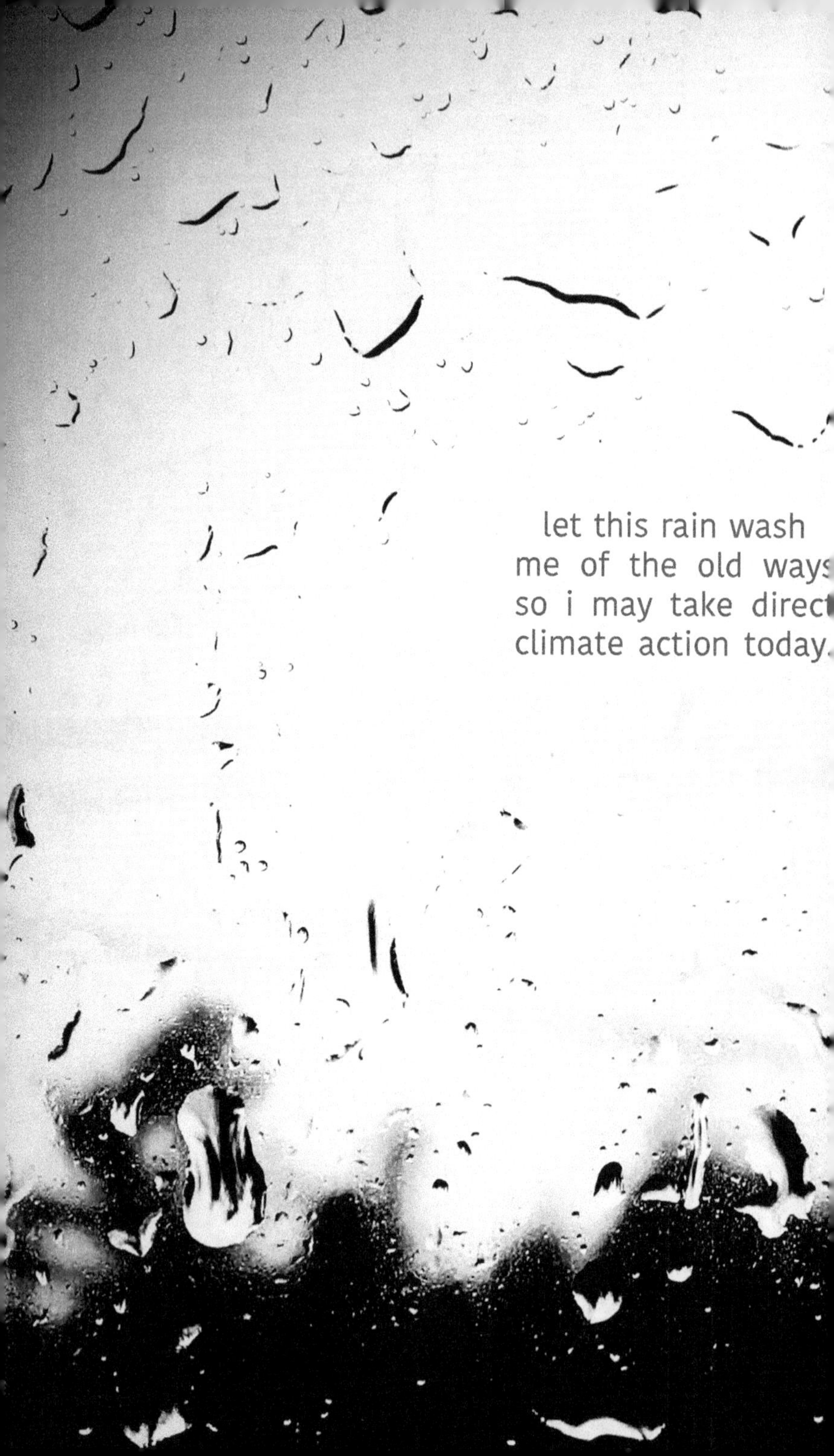
let this rain wash
me of the old ways
so i may take direct
climate action today.

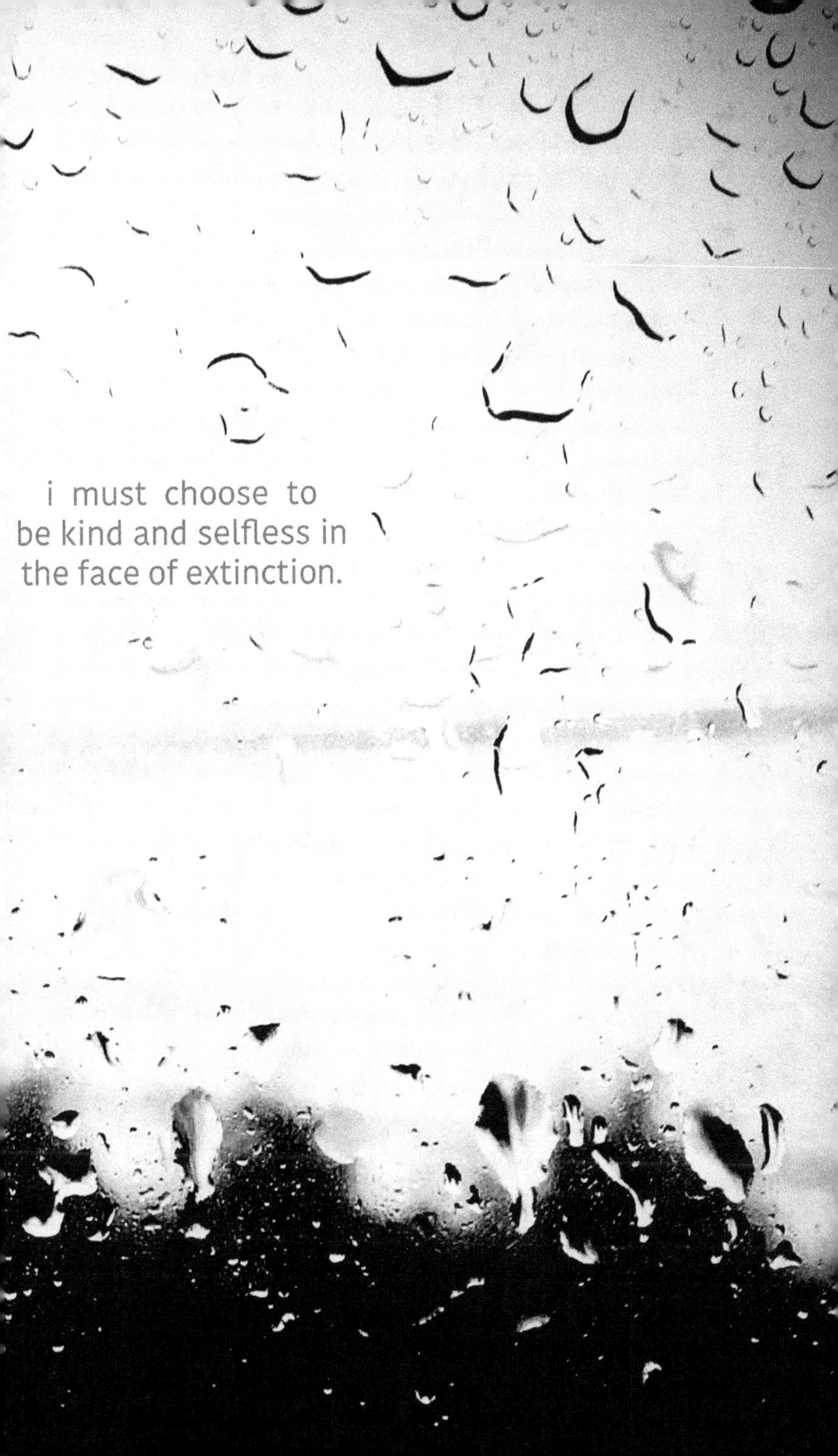
i must choose to
be kind and selfless in
the face of extinction.

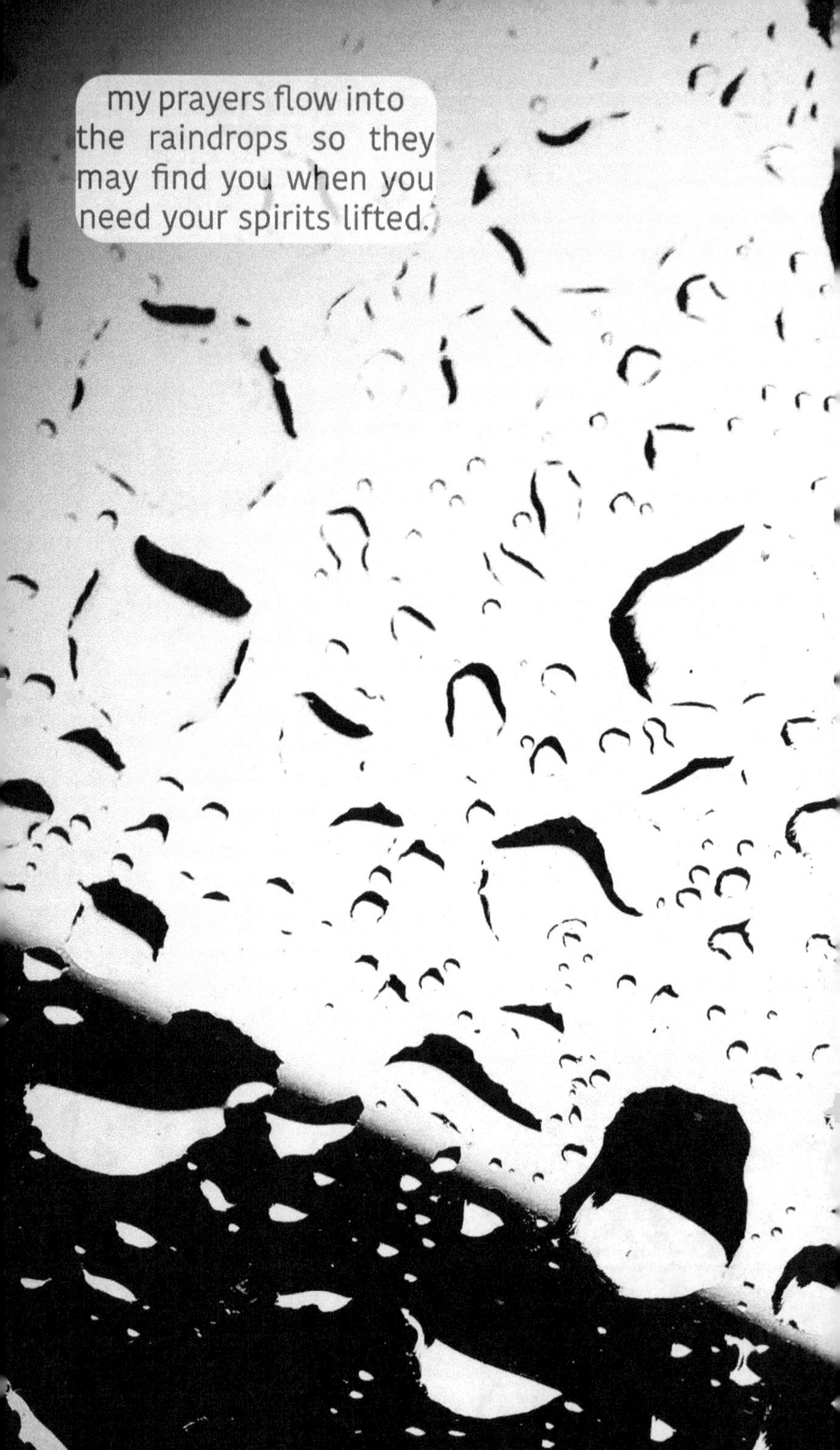
my prayers flow into
the raindrops so they
may find you when you
need your spirits lifted.

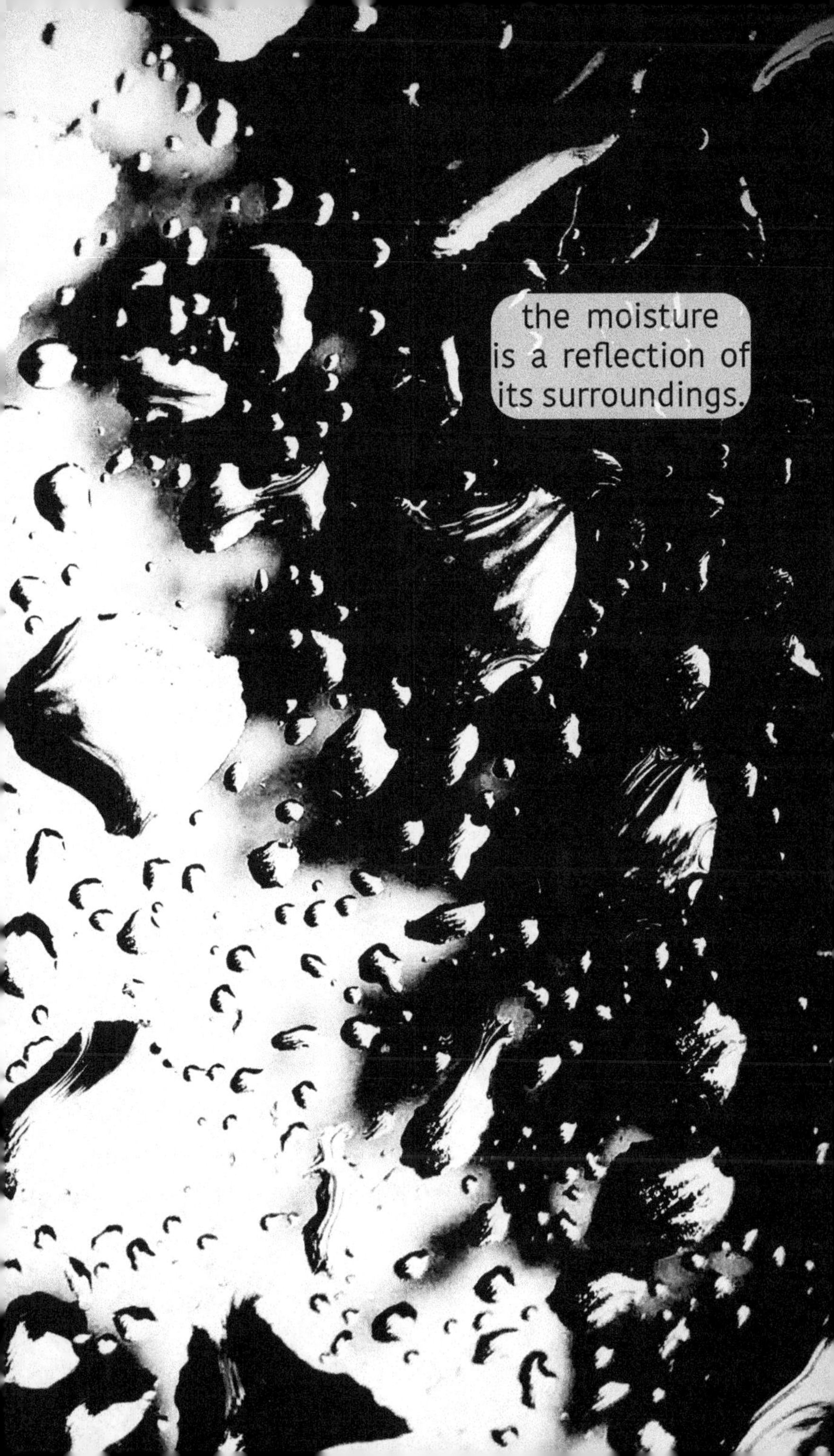
the moisture
is a reflection of
its surroundings.

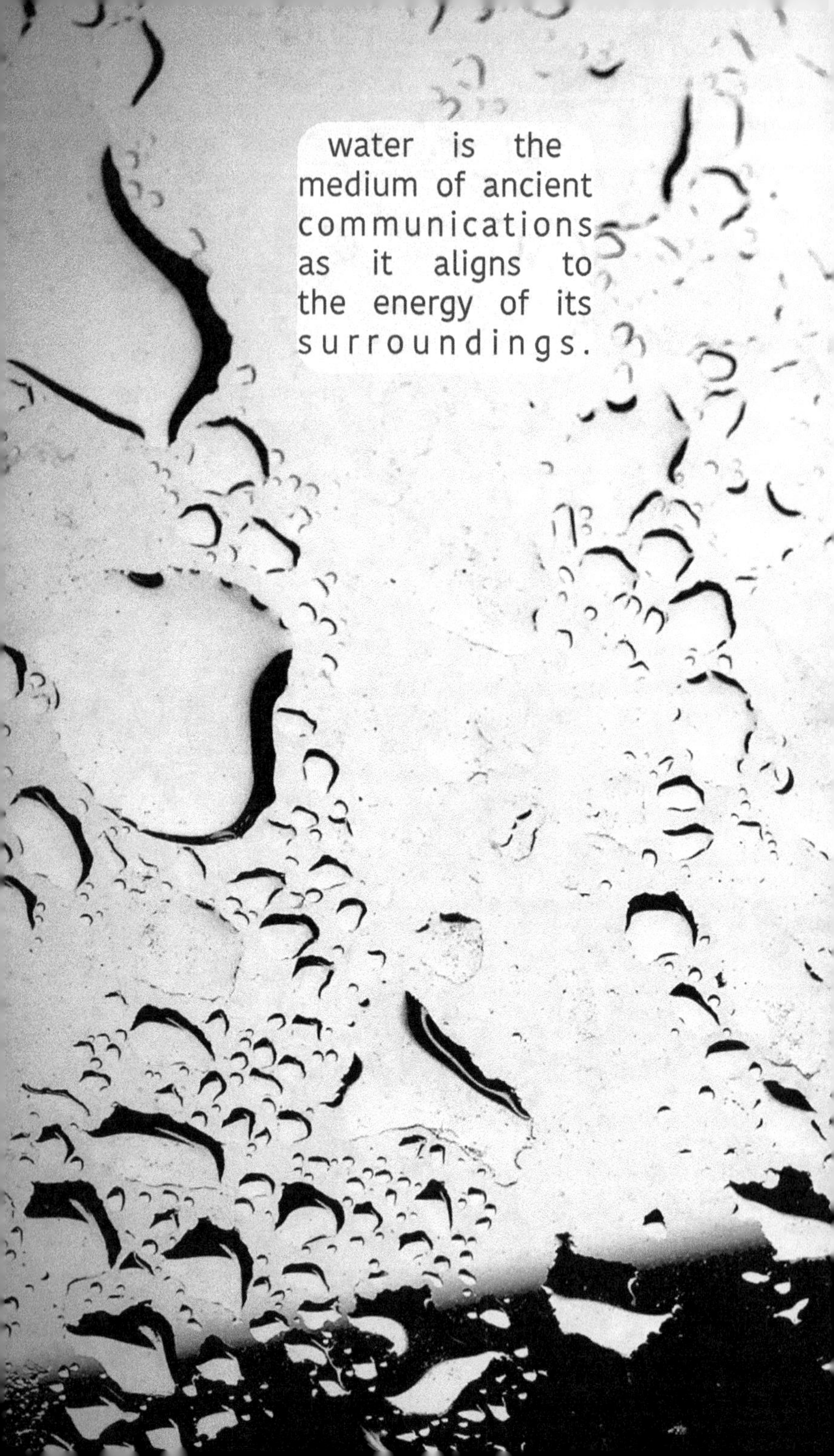
water is the
medium of ancient
communications
as it aligns to
the energy of its
surroundings.

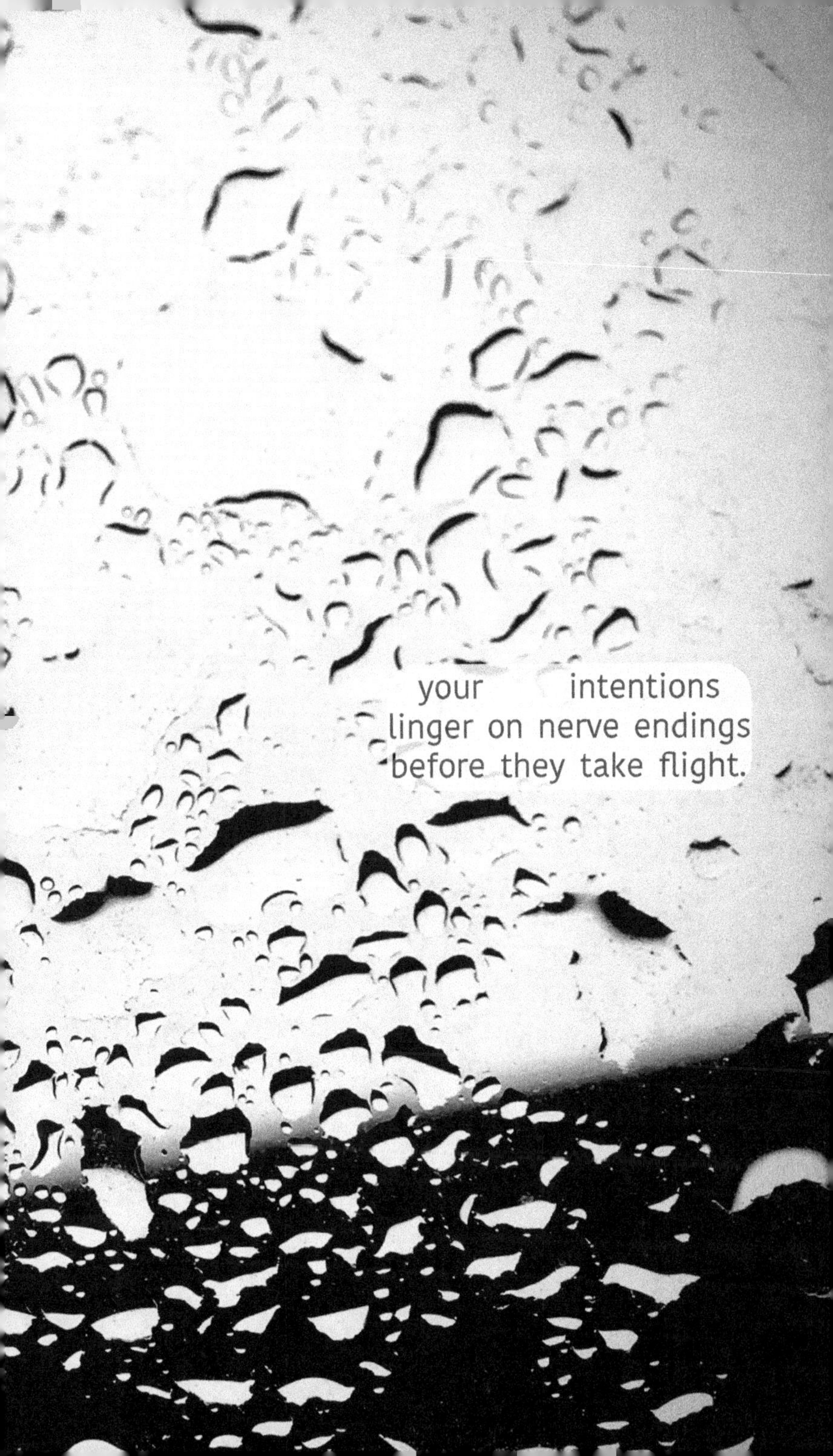
your   intentions
linger on nerve endings
before they take flight.

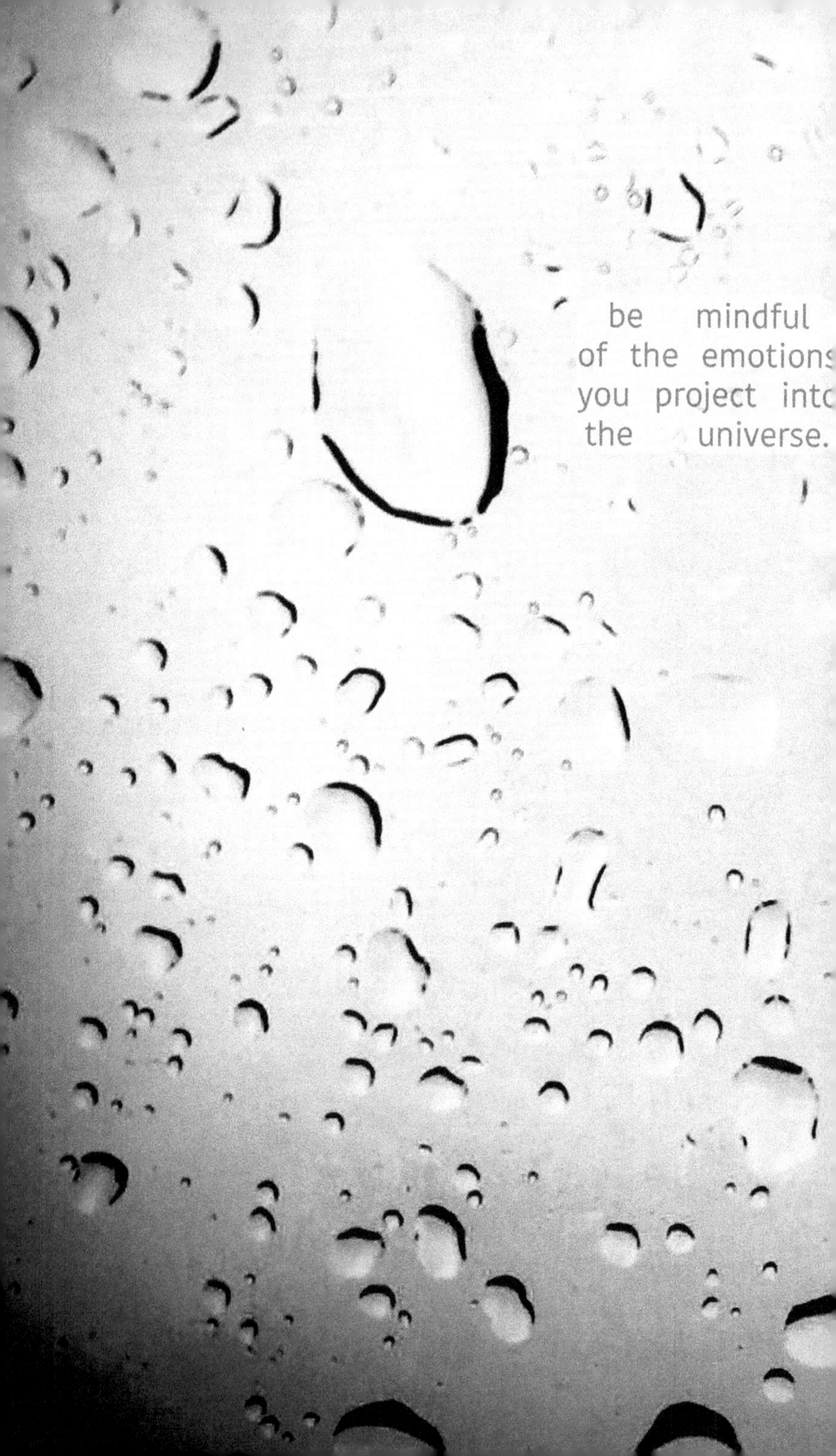

be   mindful
of the emotions
you project into
the   universe.

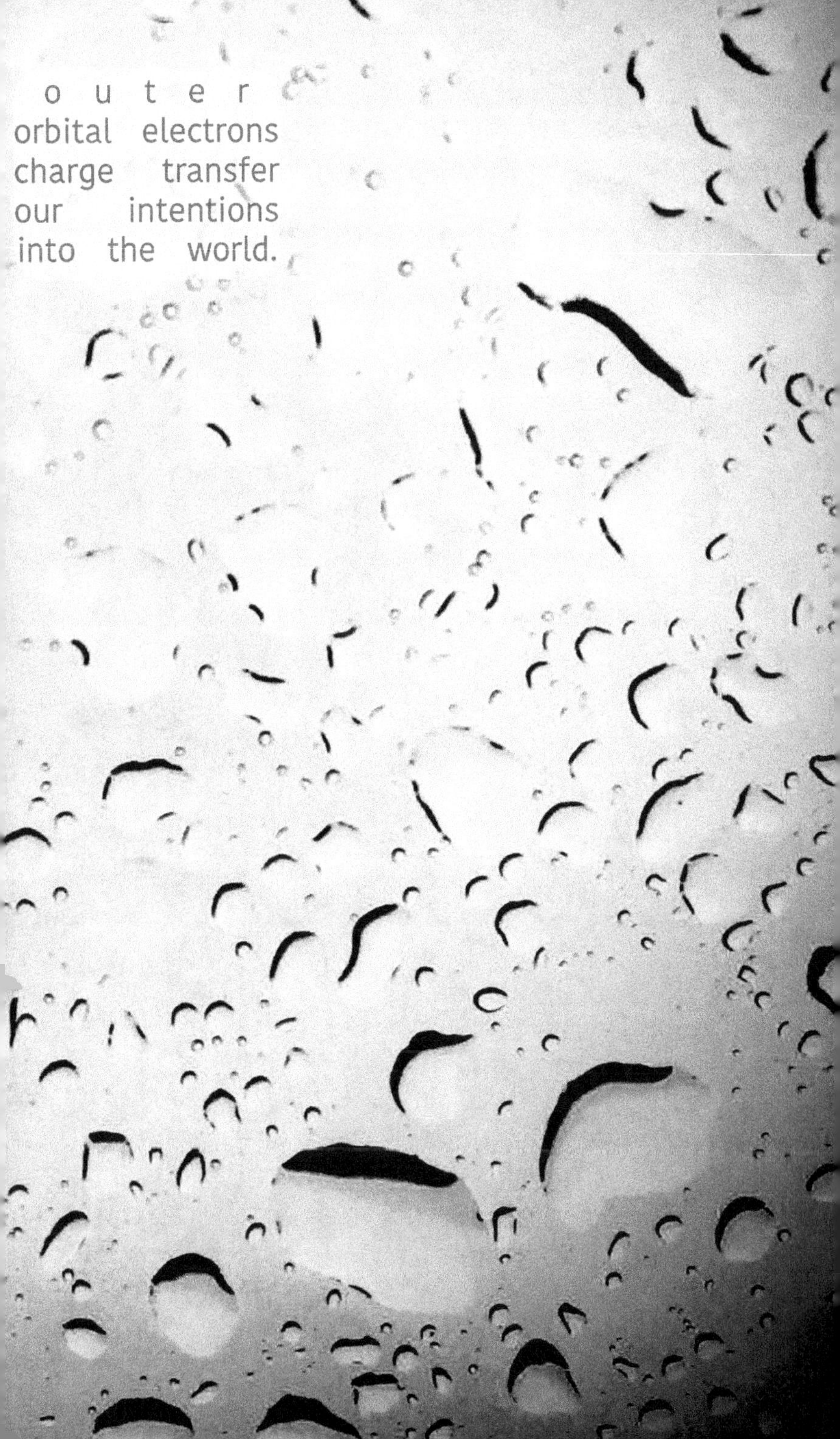
o u t e r
orbital electrons
charge   transfer
our   intentions
into the world.

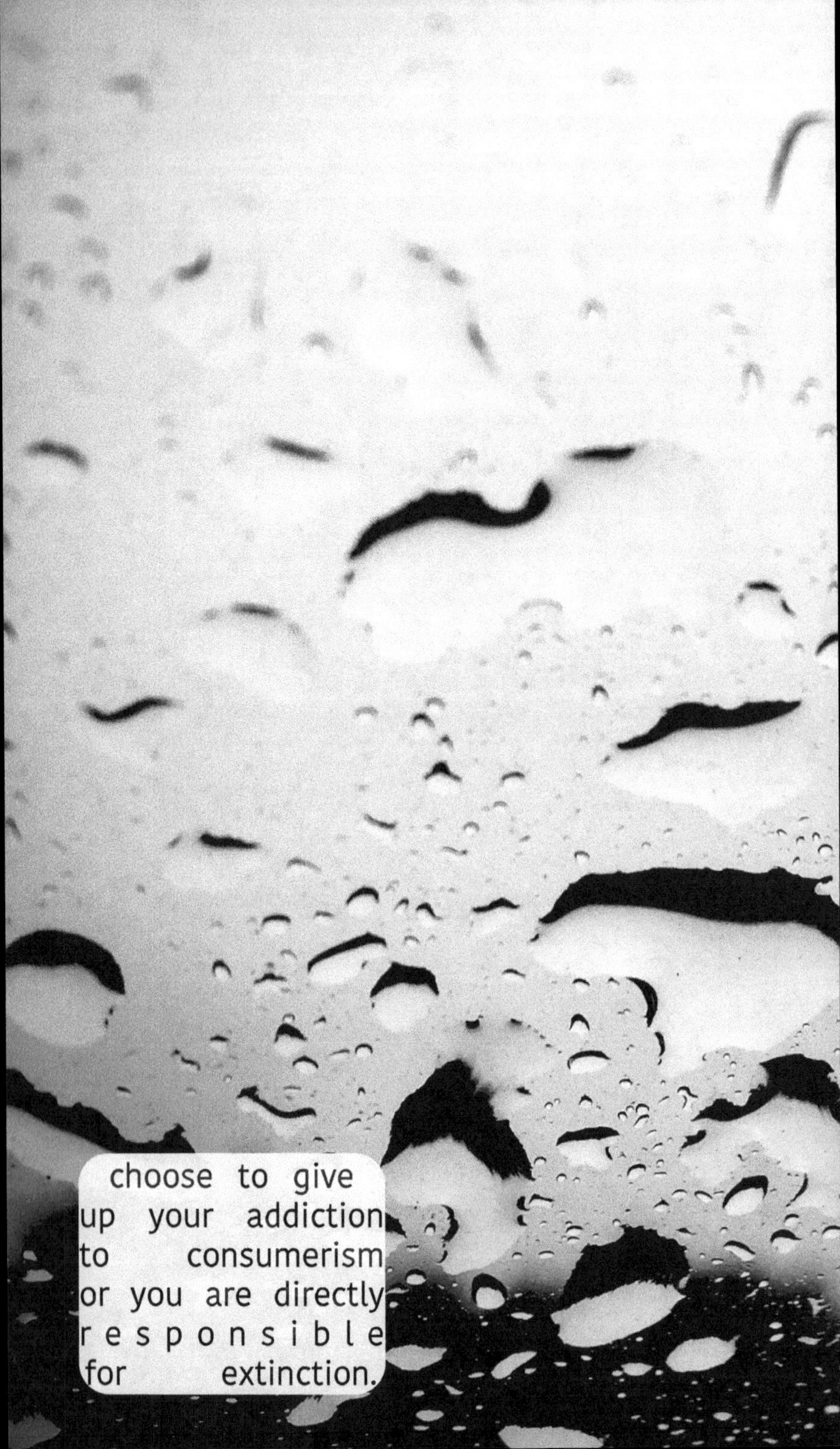
choose to give
up your addiction
to consumerism
or you are directly
responsible
for extinction.

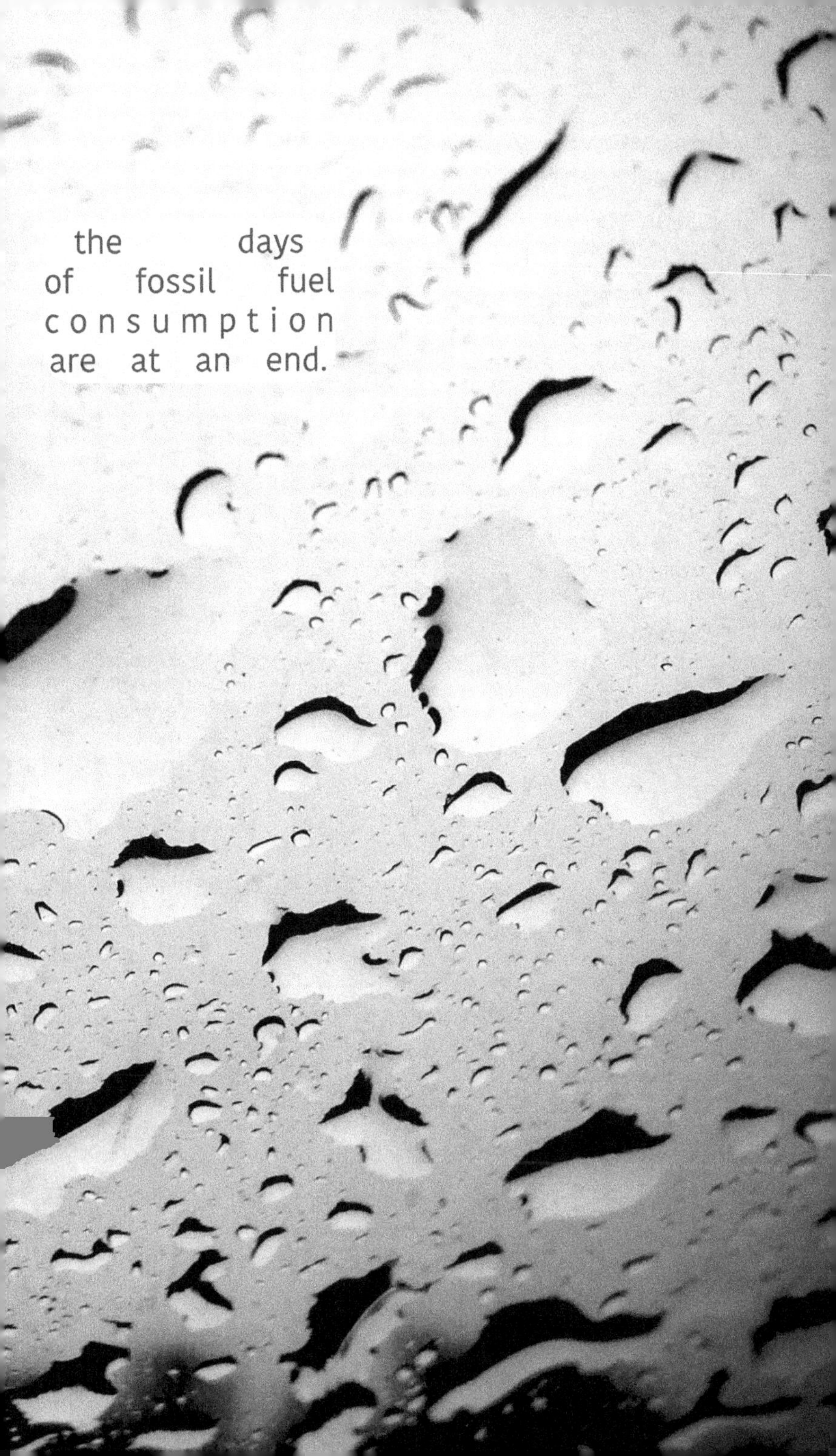

the   days
of   fossil   fuel
c o n s u m p t i o n
are   at   an   end.

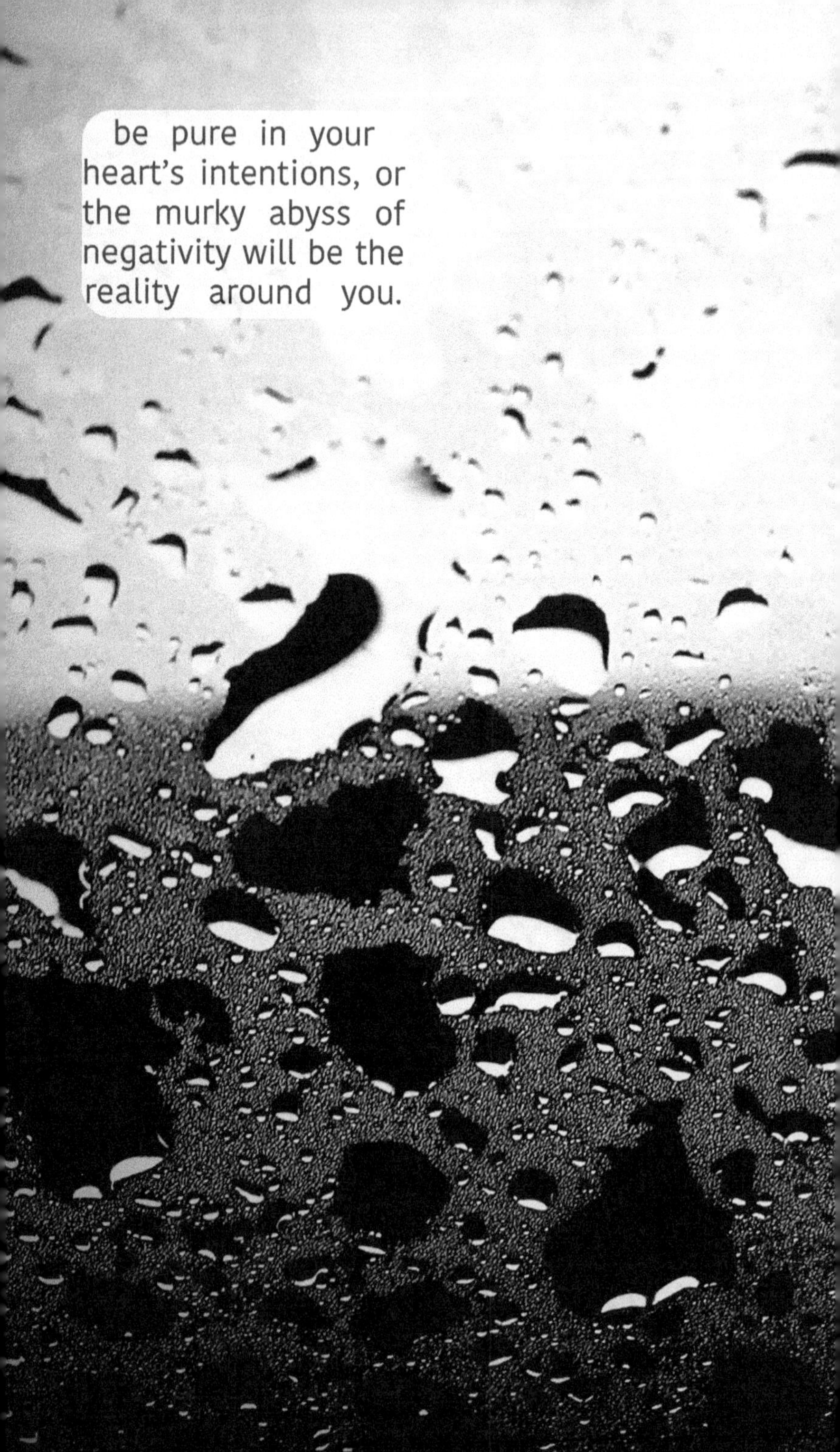
be pure in your heart's intentions, or the murky abyss of negativity will be the reality around you.

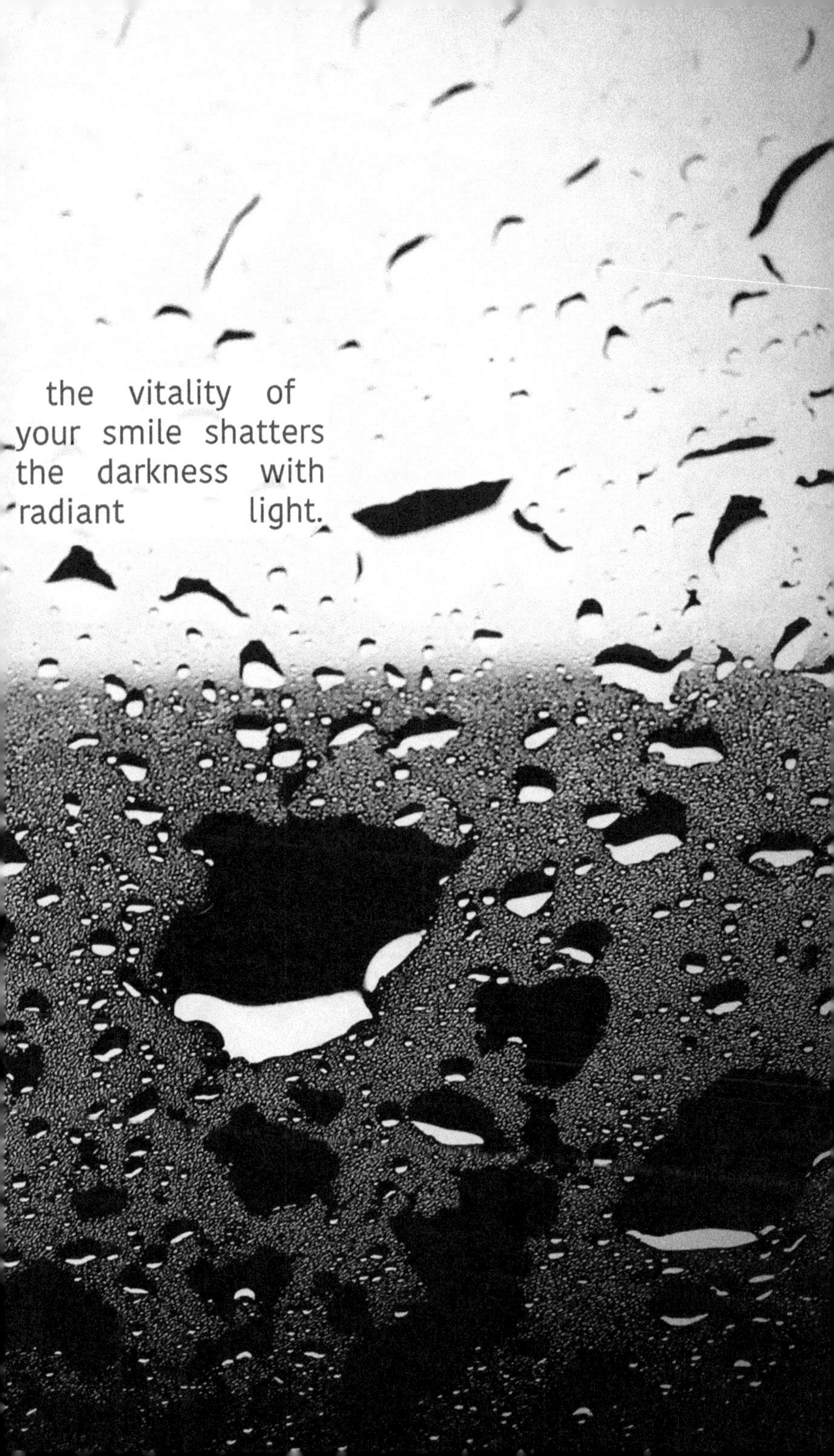

the vitality of
your smile shatters
the darkness with
radiant light.

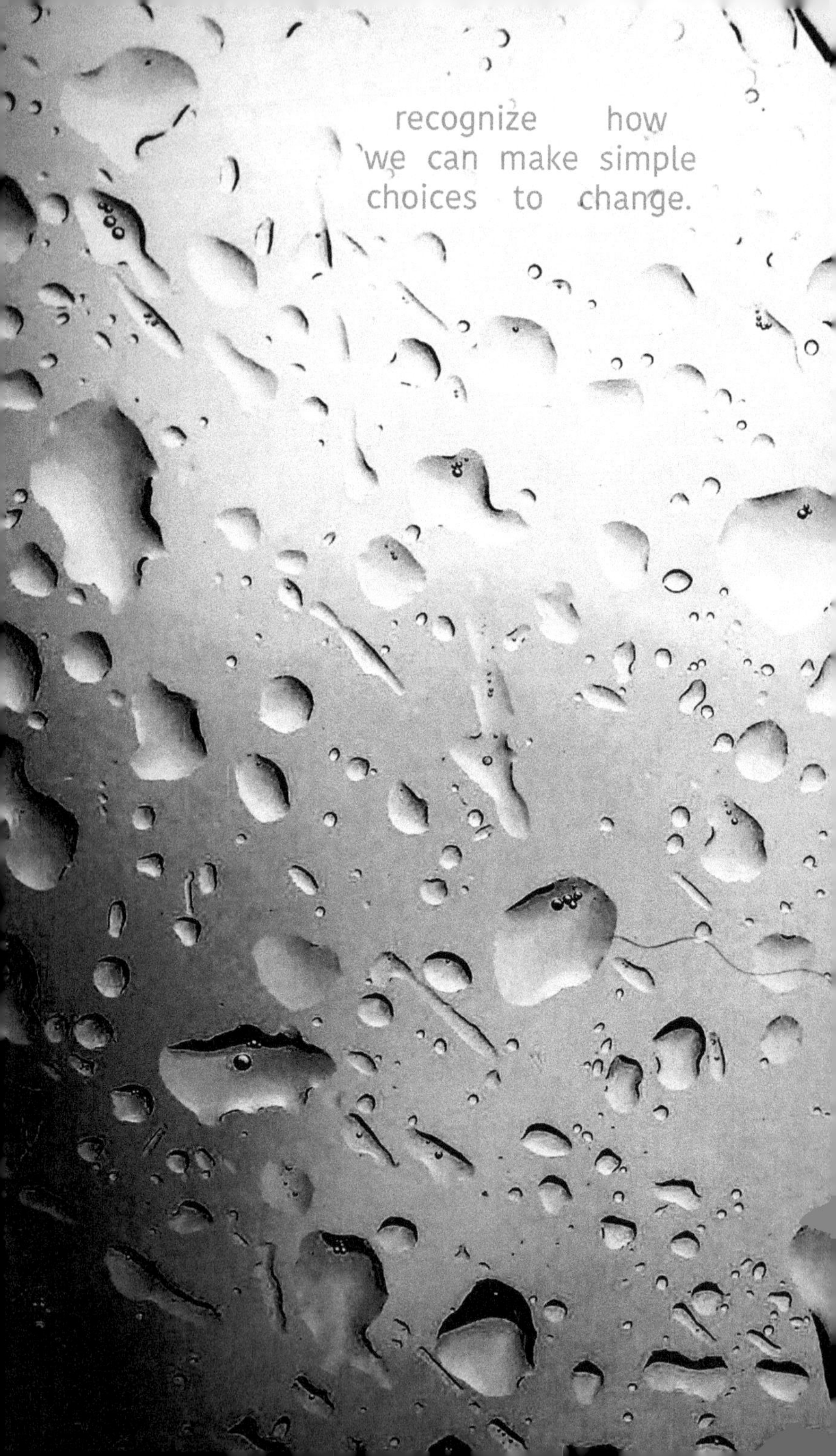

recognize   how
we can make simple
choices to change.

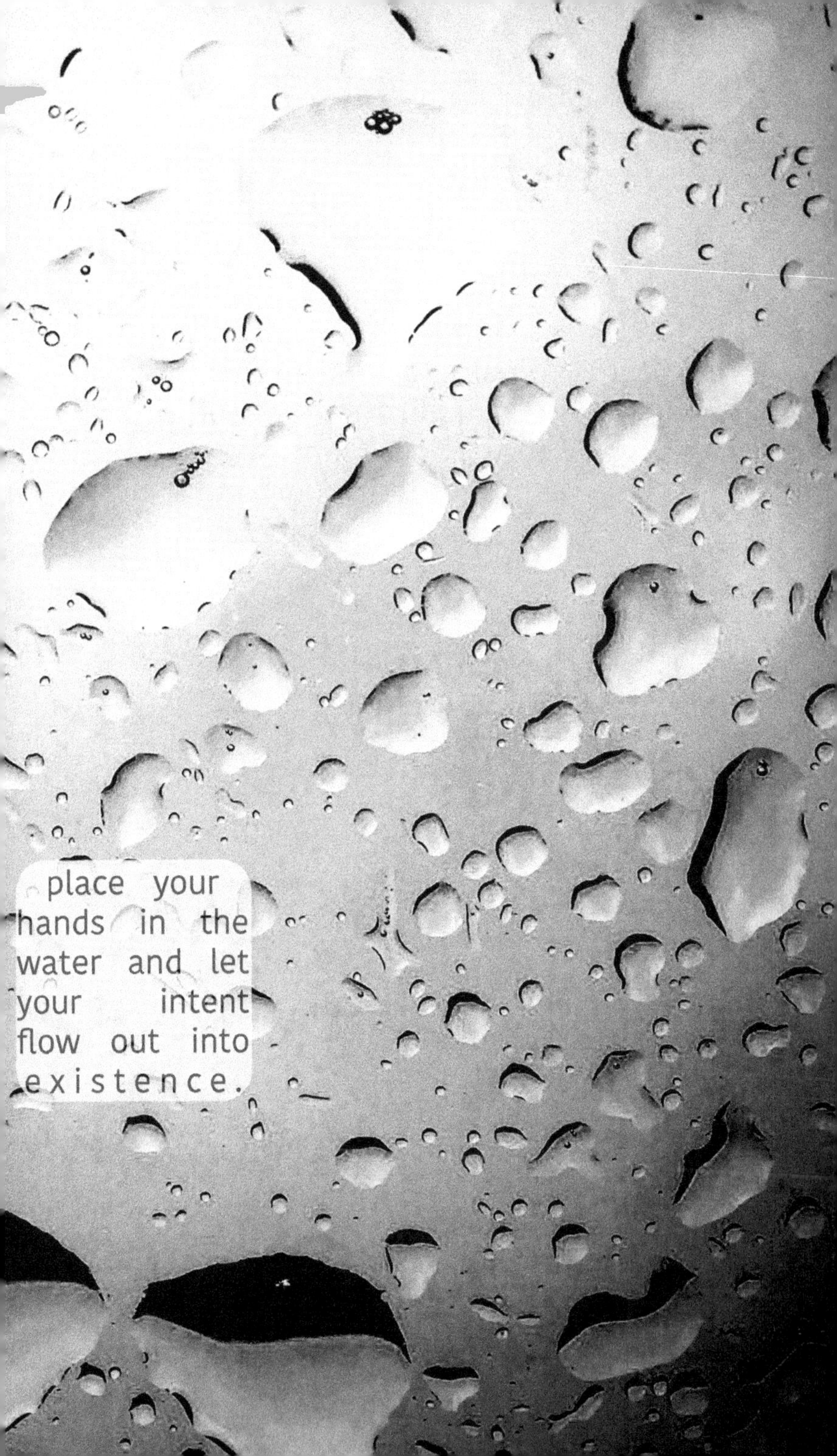
place your hands in the water and let your intent flow out into existence.

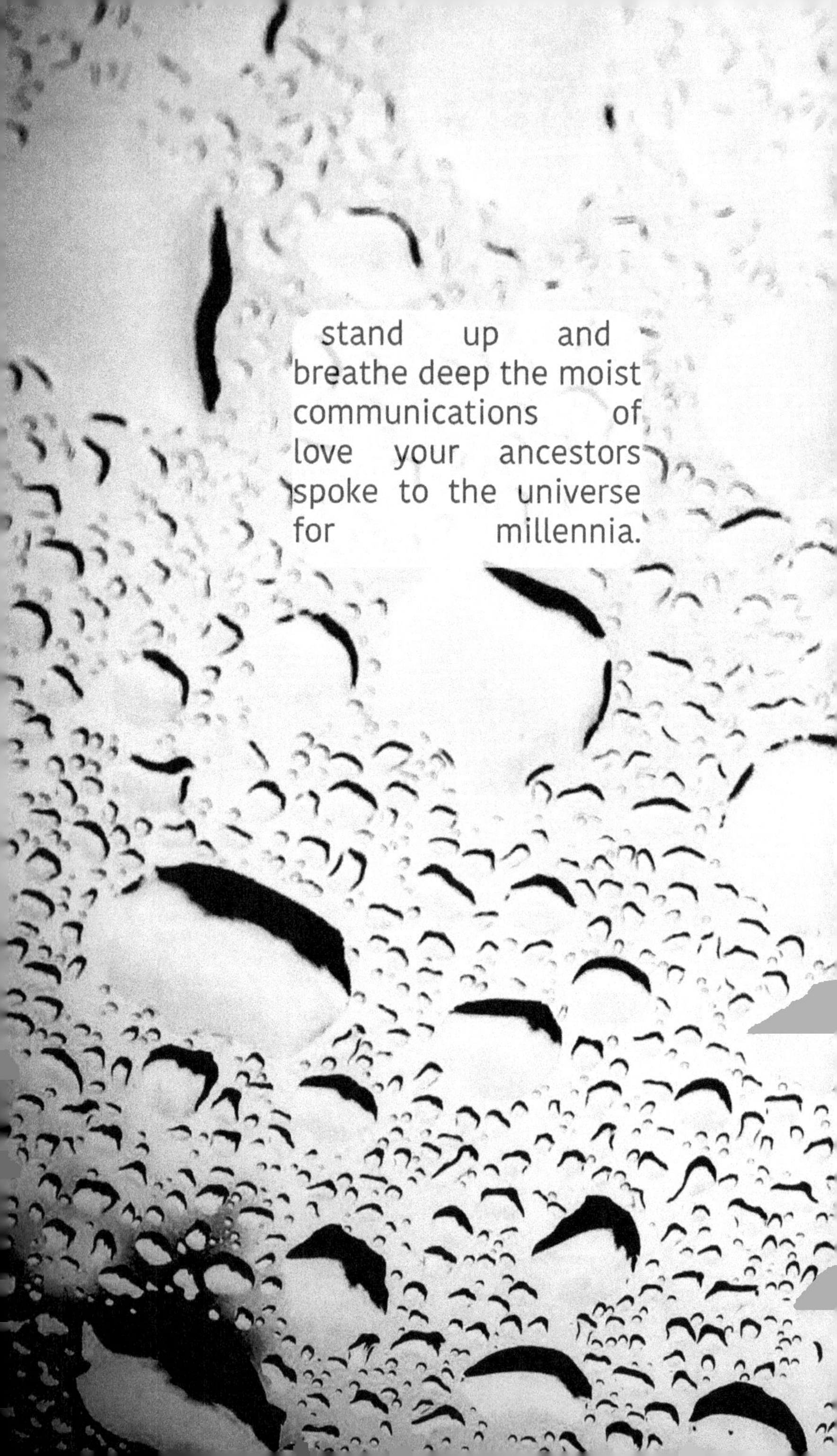
stand up and breathe deep the moist communications of love your ancestors spoke to the universe for millennia.

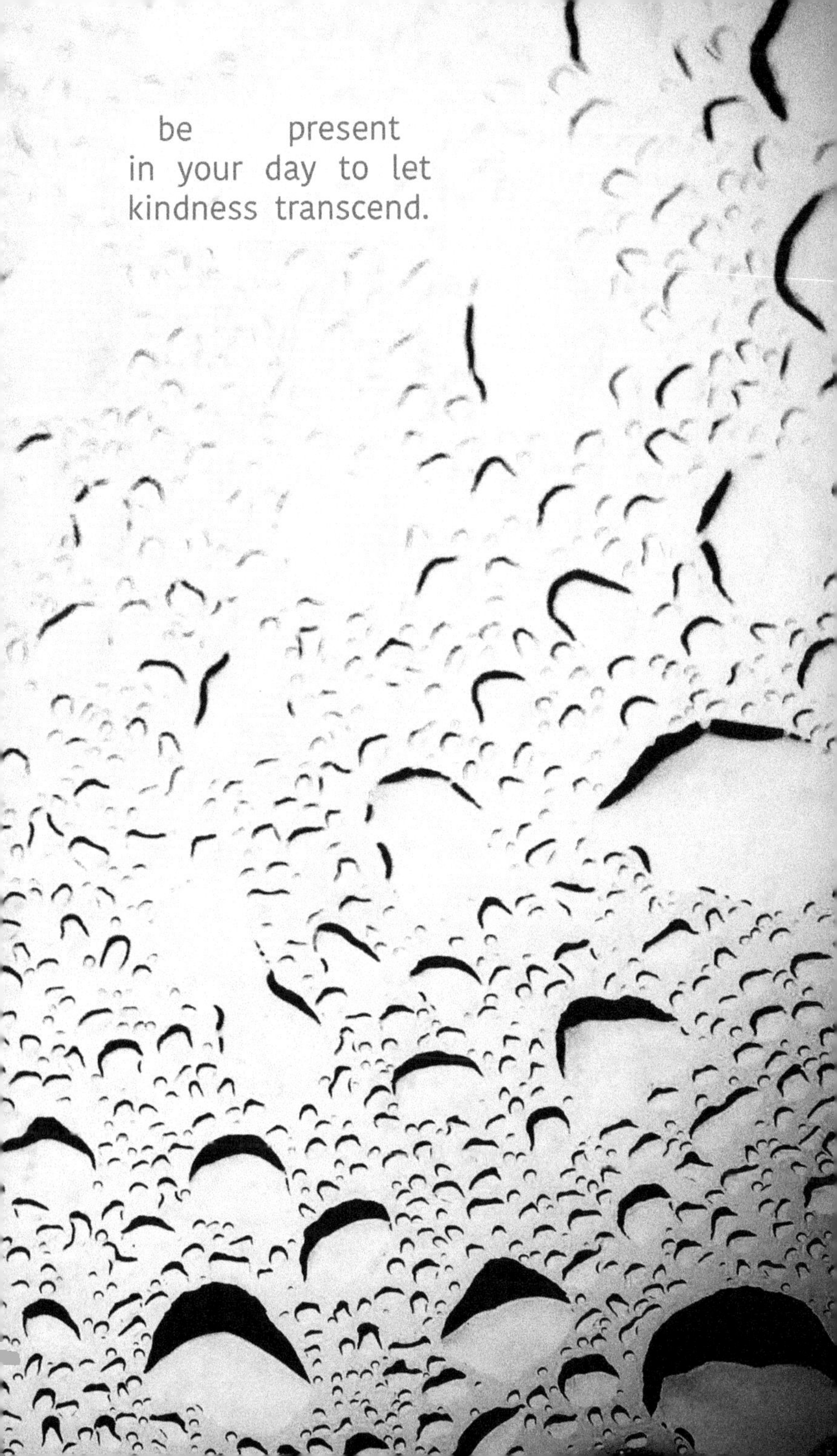

be   present
in your day to let
kindness transcend.

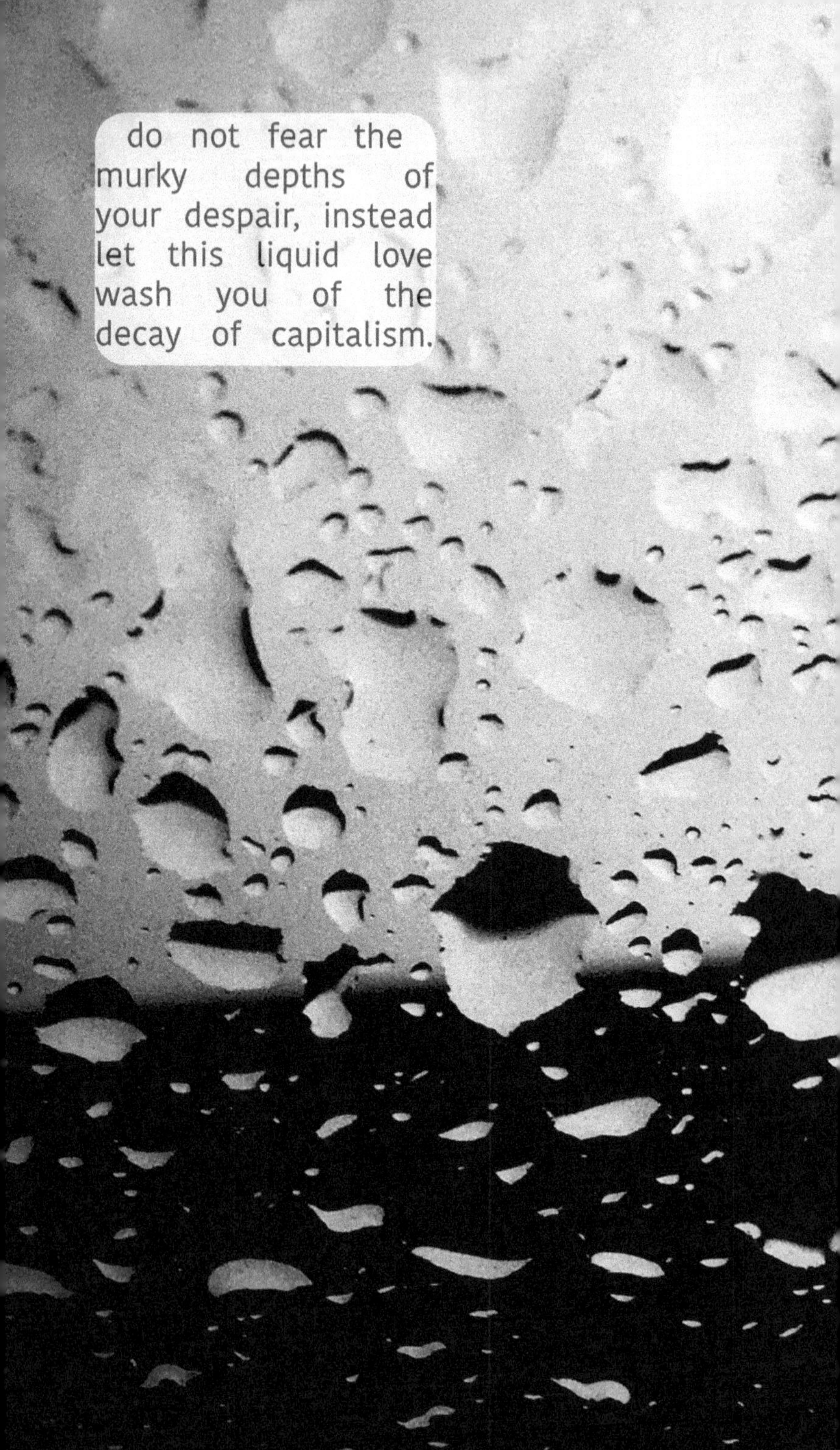

do not fear the murky depths of your despair, instead let this liquid love wash you of the decay of capitalism.

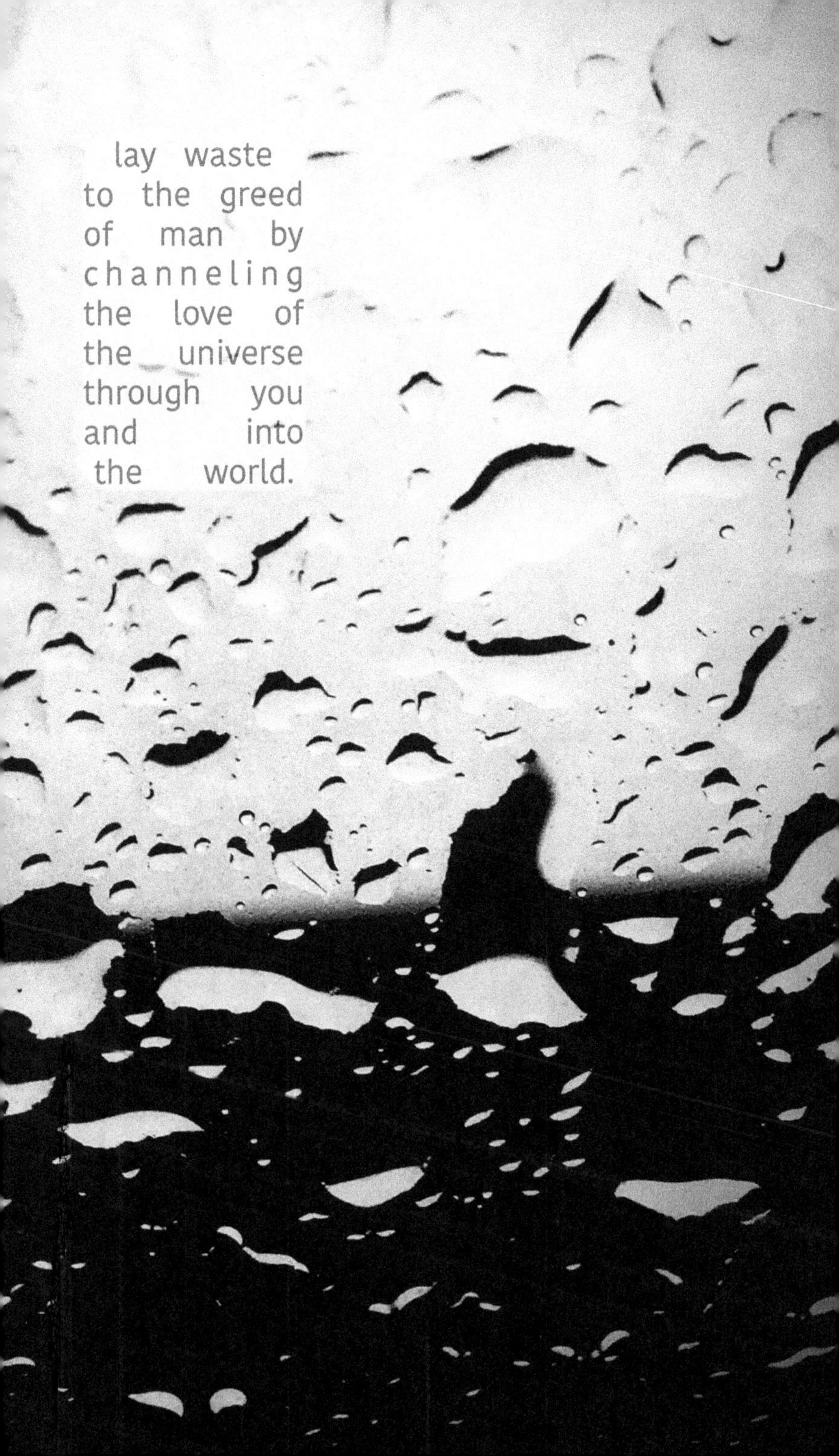

lay waste
to the greed
of man by
channeling
the love of
the universe
through you
and into
the world.

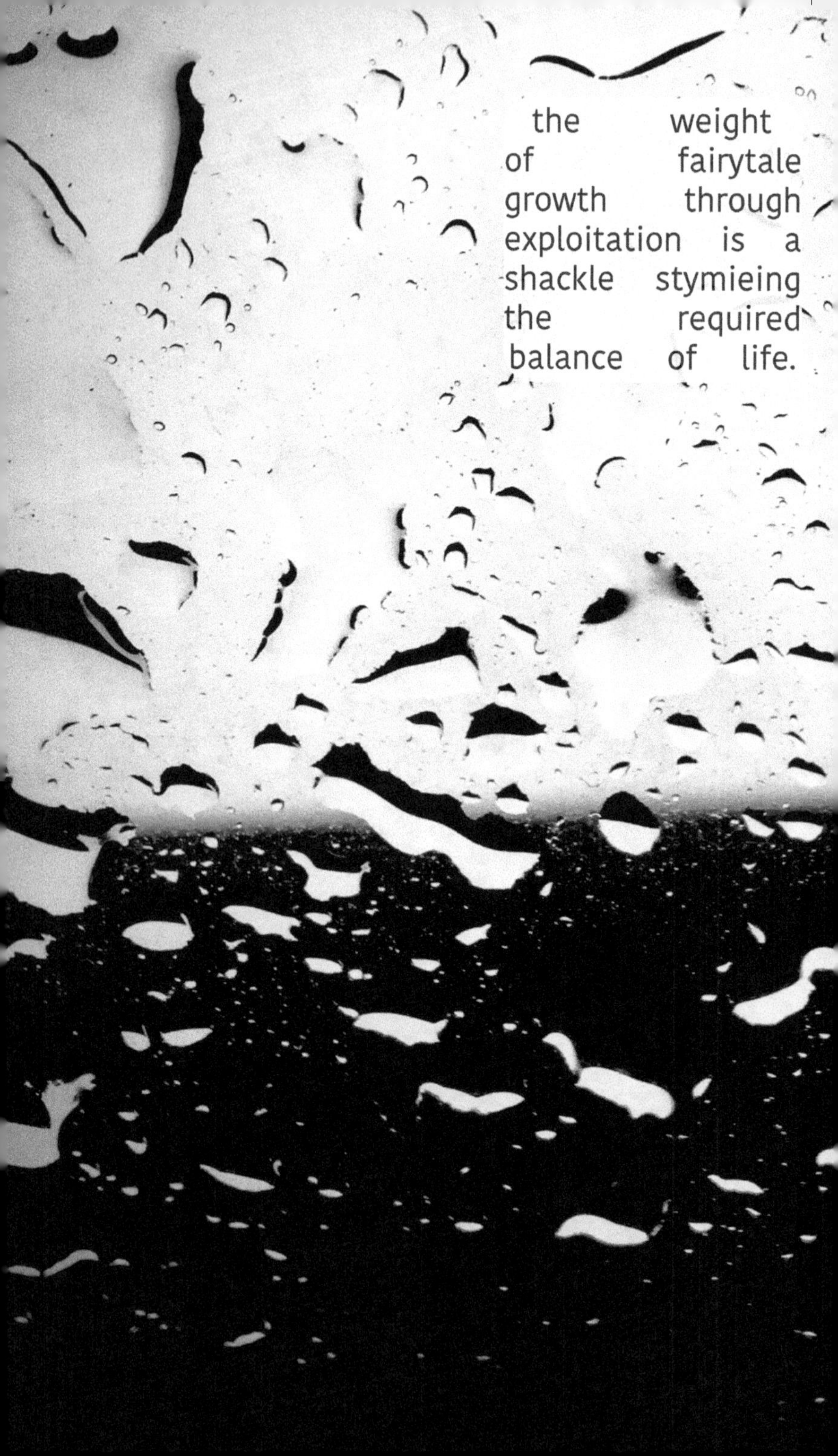
the weight of fairytale growth through exploitation is a shackle stymieing the required balance of life.

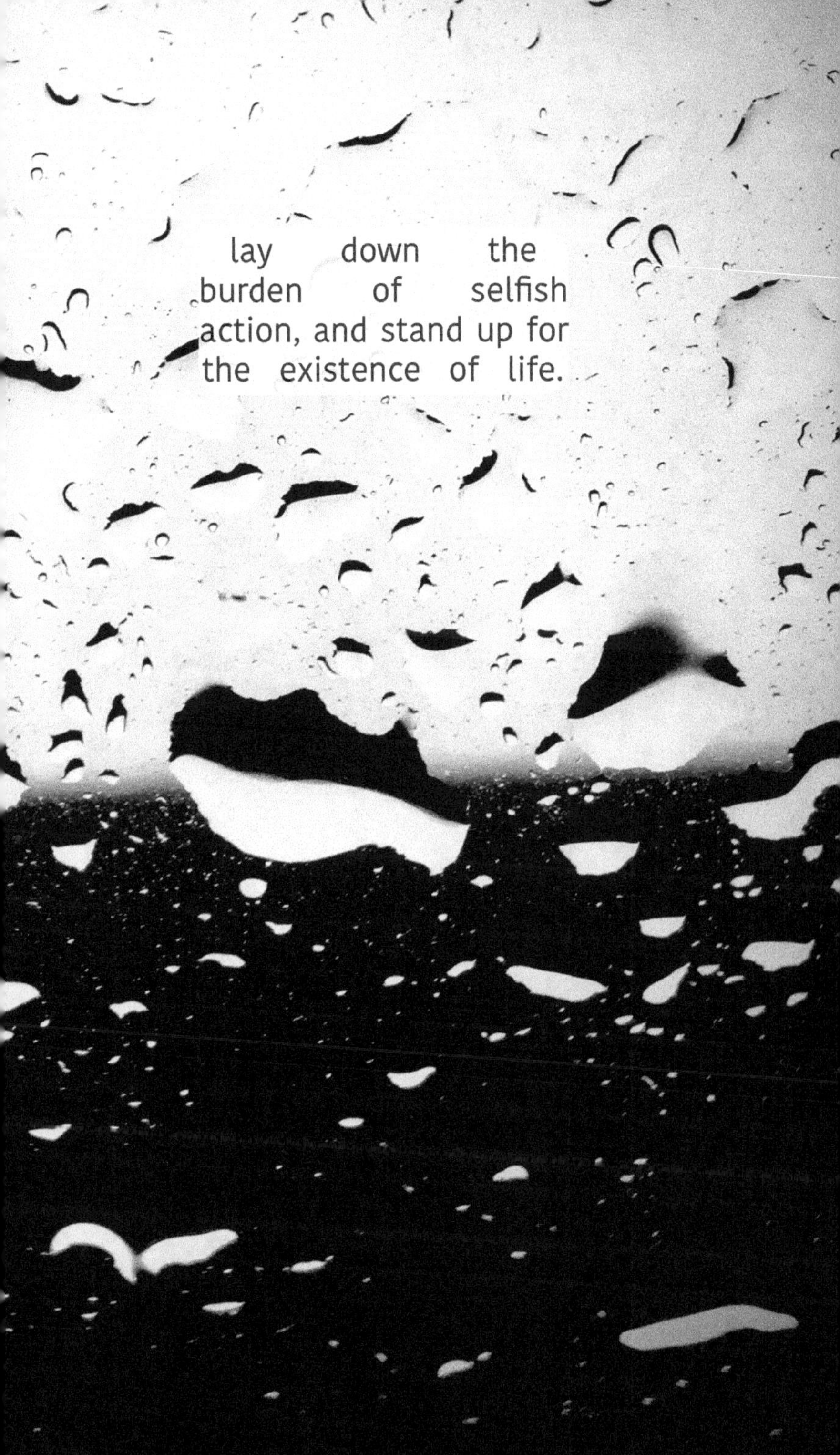
lay down the burden of selfish action, and stand up for the existence of life.

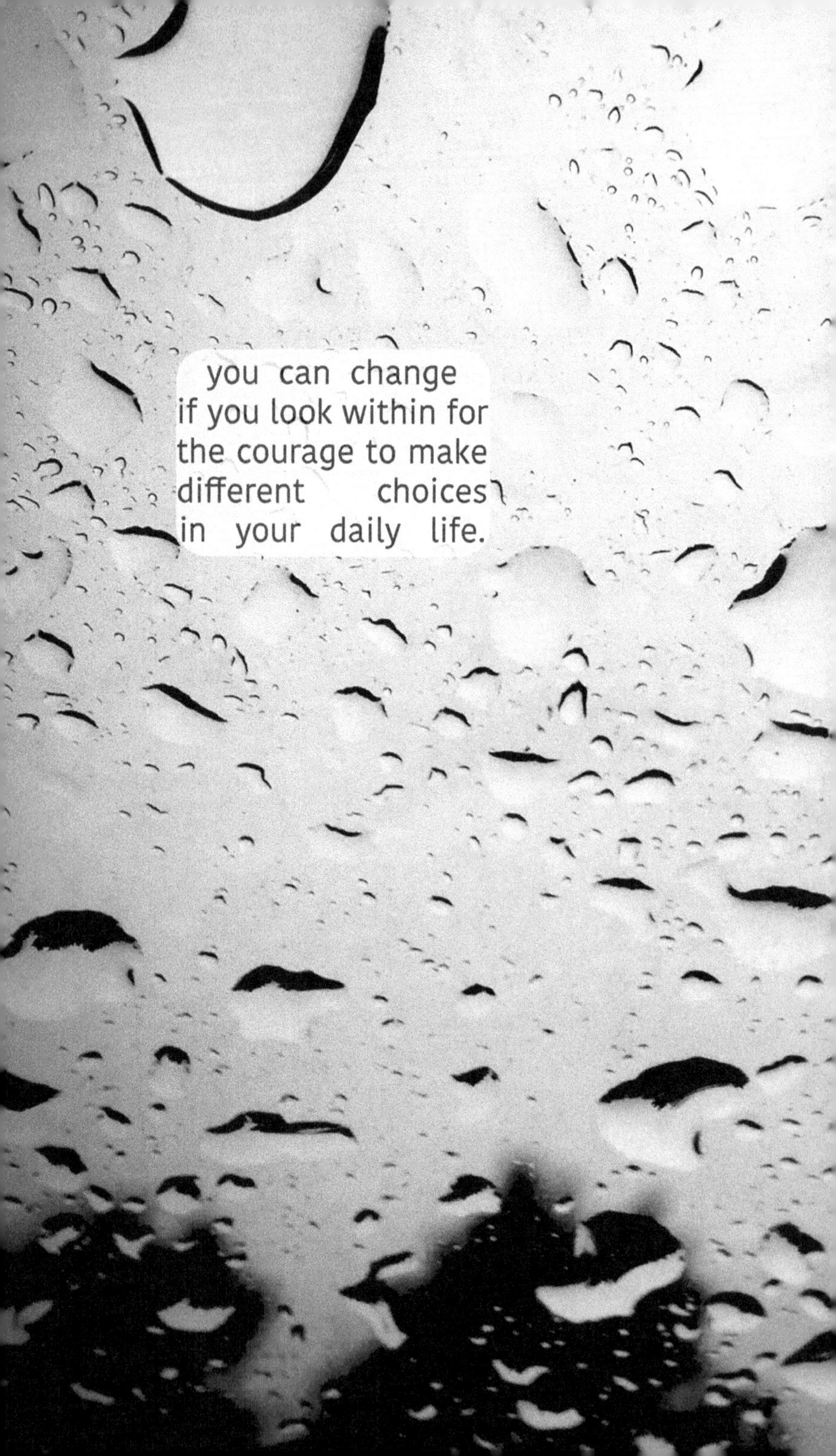
you can change
if you look within for
the courage to make
different   choices
in your daily life.

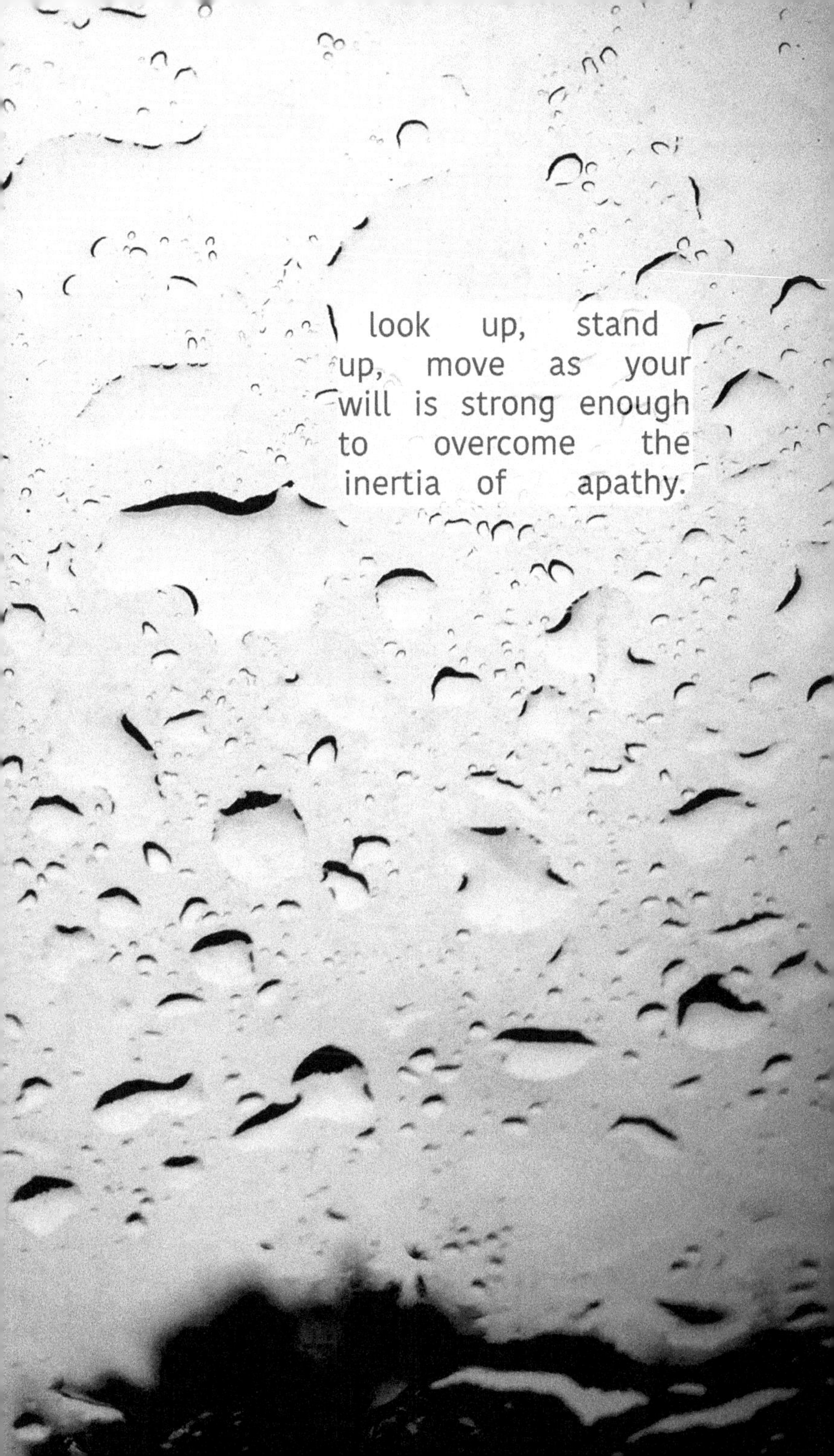
look up, stand up, move as your will is strong enough to overcome the inertia of apathy.

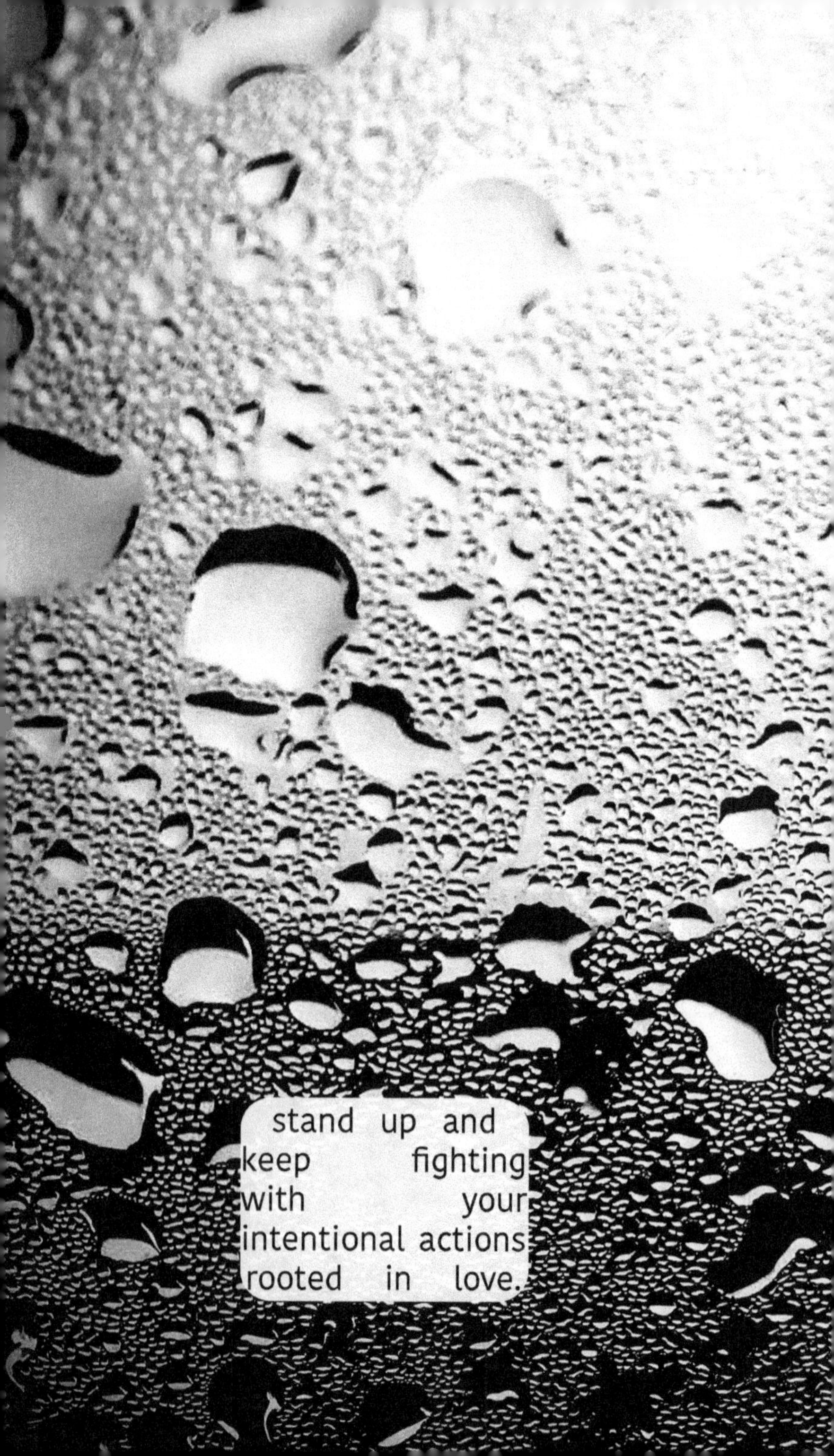

stand up and
keep   fighting
with   your
intentional actions
rooted   in   love.

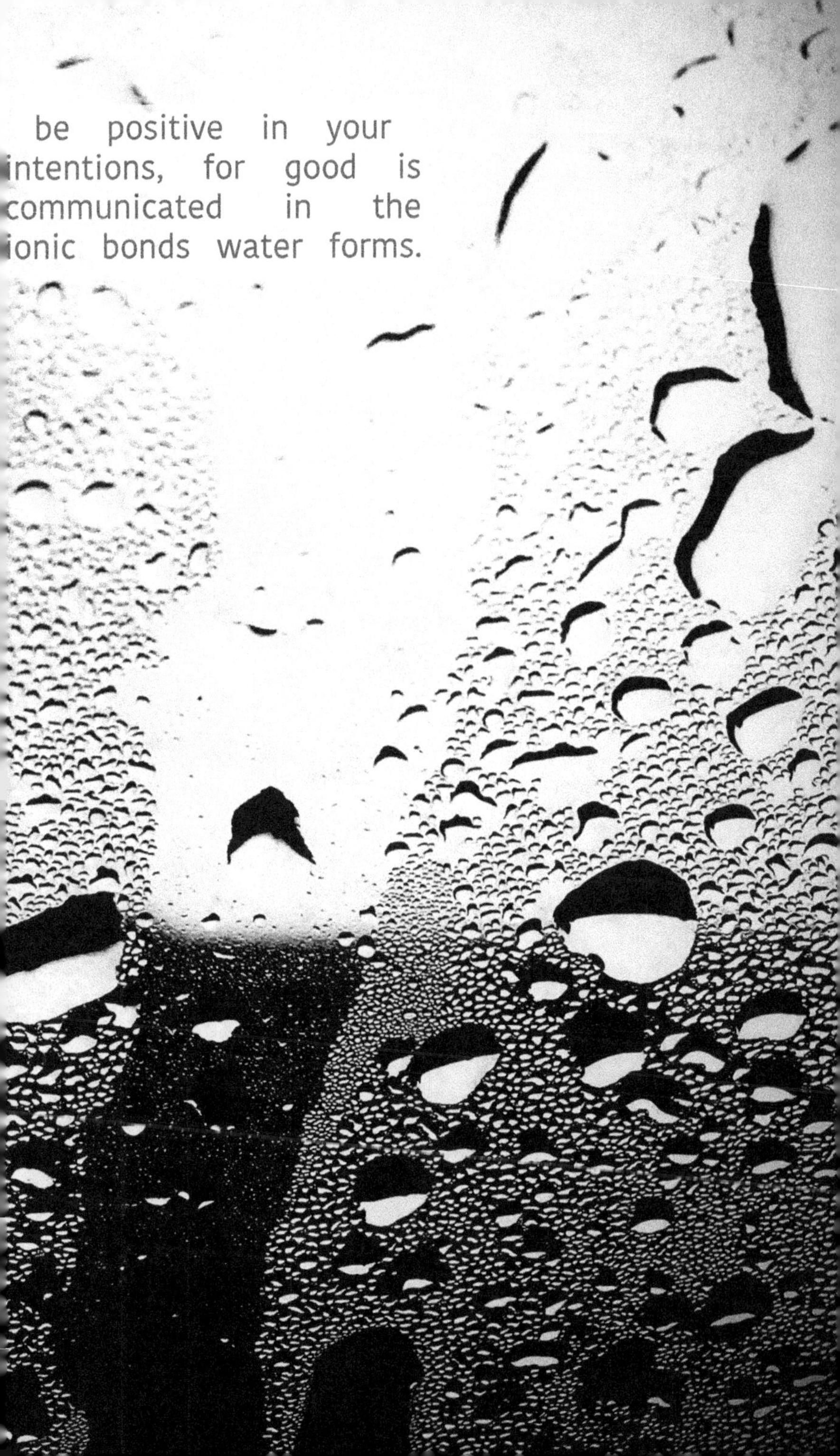
be positive in your
intentions, for good is
communicated in the
ionic bonds water forms.

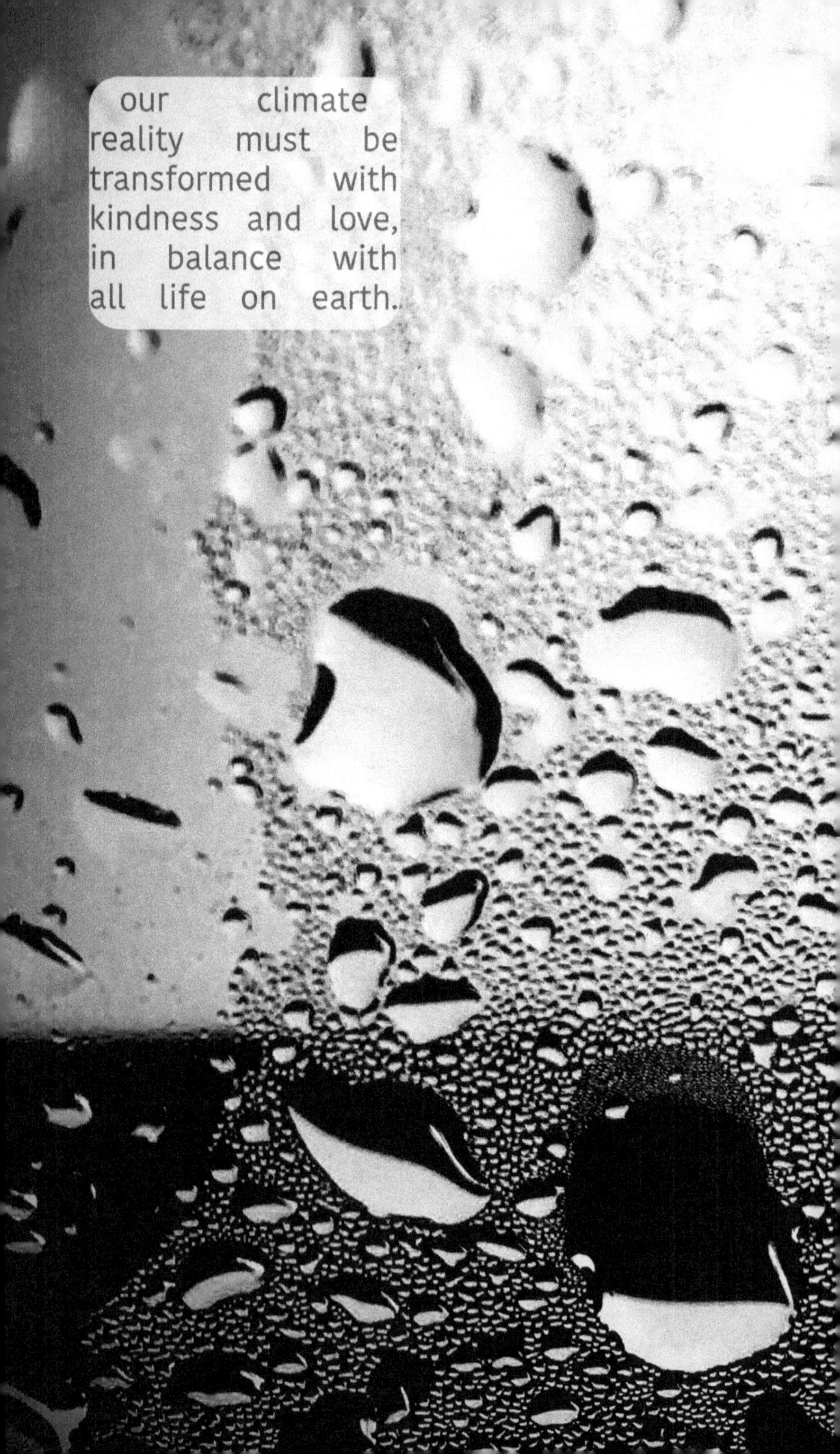
our climate reality must be transformed with kindness and love, in balance with all life on earth.

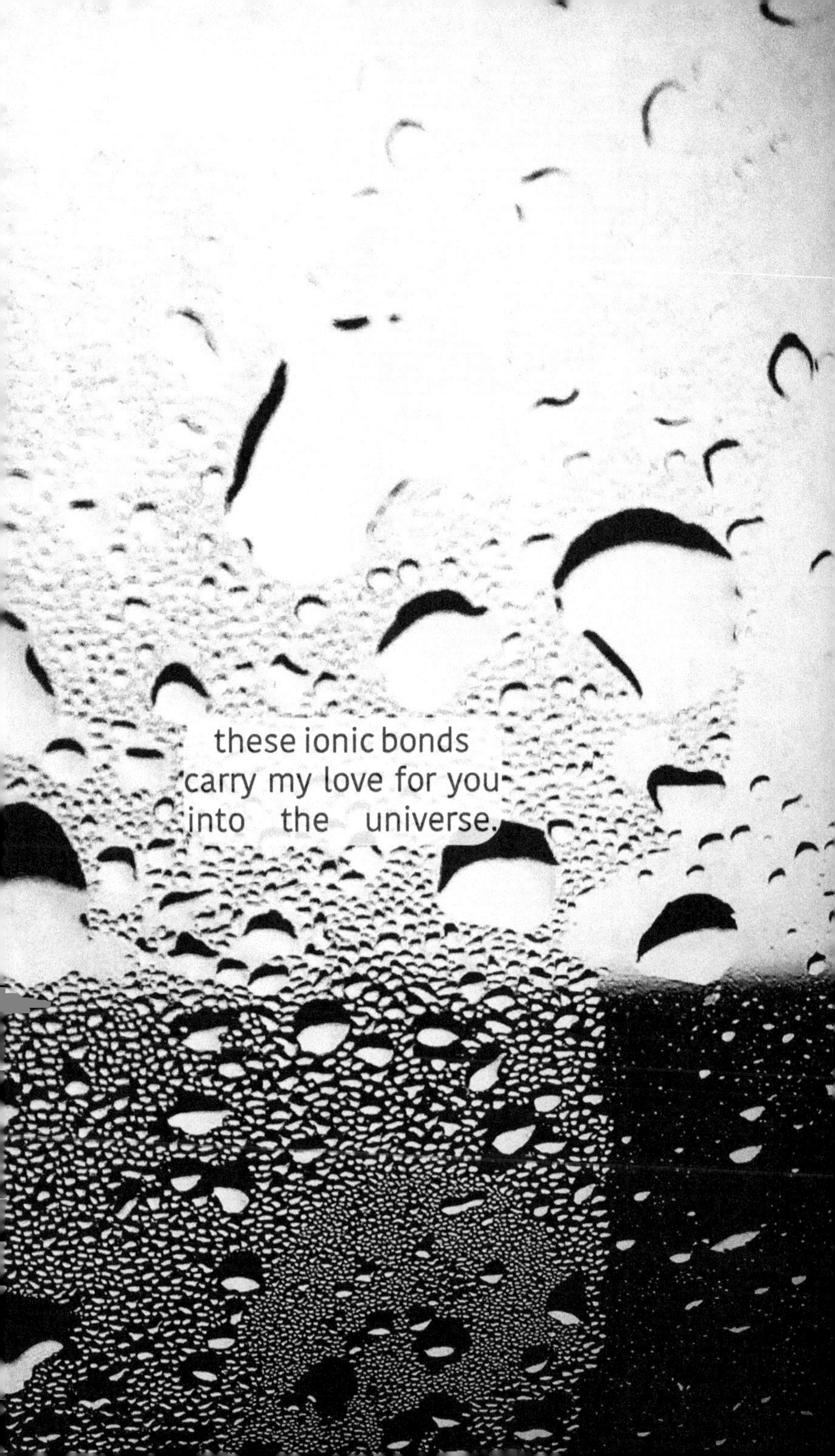
these ionic bonds
carry my love for you
into   the   universe.

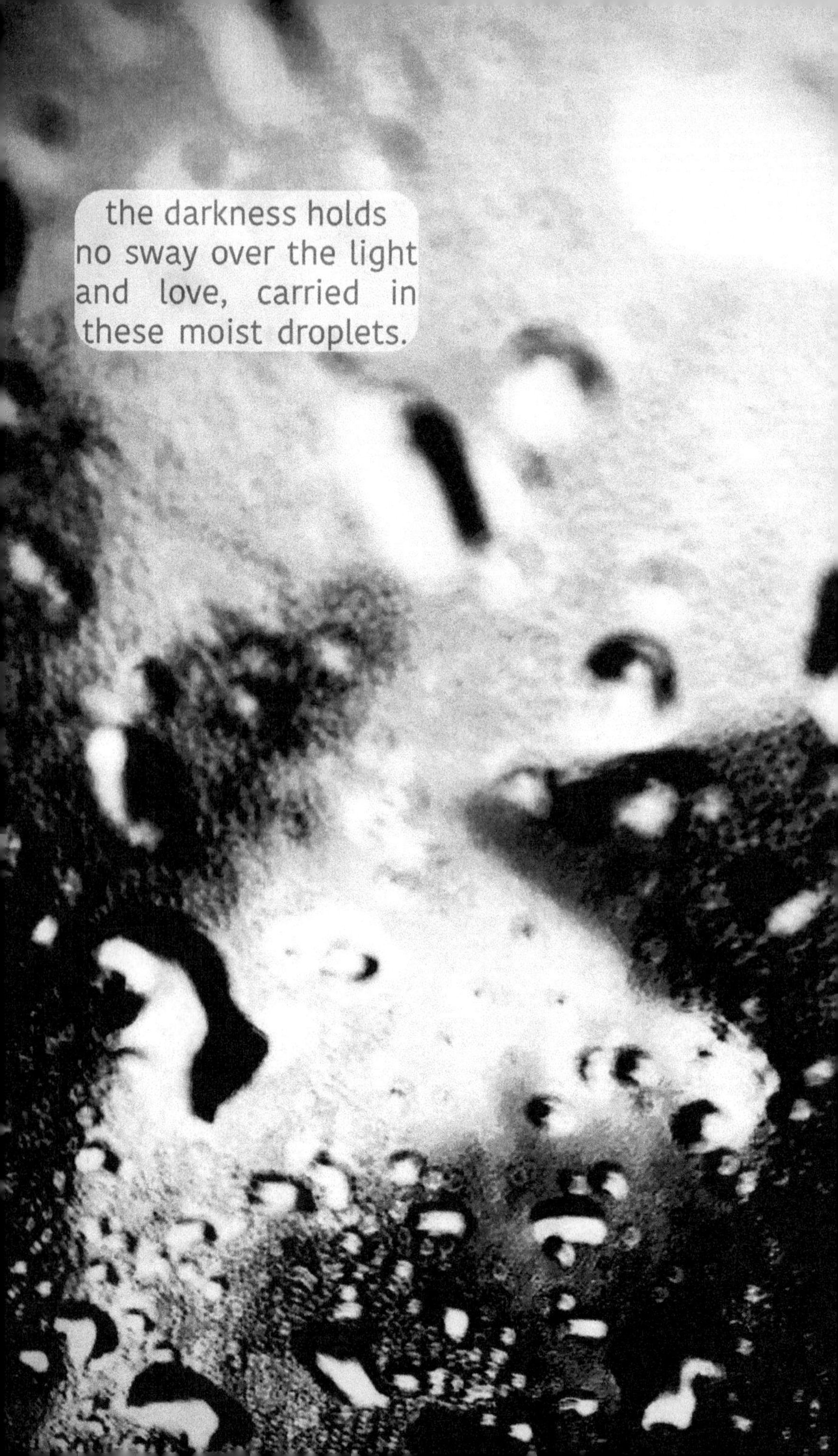
the darkness holds
no sway over the light
and love, carried in
these moist droplets.

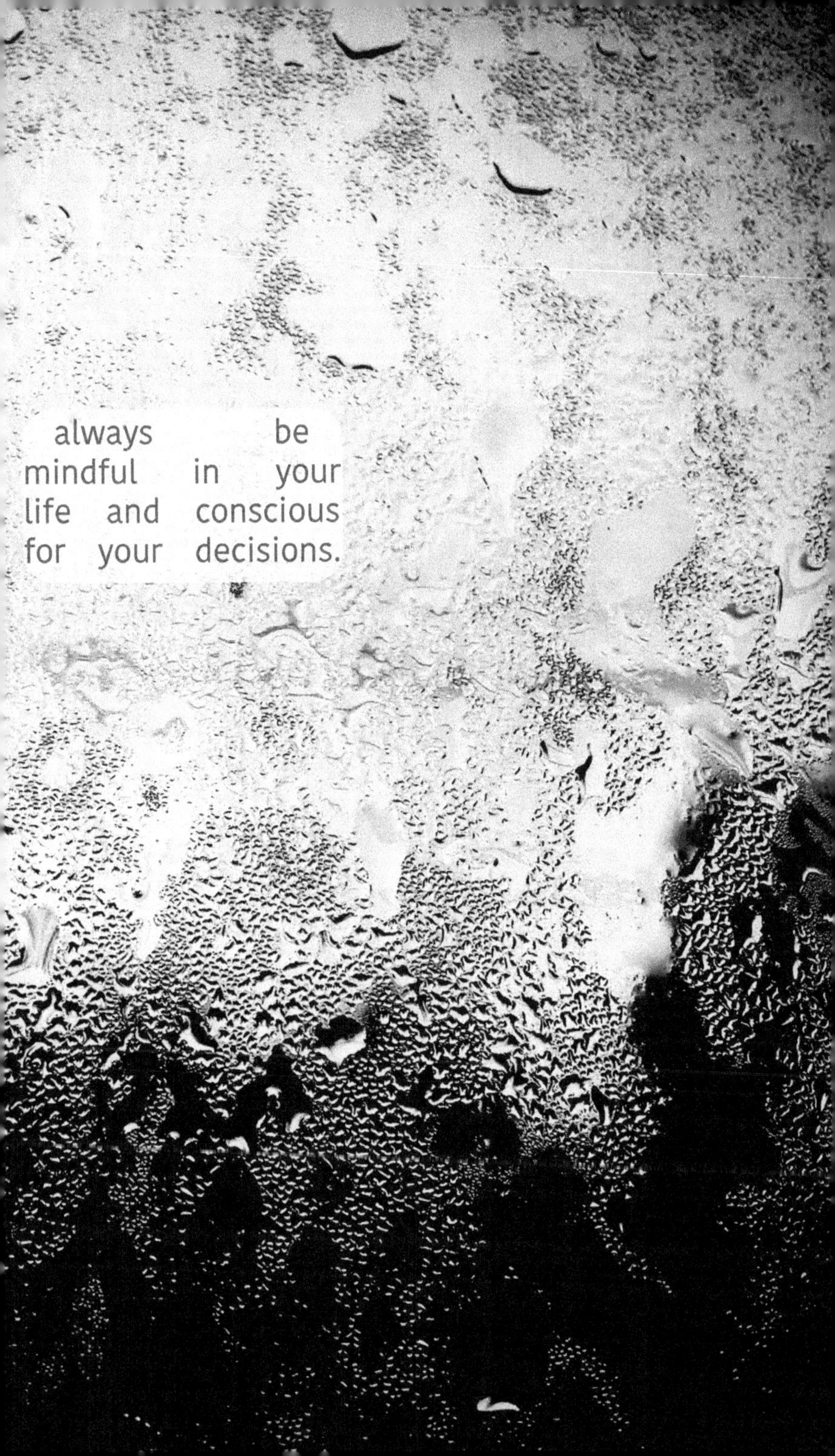

always   be
mindful   in   your
life   and   conscious
for   your   decisions.

breathe in the messages from your ancestors as the rain falls.

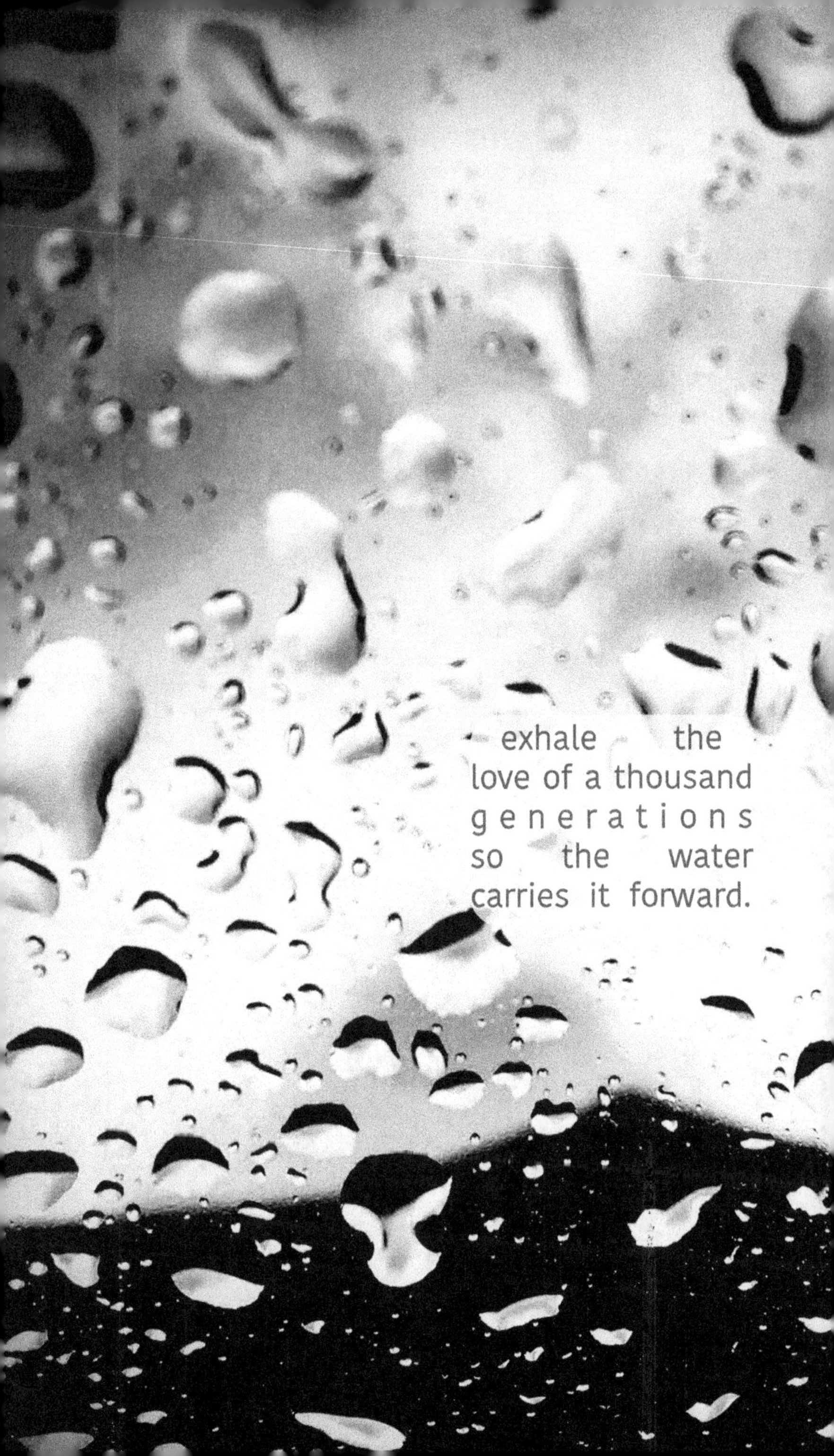
exhale the
love of a thousand
g e n e r a t i o n s
so the water
carries it forward.

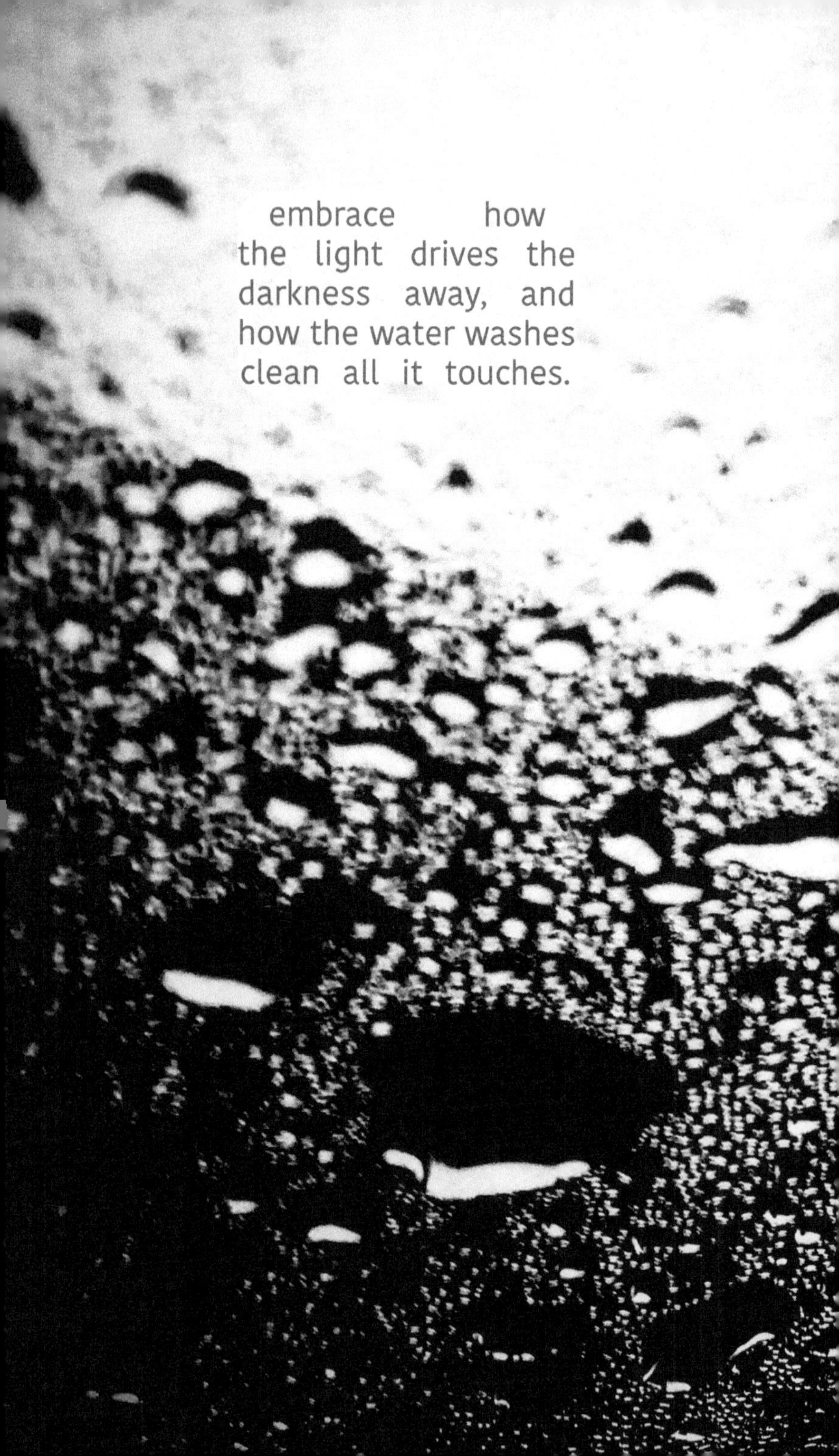

embrace   how
the light drives the
darkness   away,   and
how the water washes
clean all it touches.

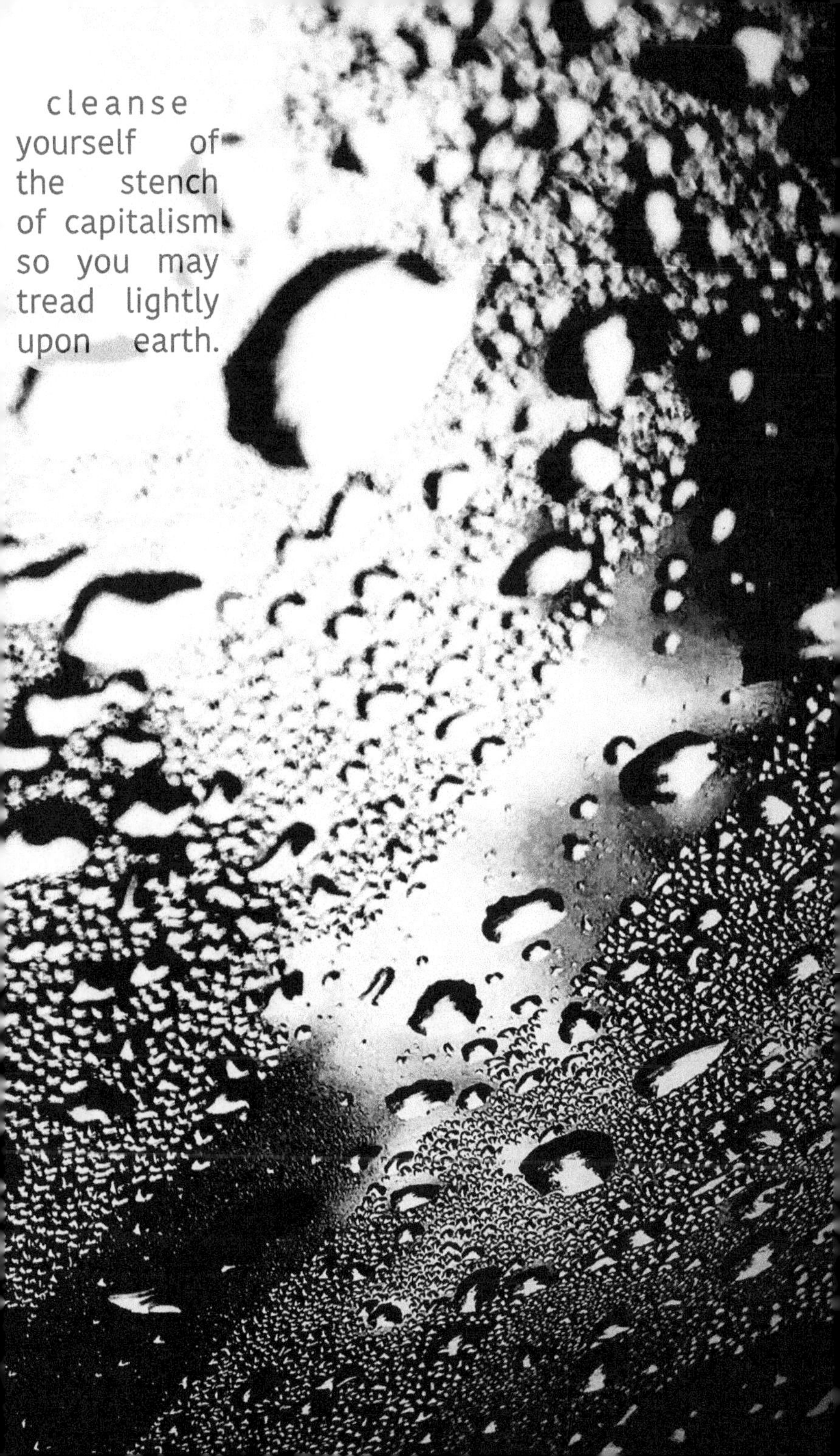
cleanse
yourself of
the stench
of capitalism
so you may
tread lightly
upon earth.

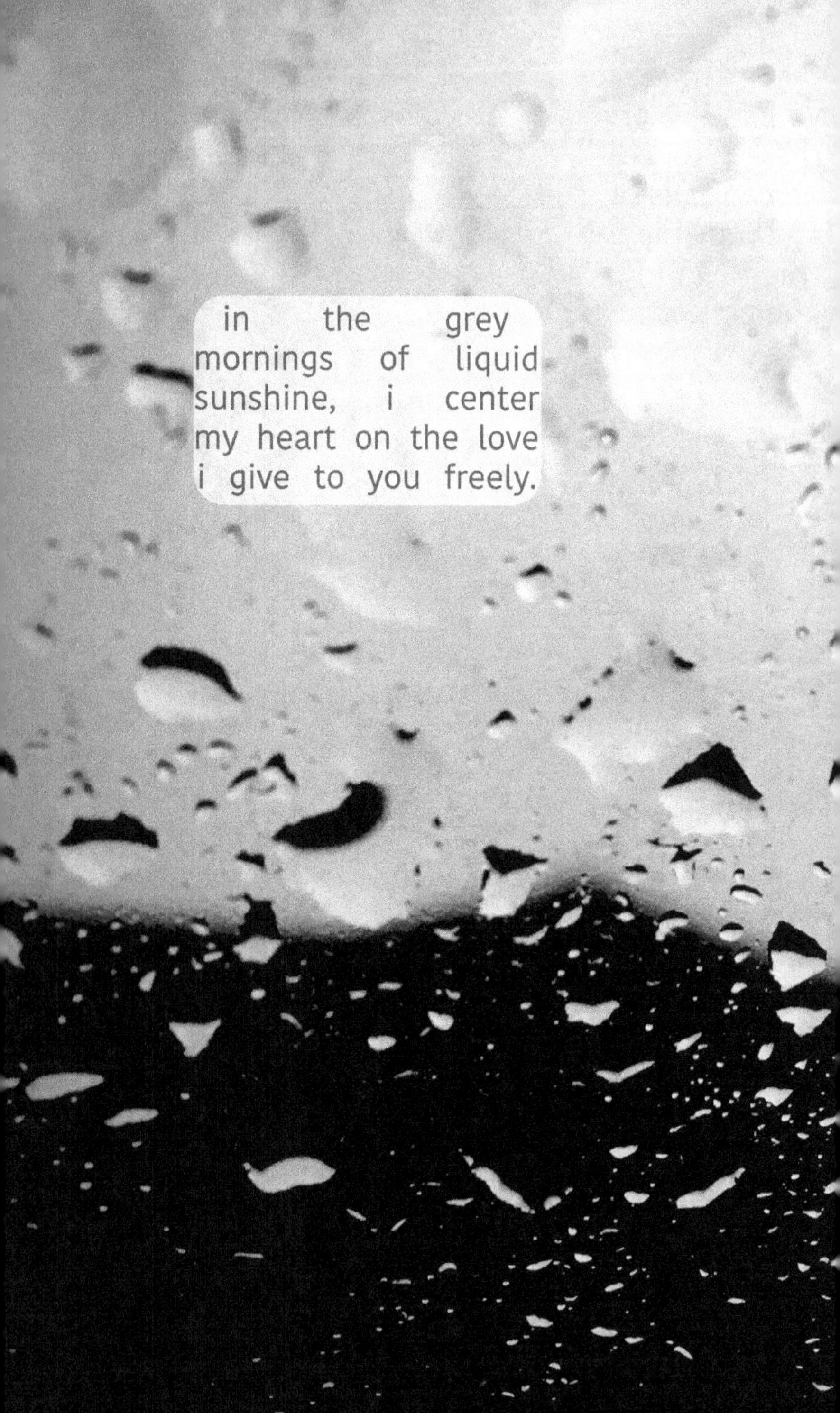

in the grey mornings of liquid sunshine, i center my heart on the love i give to you freely.

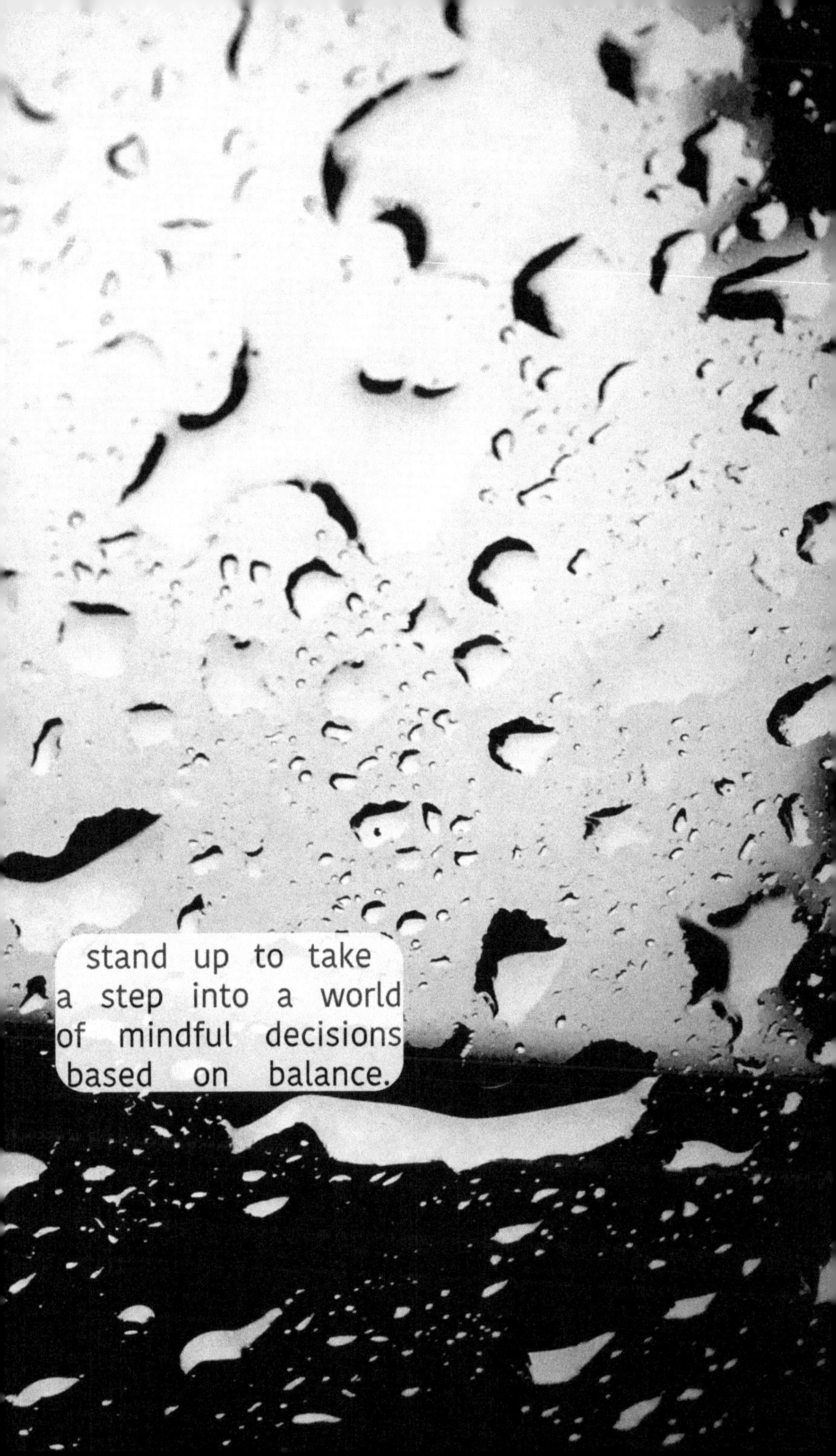

stand up to take
a step into a world
of mindful decisions
based on balance.

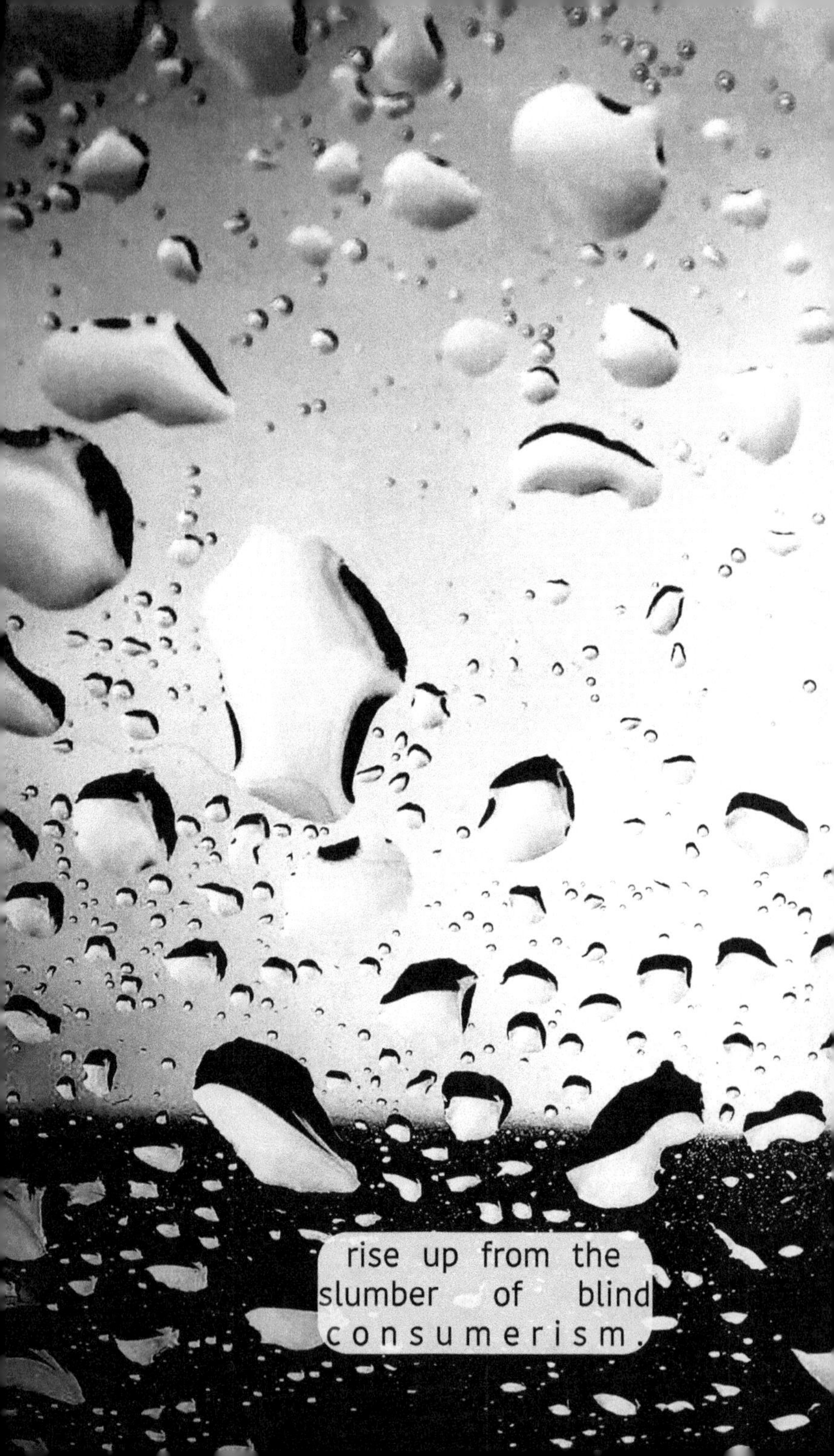
rise up from the
slumber of blind
consumerism.

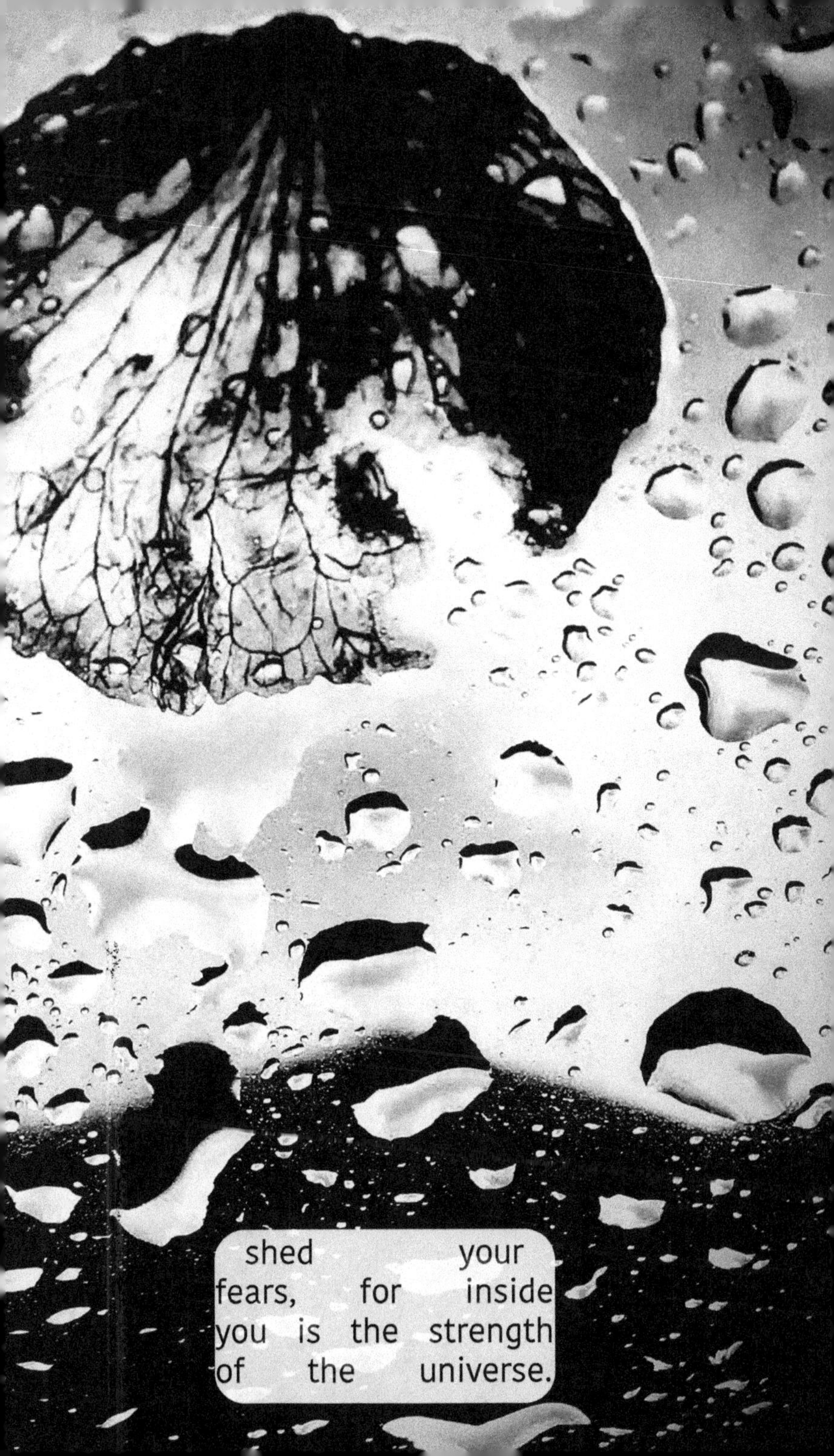

shed   your
fears,   for   inside
you   is   the strength
of   the   universe.

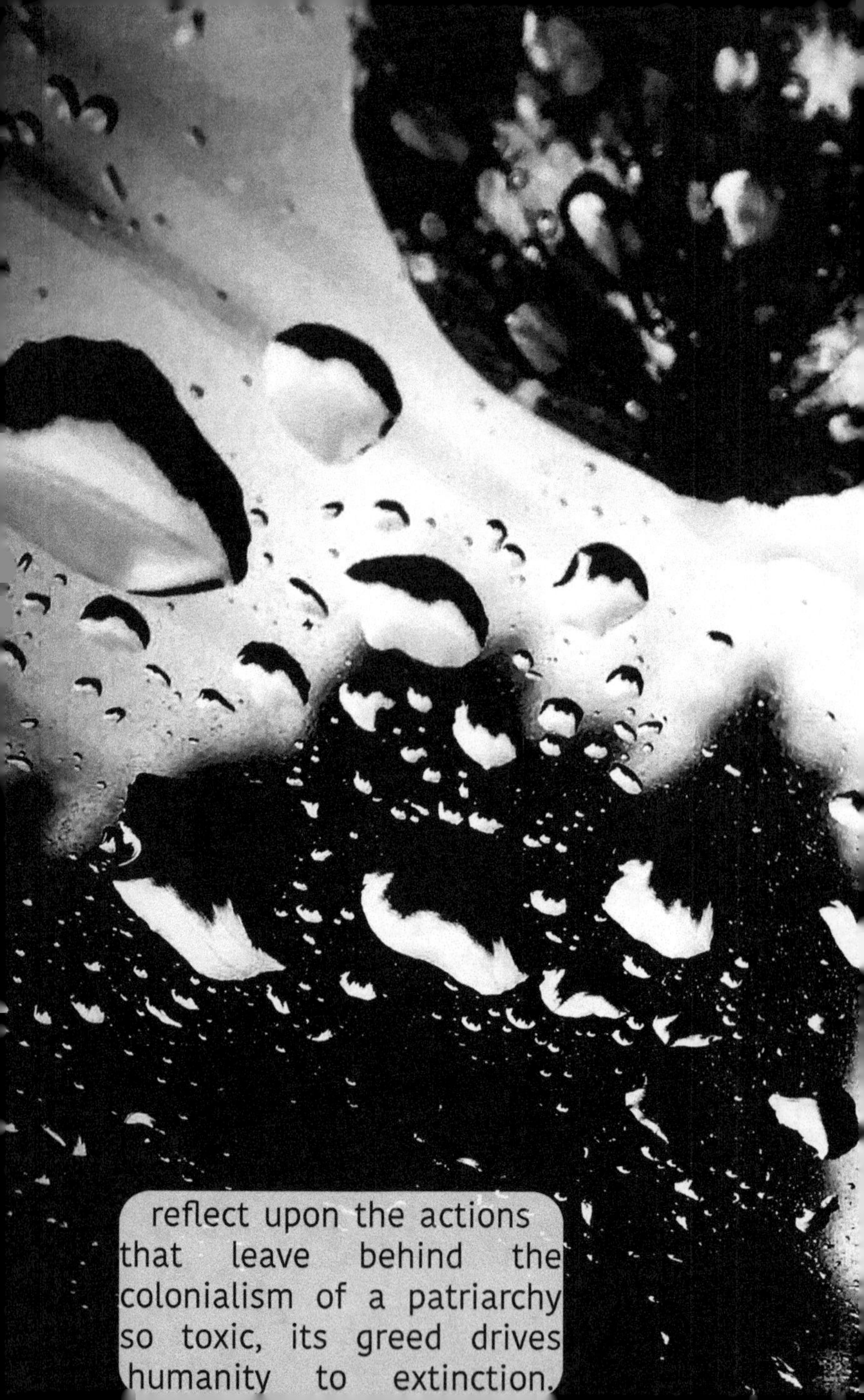

reflect upon the actions
that leave behind the
colonialism of a patriarchy
so toxic, its greed drives
humanity to extinction.

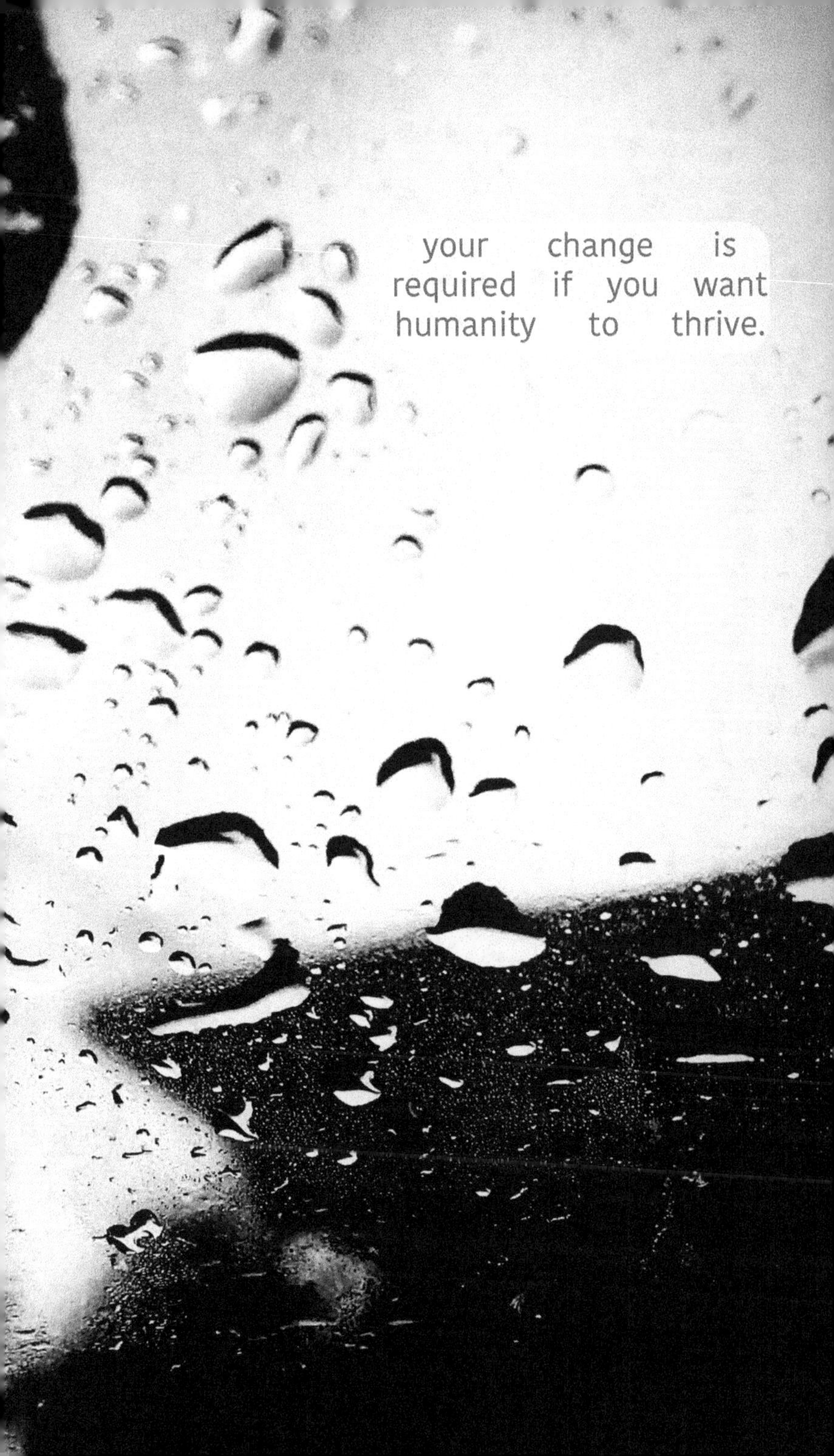
your change is
required if you want
humanity to thrive.

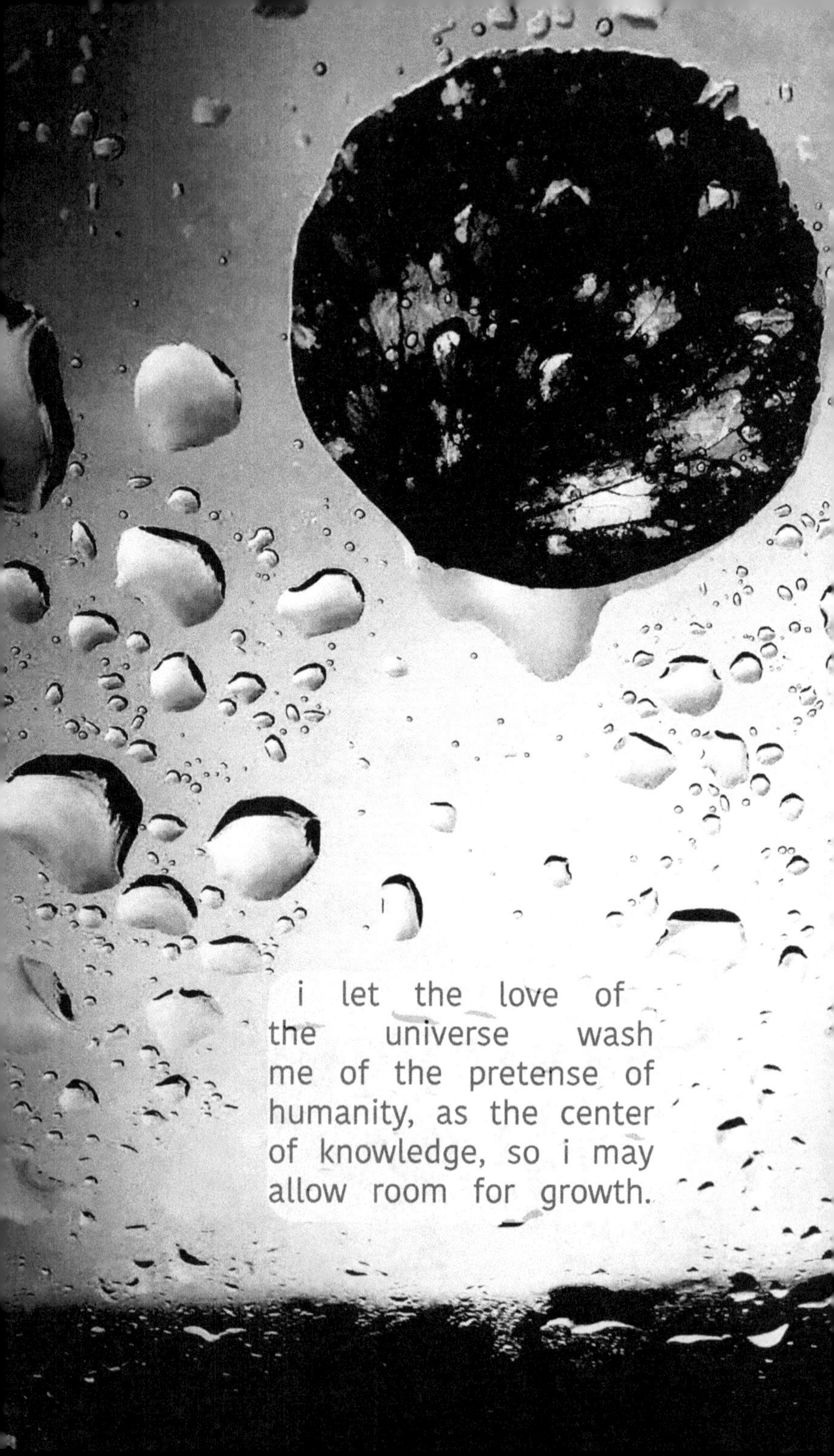

i let the love of the universe wash me of the pretense of humanity, as the center of knowledge, so i may allow room for growth.

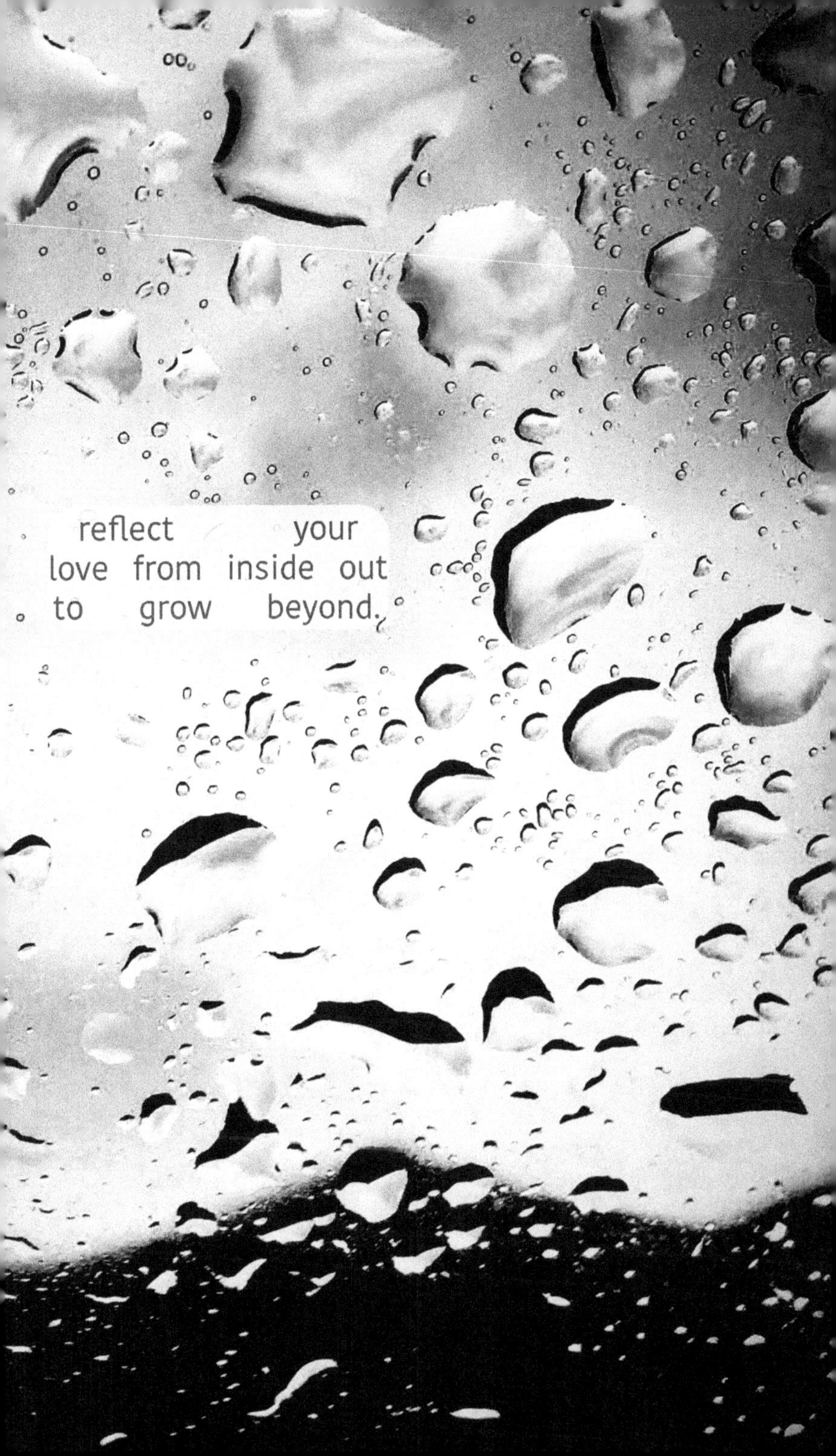

reflect   your
love from inside out
to   grow   beyond.

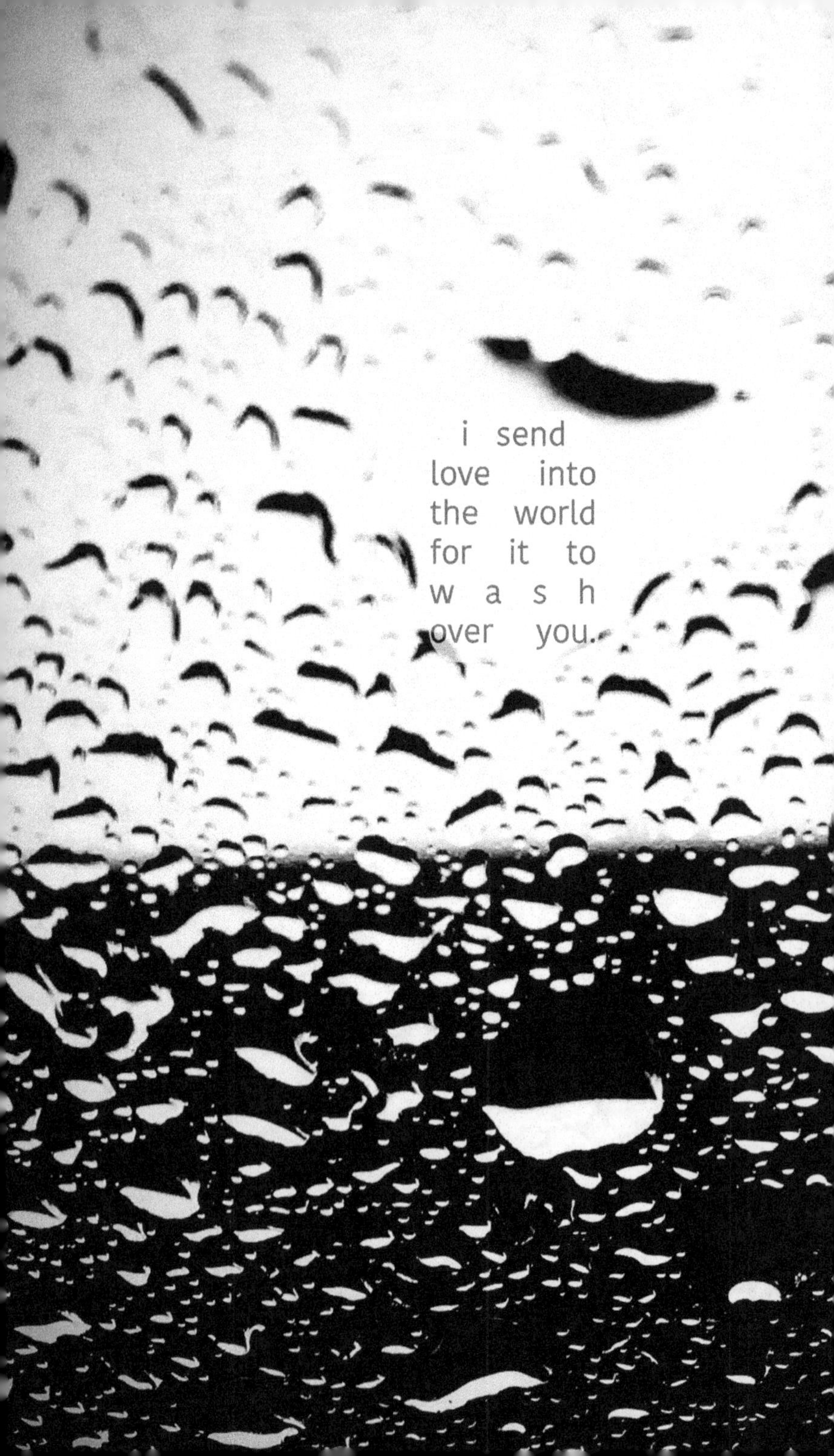

i send
love   into
the   world
for it to
w a s h
over   you.

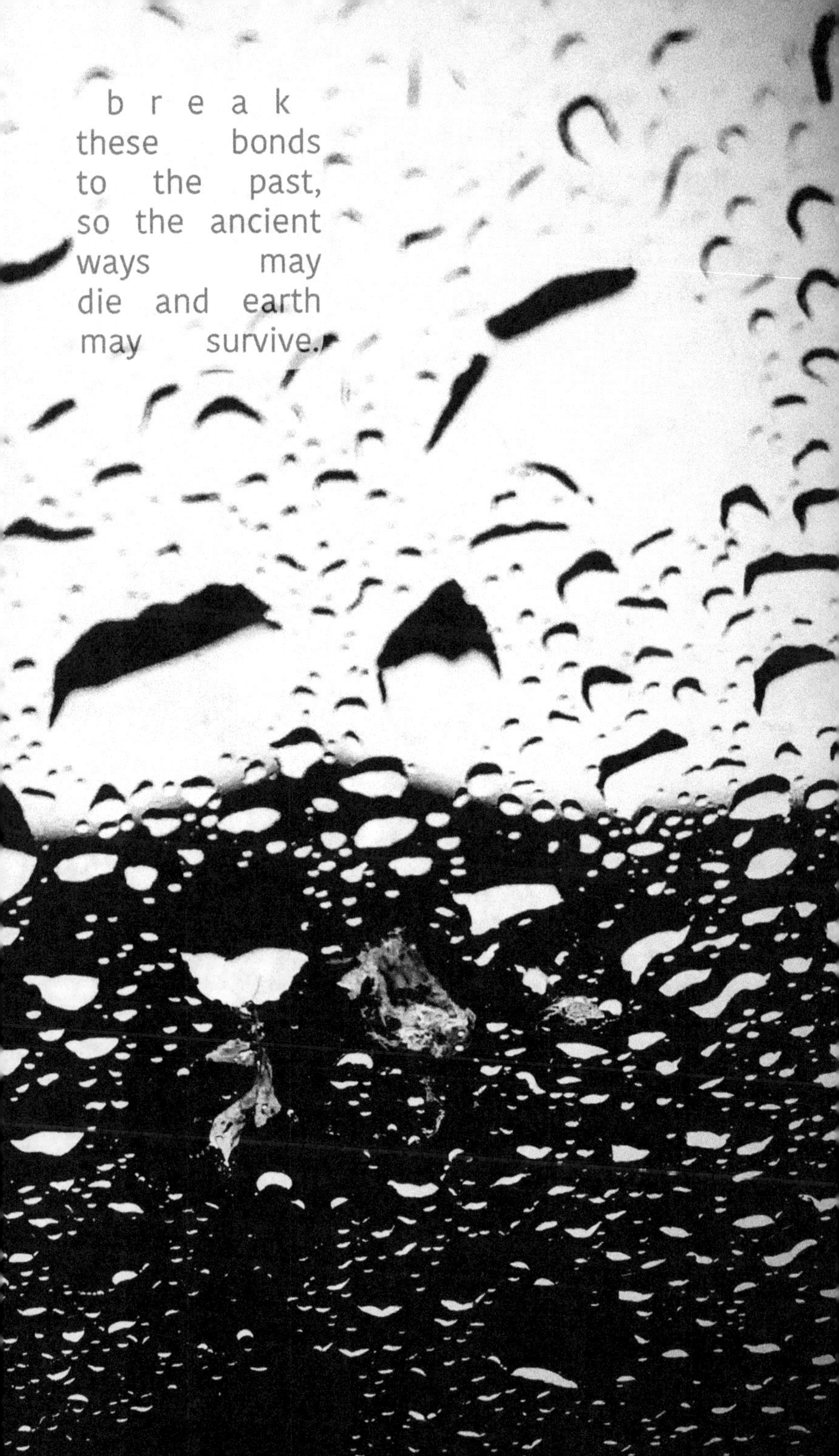
break
these bonds
to the past,
so the ancient
ways may
die and earth
may survive.

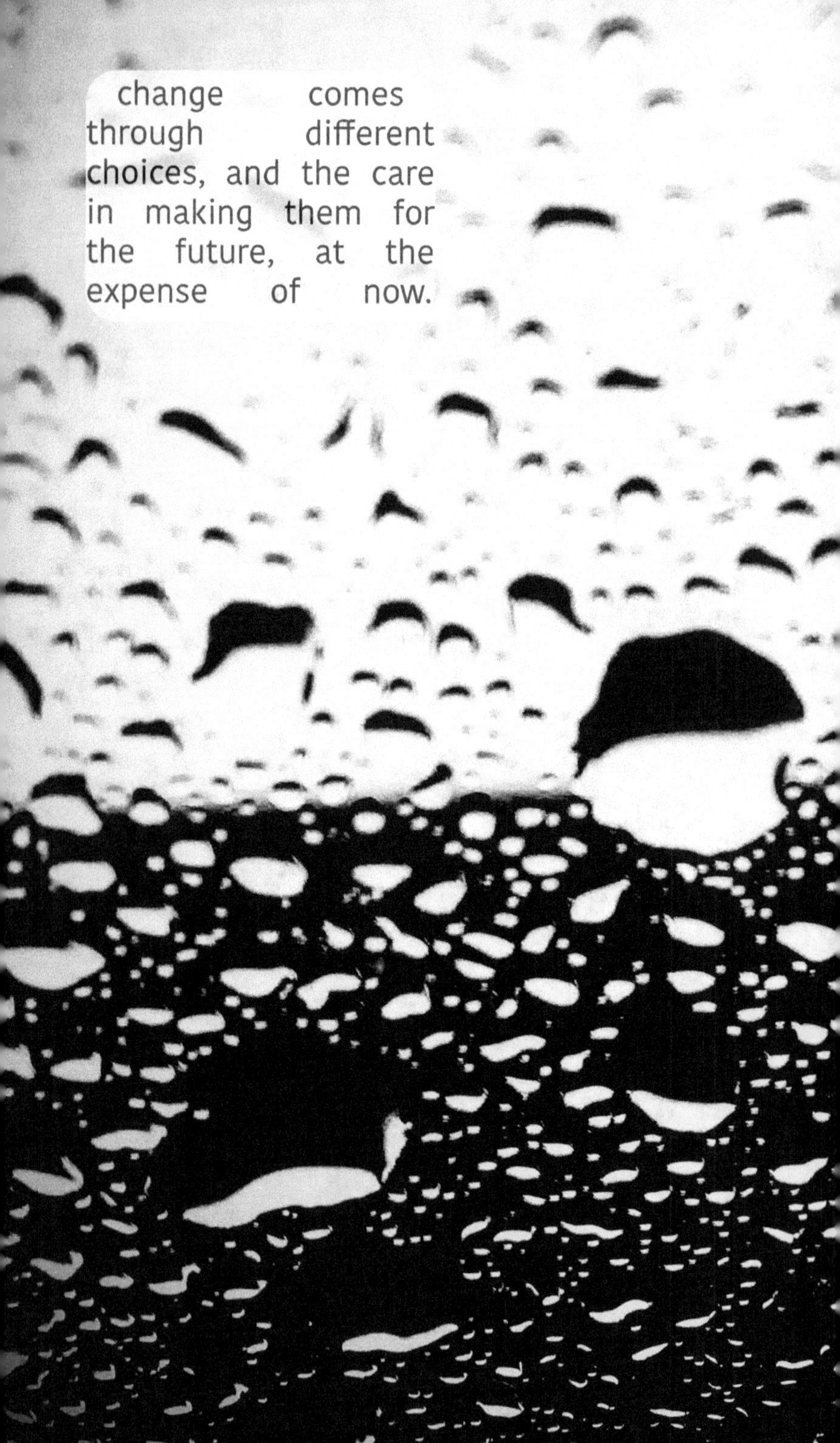
change comes through different choices, and the care in making them for the future, at the expense of now.

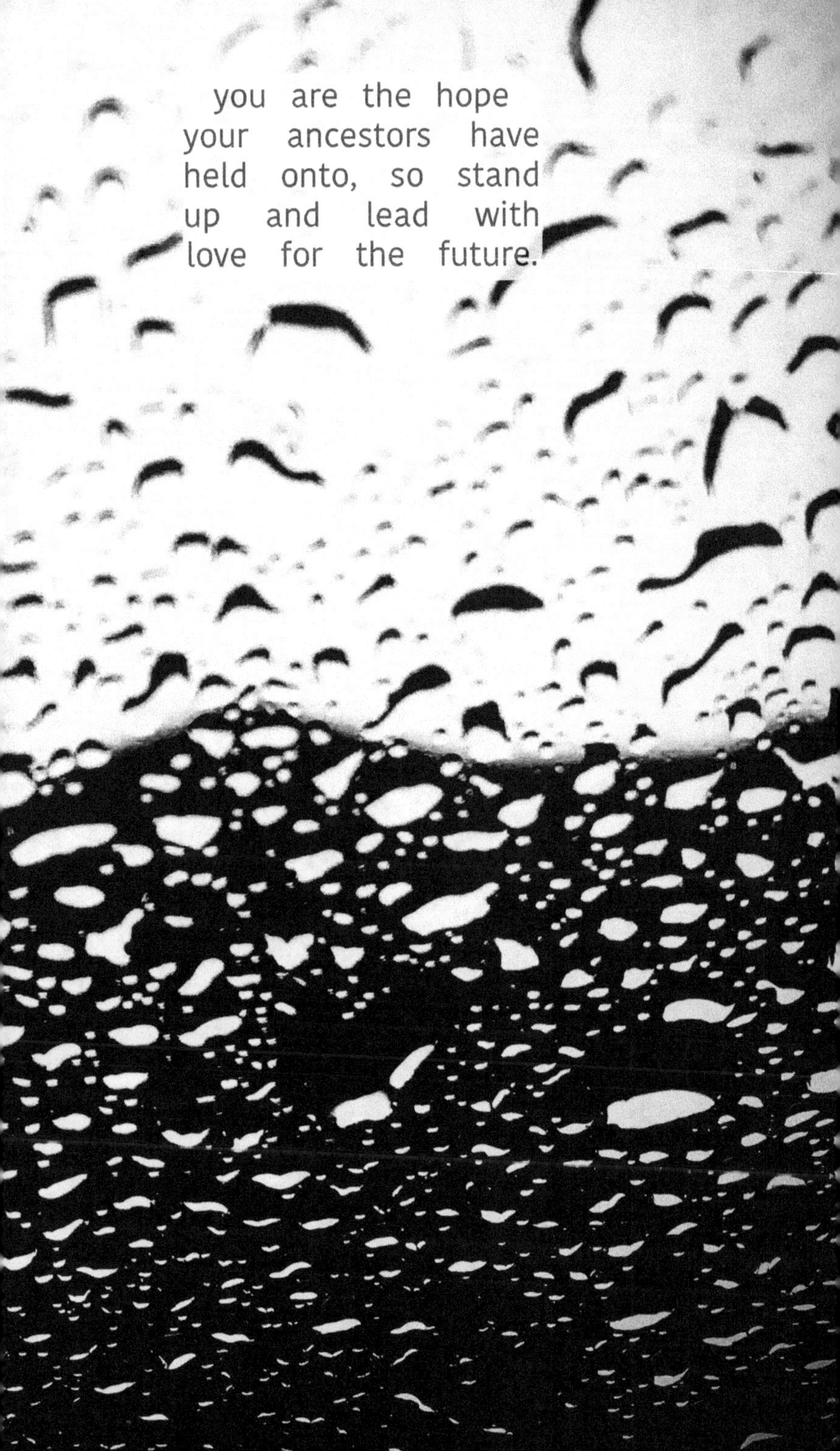

you are the hope
your ancestors have
held onto, so stand
up and lead with
love for the future.

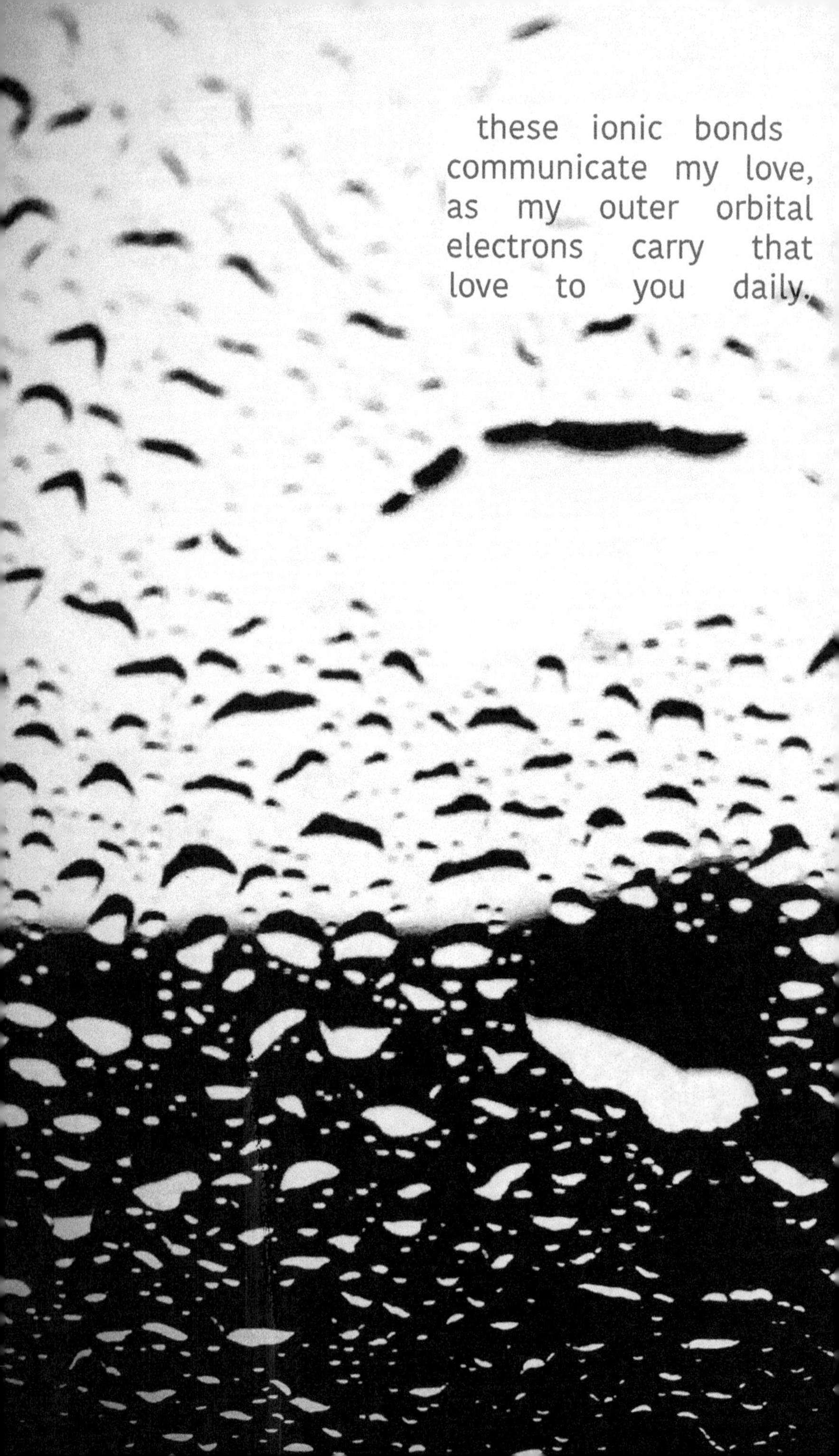
these ionic bonds
communicate my love,
as my outer orbital
electrons carry that
love to you daily.

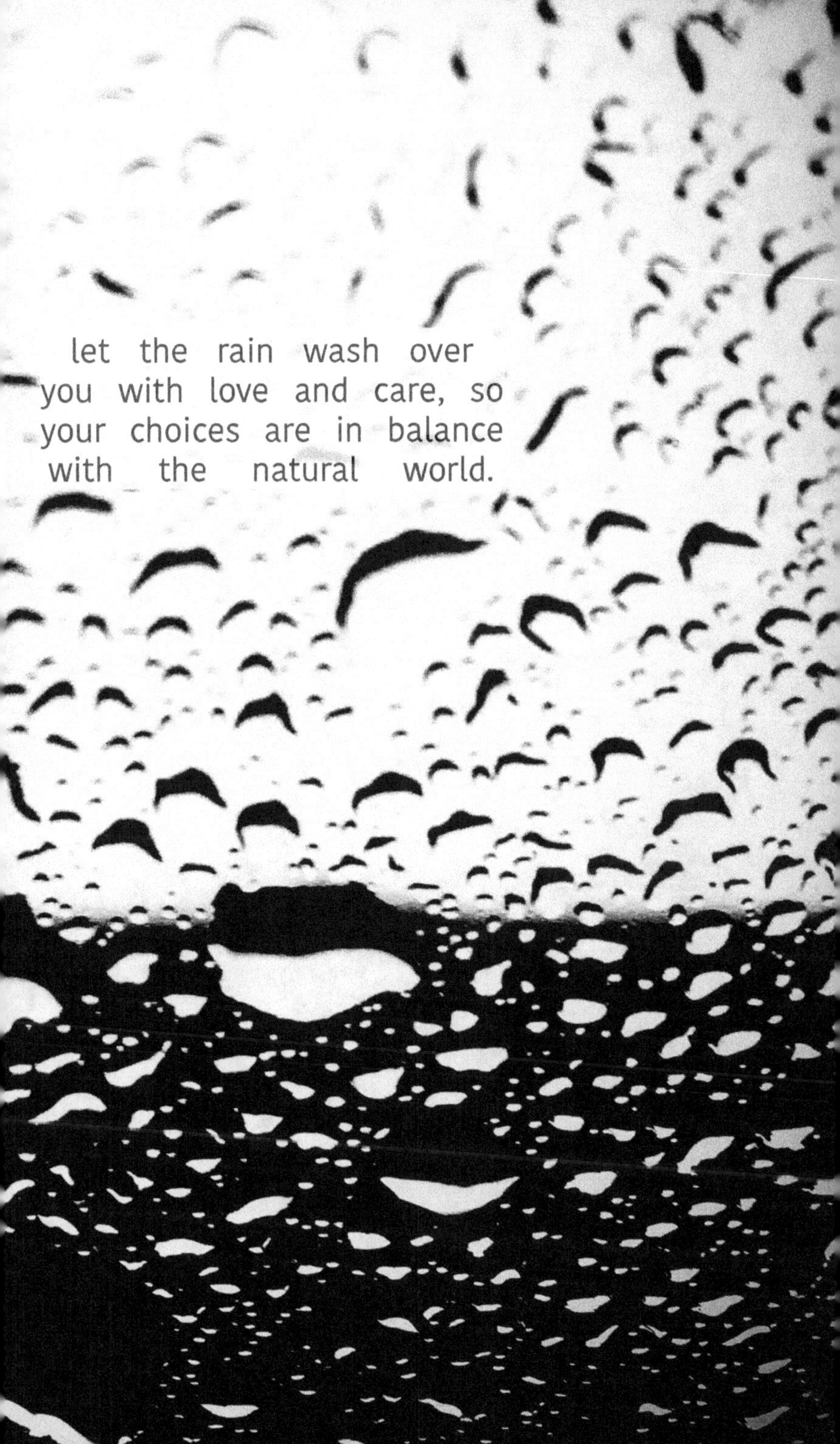

let the rain wash over
you with love and care, so
your choices are in balance
with the natural world.

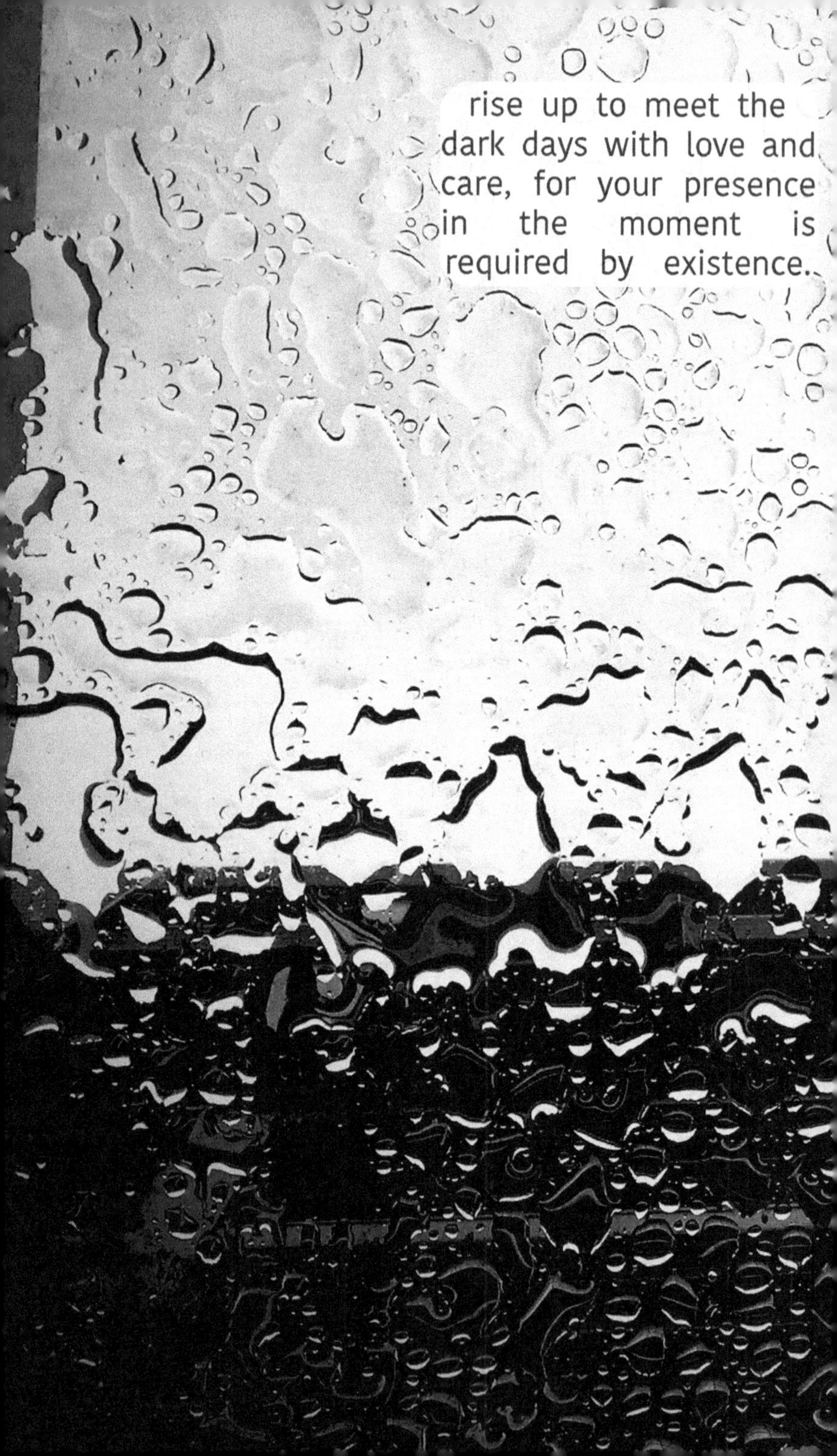
rise up to meet the
dark days with love and
care, for your presence
in the moment is
required by existence.

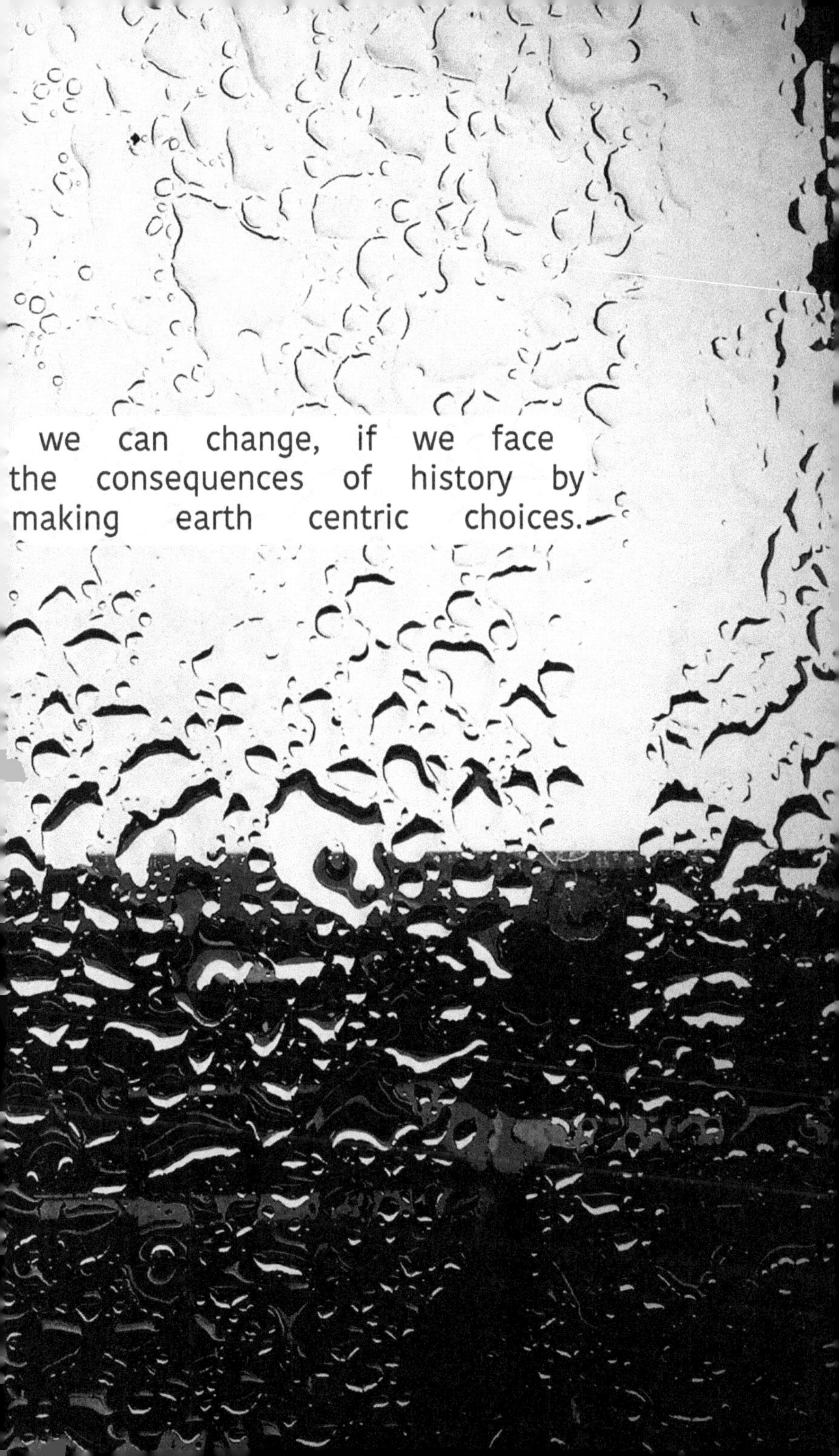

we can change, if we face
the consequences of history by
making earth centric choices.

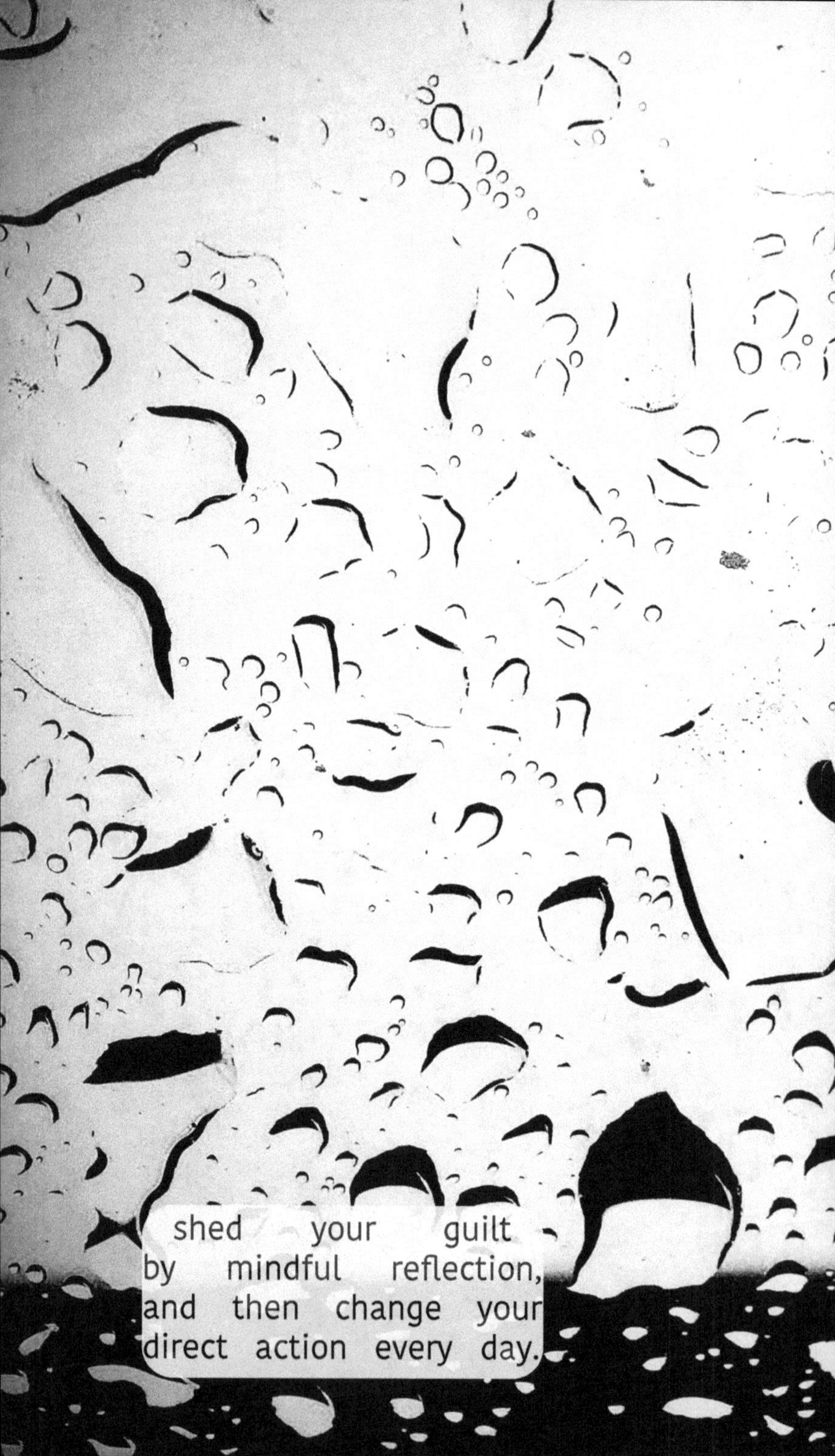

shed   your   guilt
by   mindful   reflection,
and   then   change   your
direct   action   every   day.

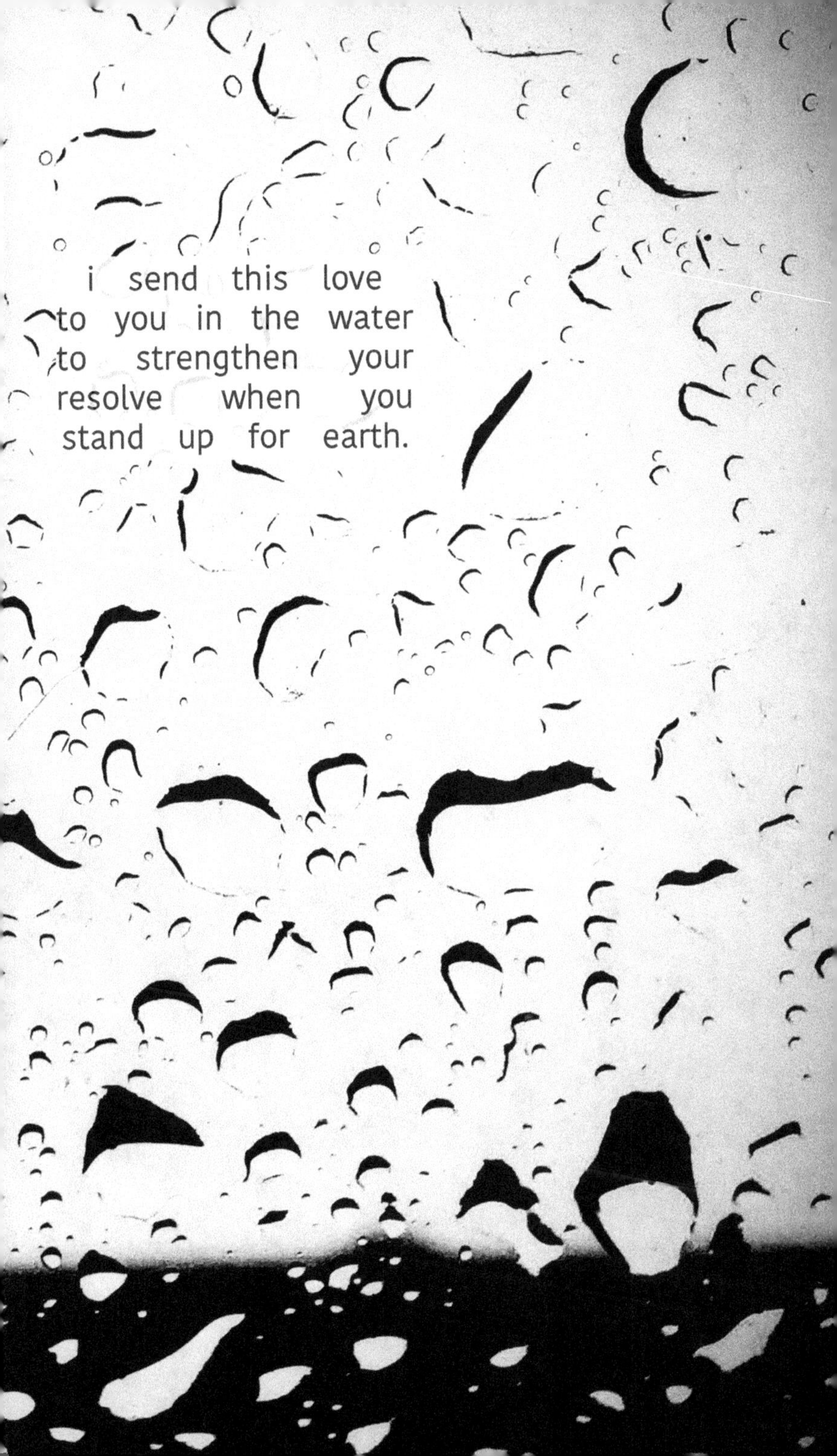

i send this love
to you in the water
to strengthen your
resolve when you
stand up for earth.

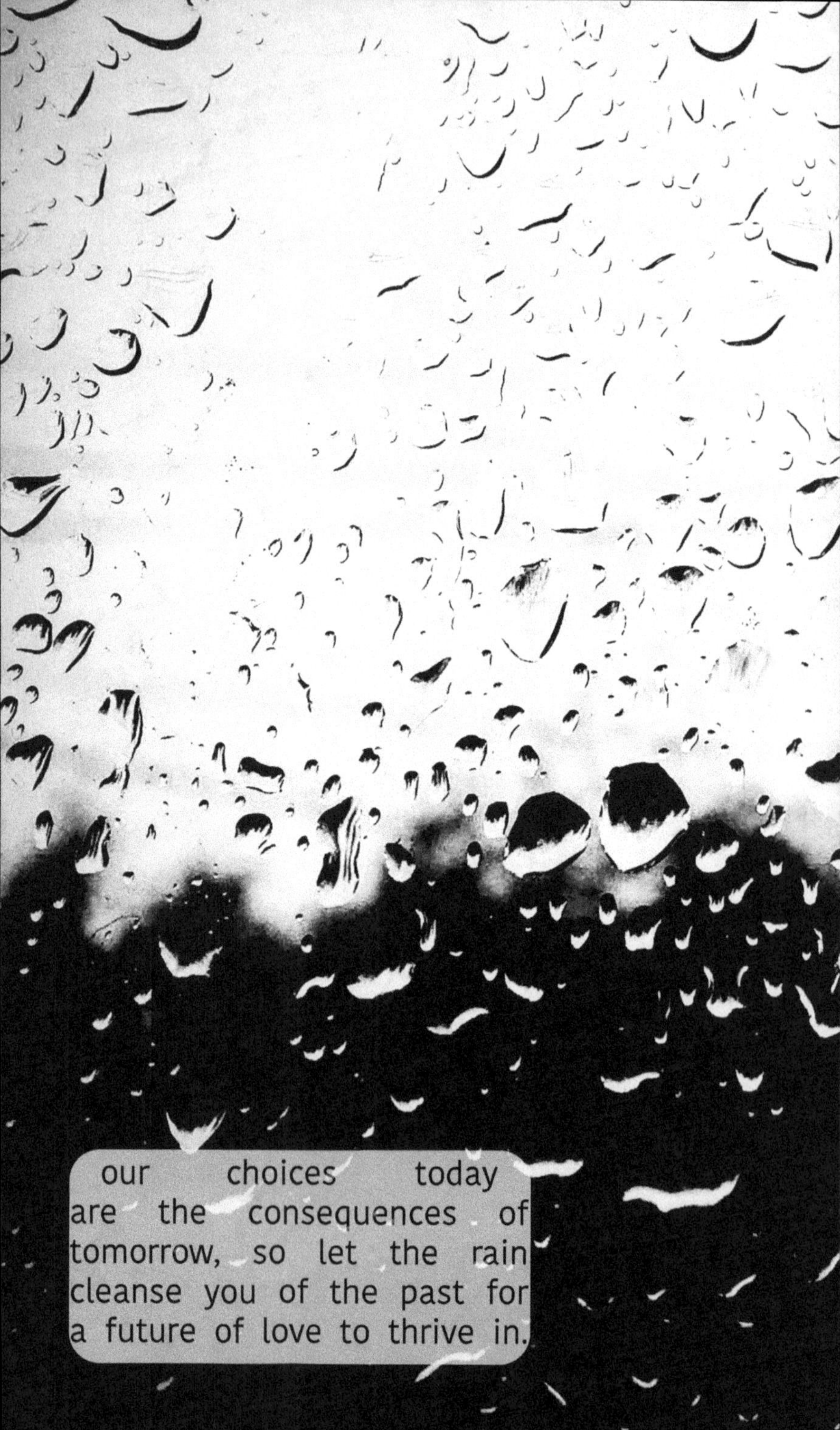

our choices today are the consequences of tomorrow, so let the rain cleanse you of the past for a future of love to thrive in.

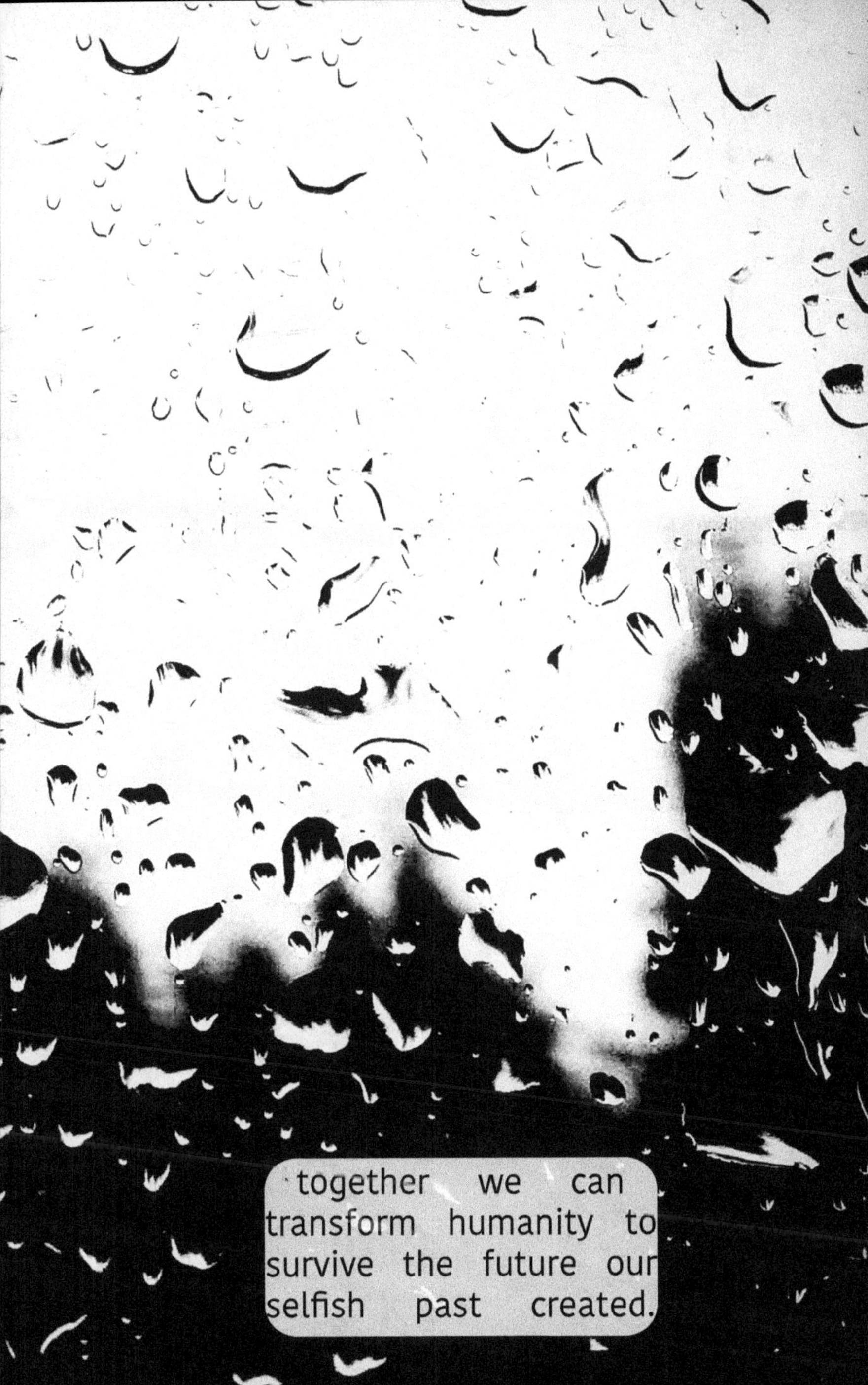
together we can
transform humanity to
survive the future our
selfish past created.

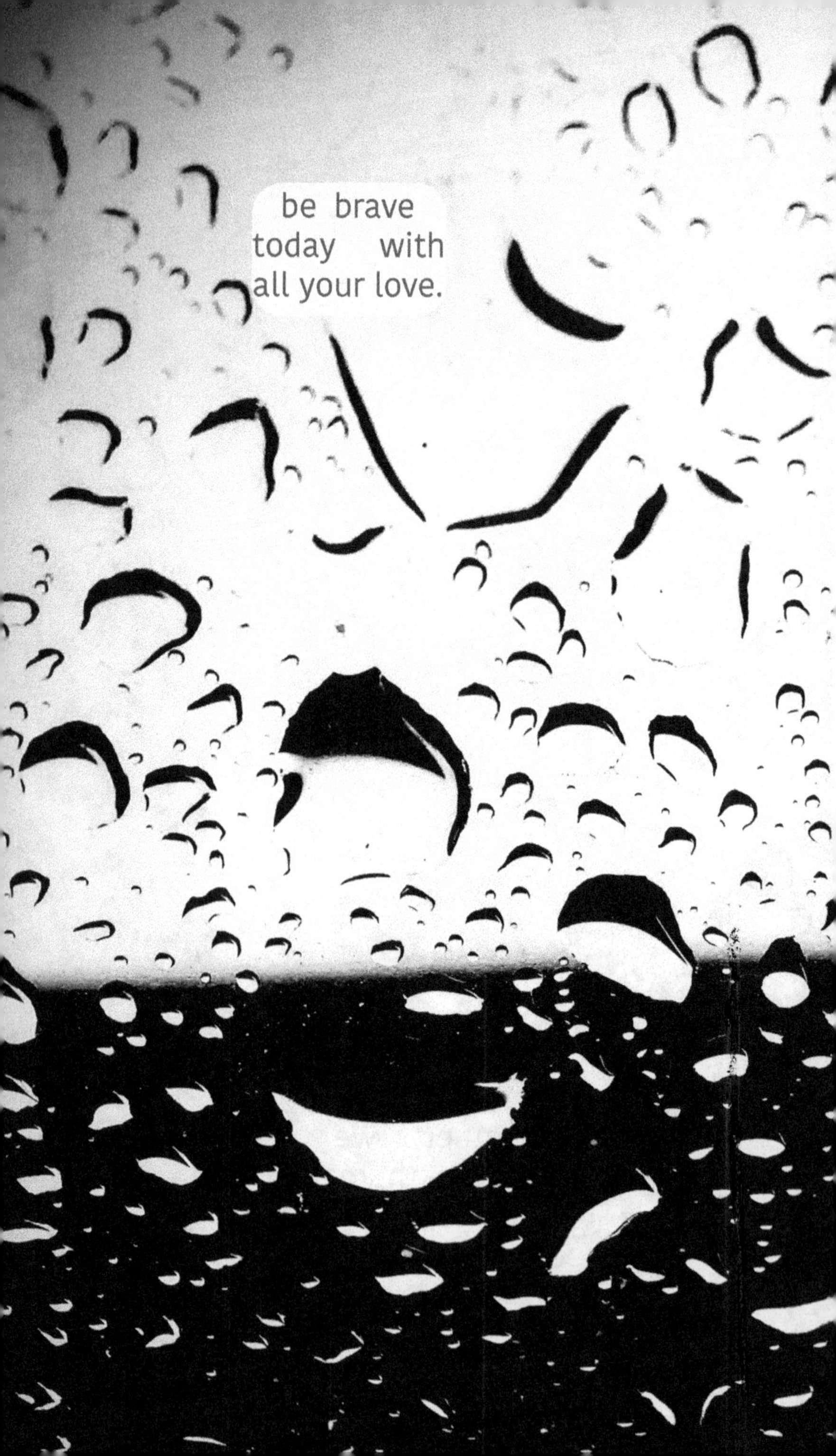
be brave
today with
all your love.

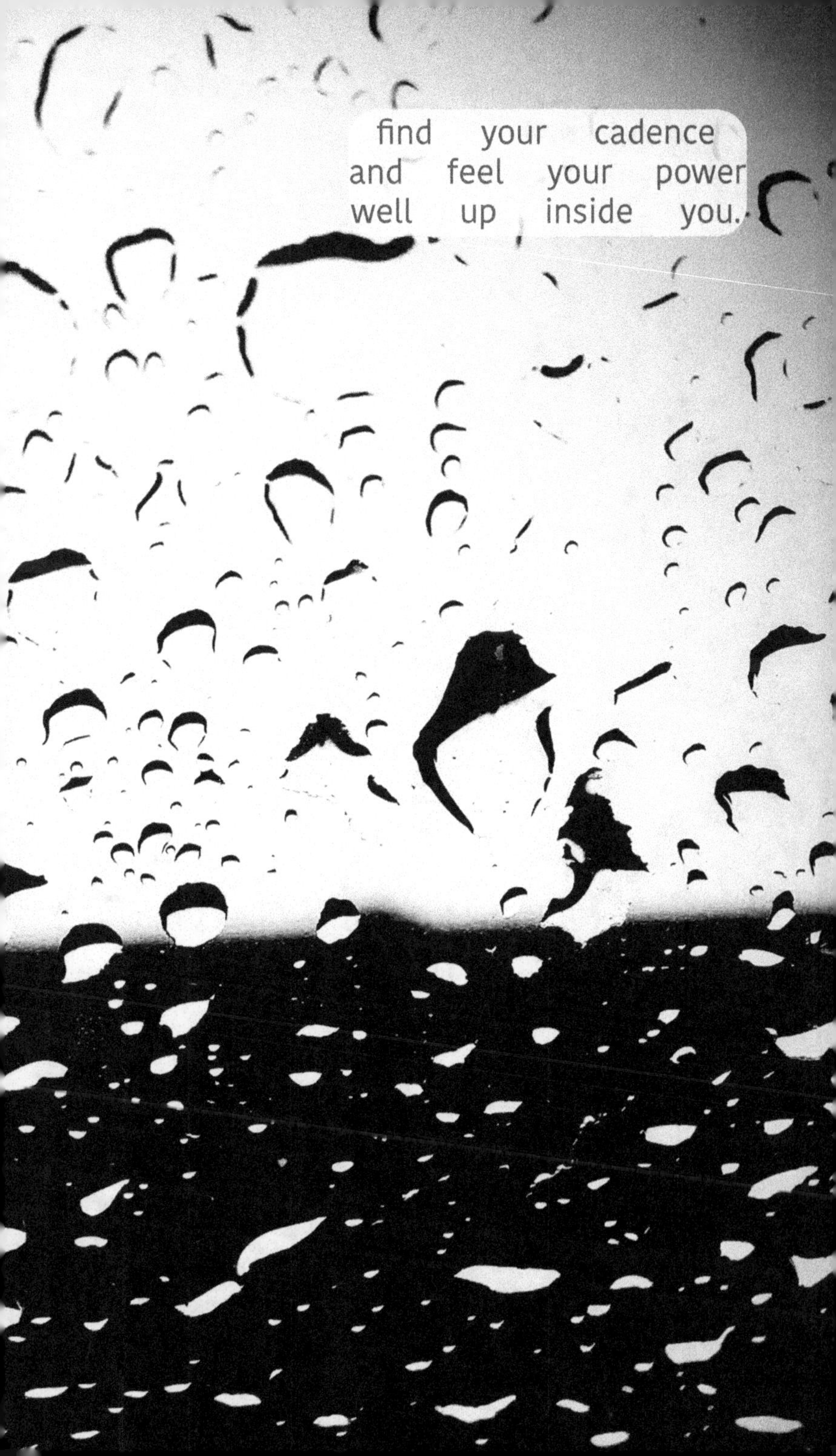

find   your   cadence
and   feel   your   power
well   up   inside   you.

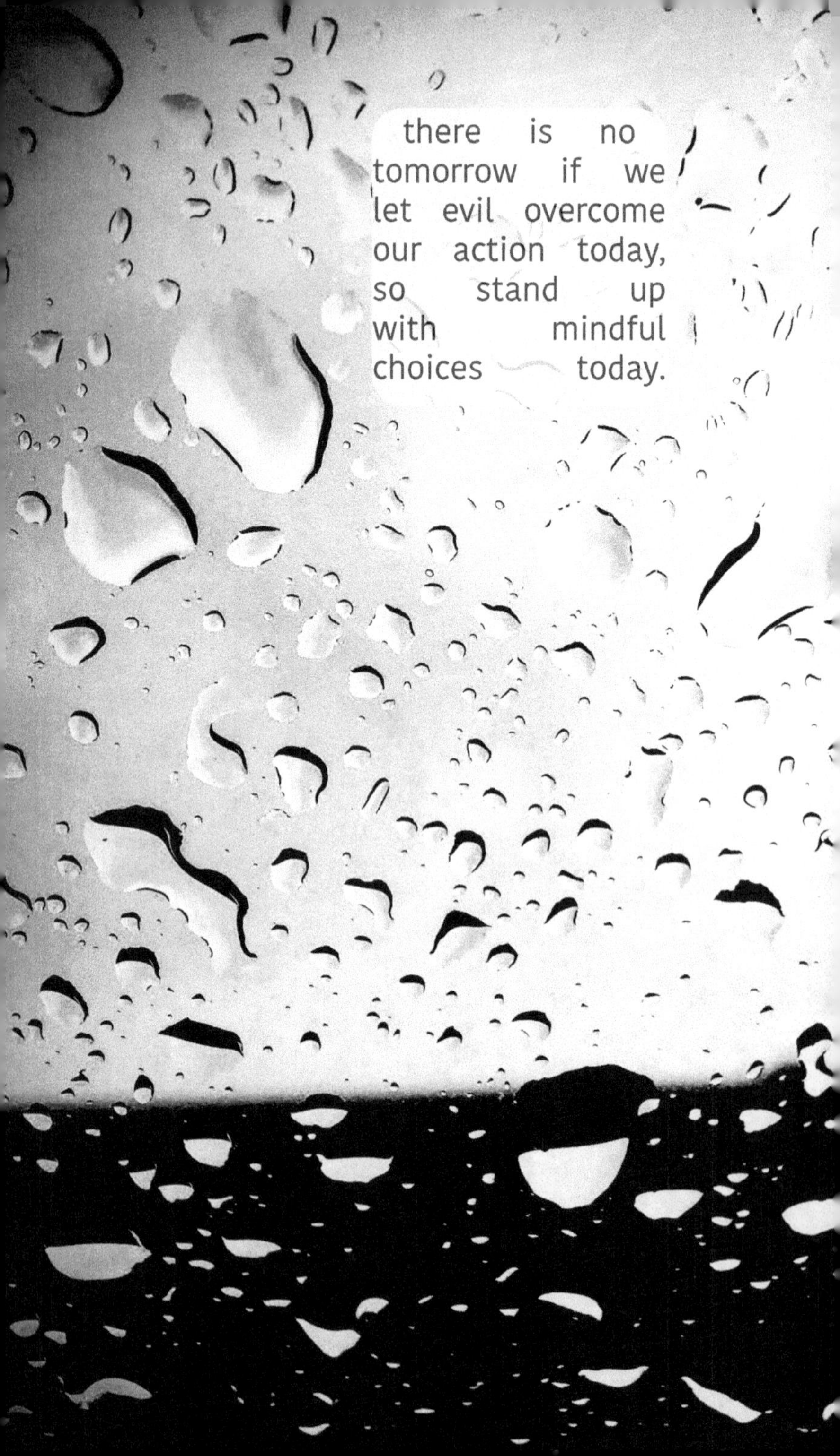

there is no tomorrow if we let evil overcome our action today, so stand up with mindful choices today.

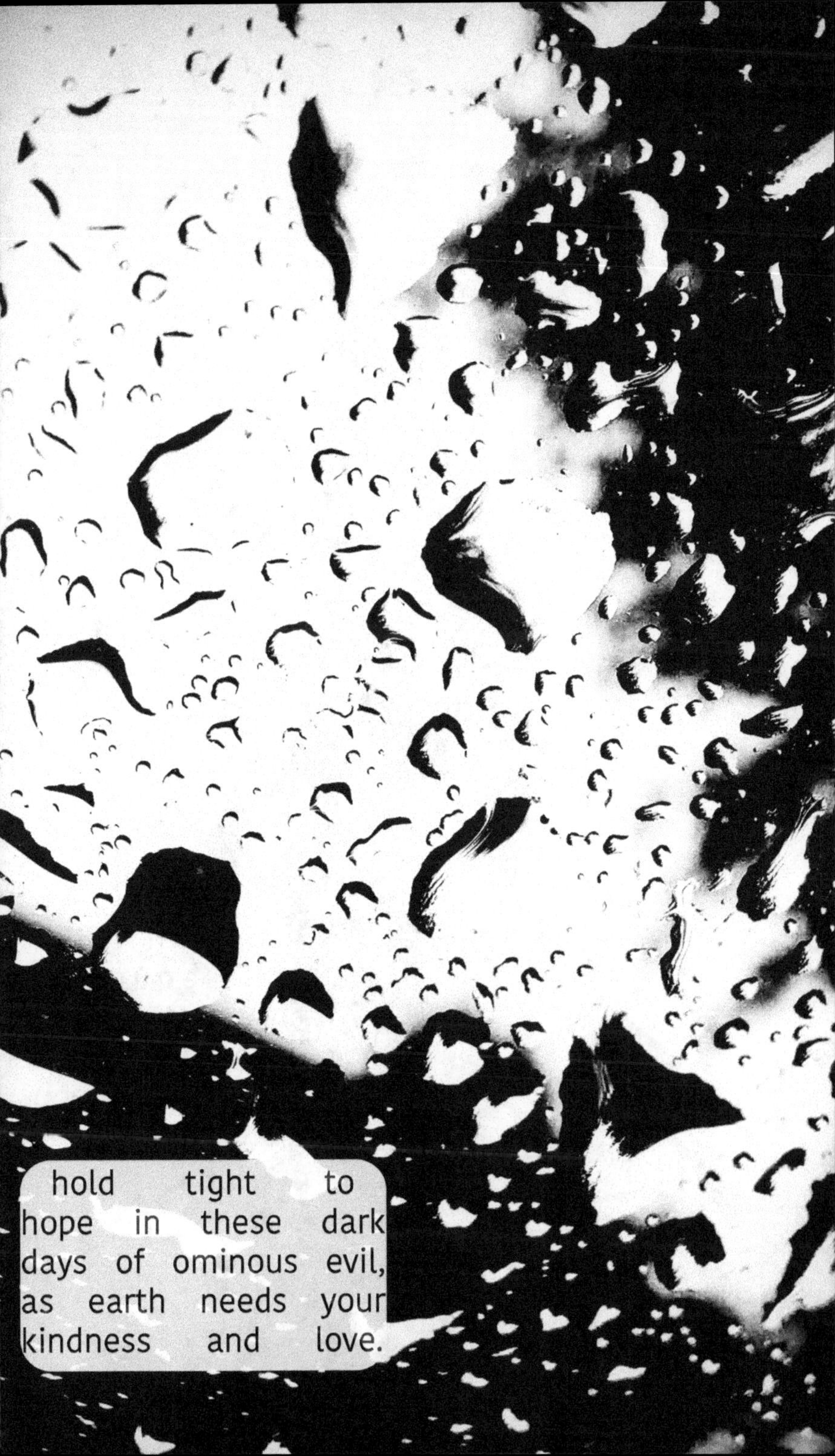

hold tight to hope in these dark days of ominous evil, as earth needs your kindness and love.

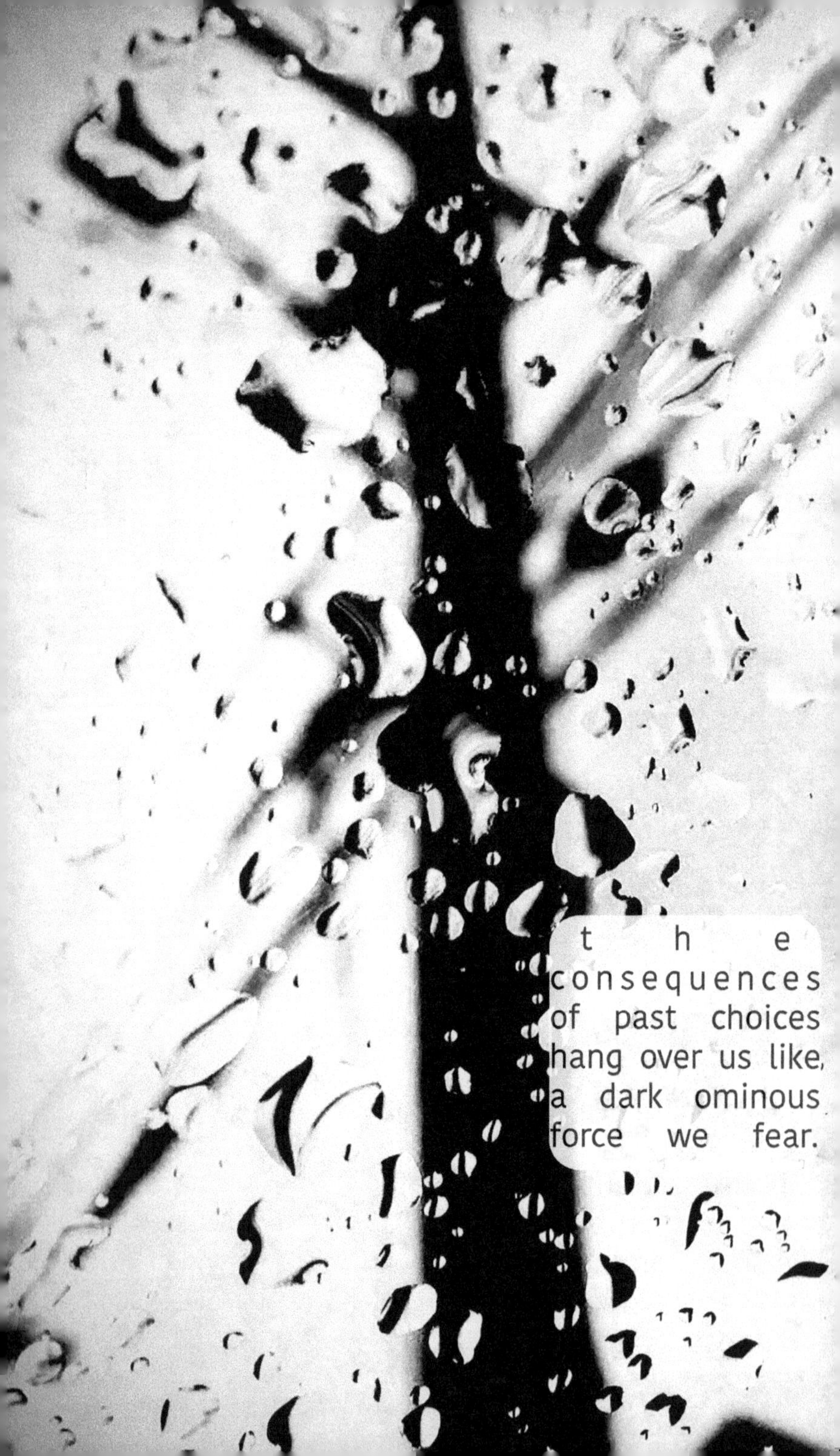
t h e
consequences
of past choices
hang over us like,
a dark ominous
force we fear.

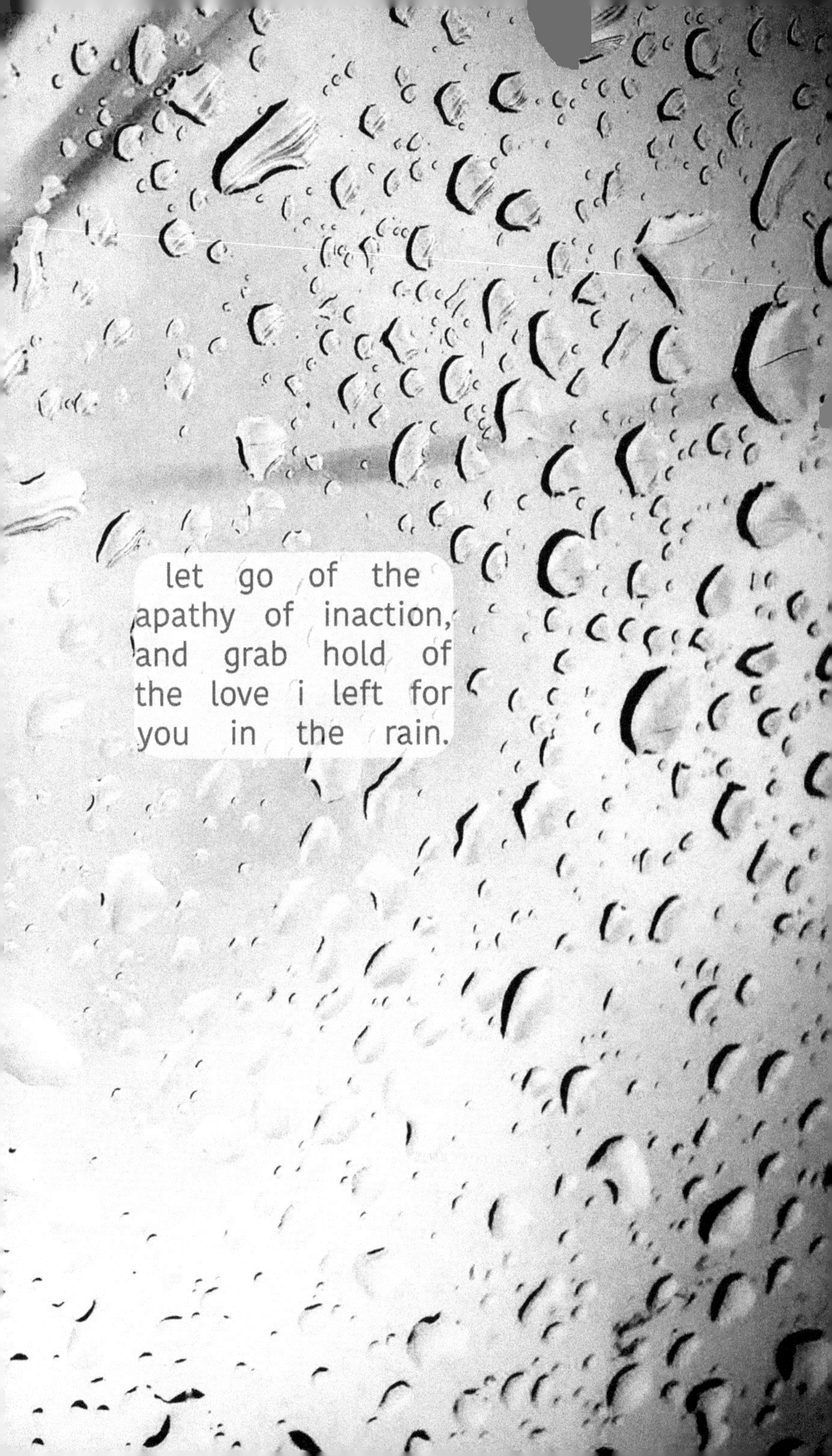
let go of the
apathy of inaction,
and grab hold of
the love i left for
you in the rain.

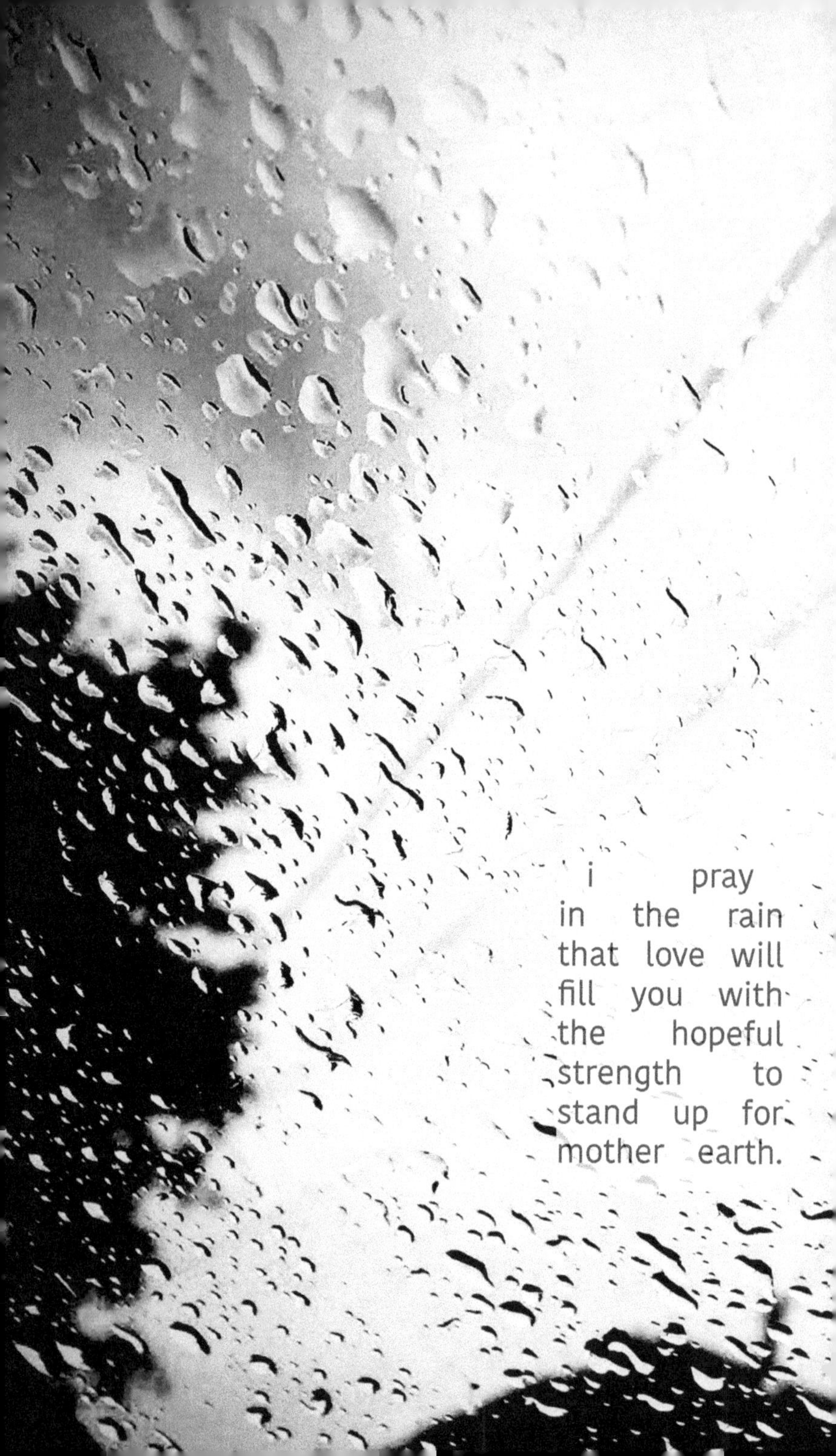

i   pray
in   the   rain
that love will
fill you with
the   hopeful
strength   to
stand up for
mother earth.

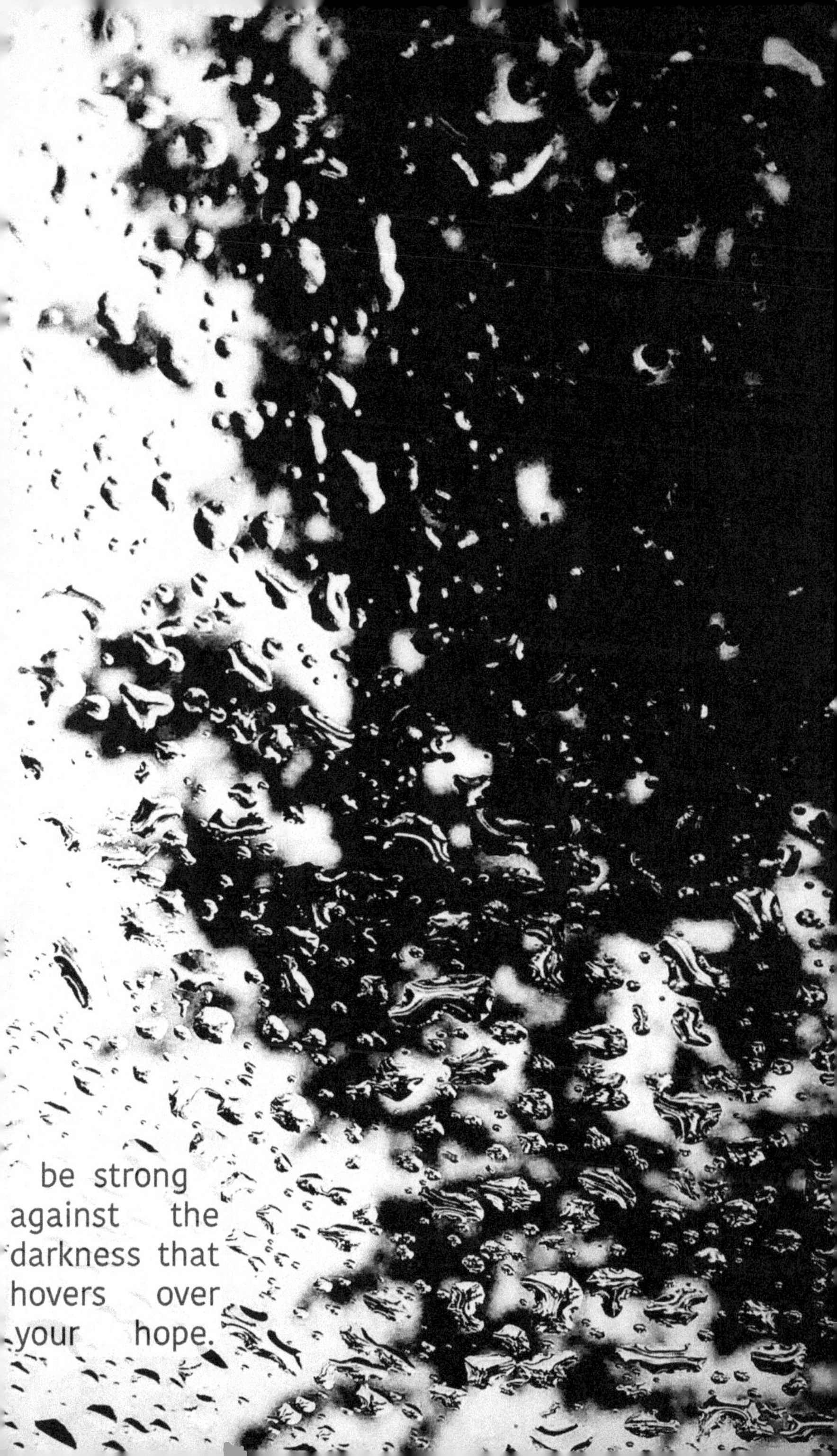
be strong
against the
darkness that
hovers over
your hope.

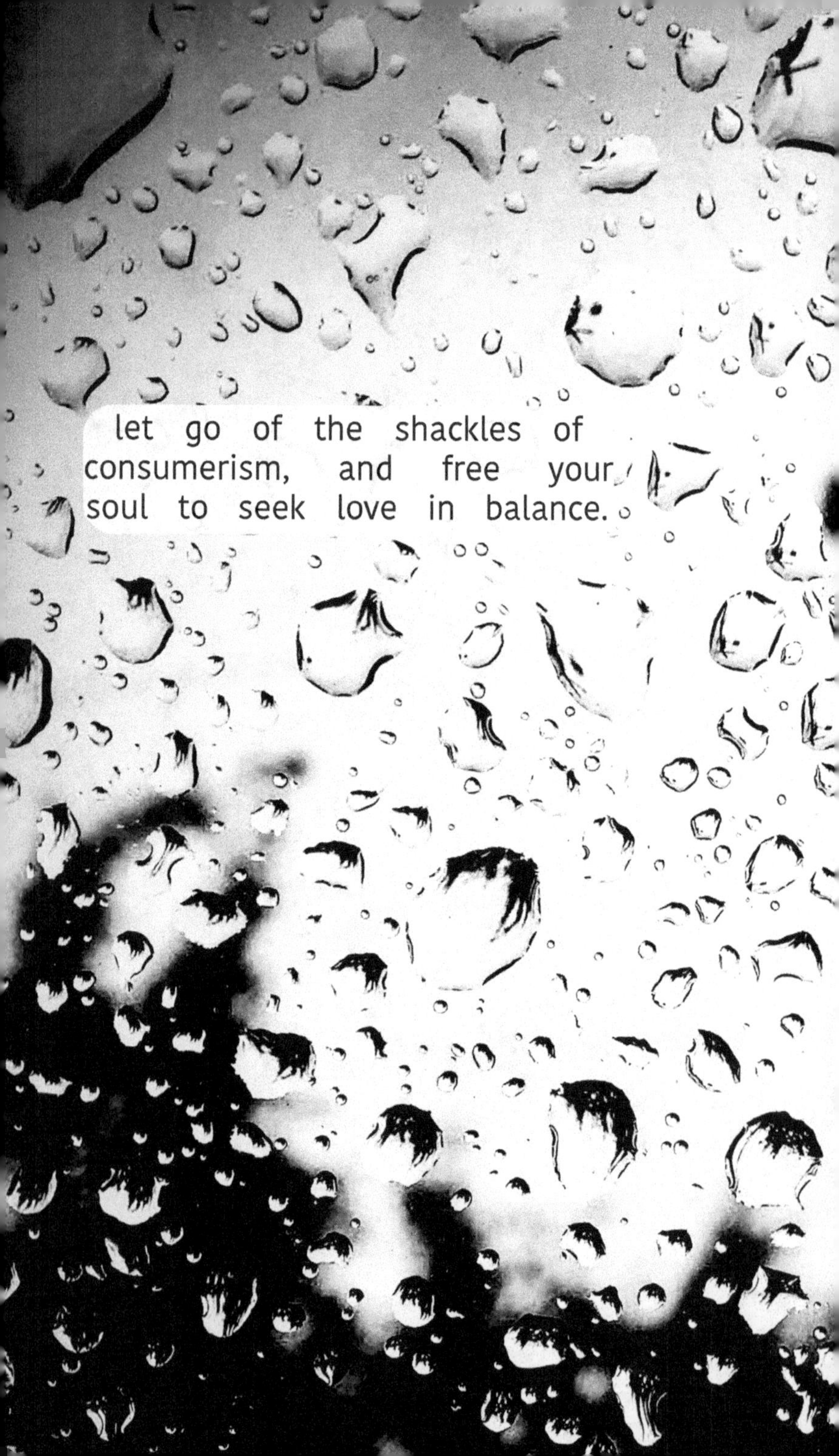
let go of the shackles of
consumerism, and free your
soul to seek love in balance.

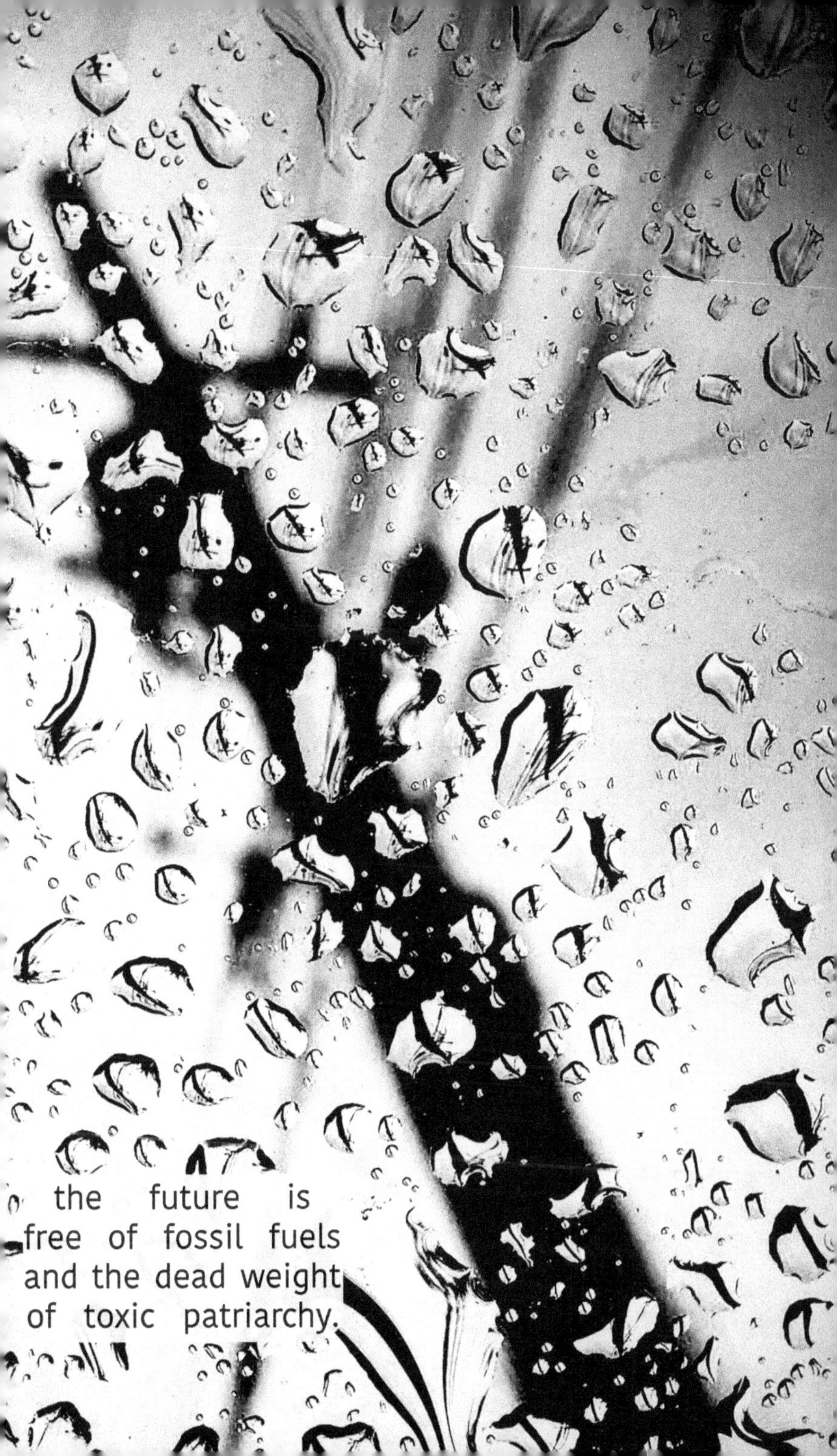
the future is
free of fossil fuels
and the dead weight
of toxic patriarchy.

strip me of the pretense
of a selfish past, so i may
run wild in my daily actions
for a balanced way of
life, in love with earth.

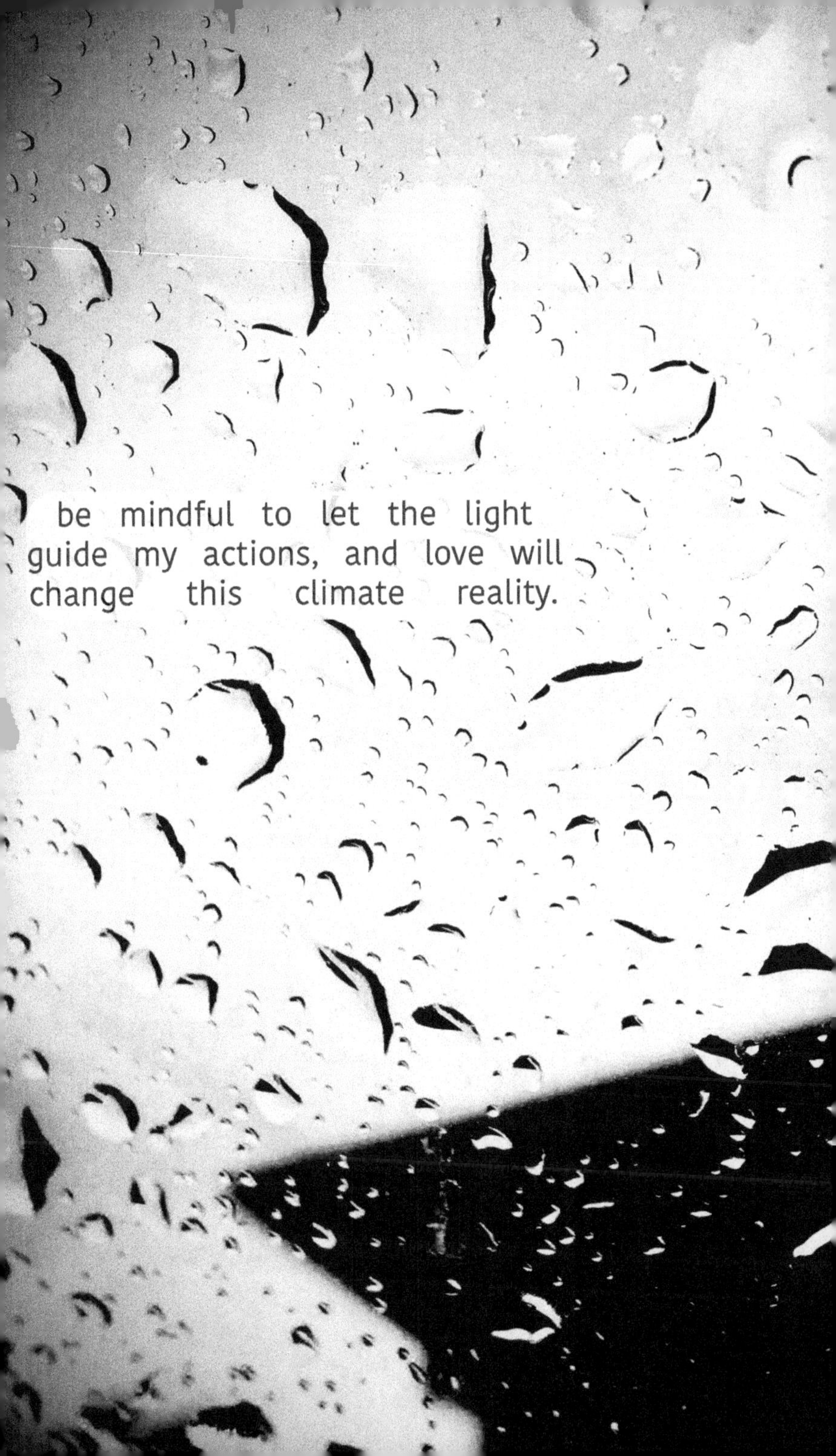
be mindful to let the light
guide my actions, and love will
change this climate reality.

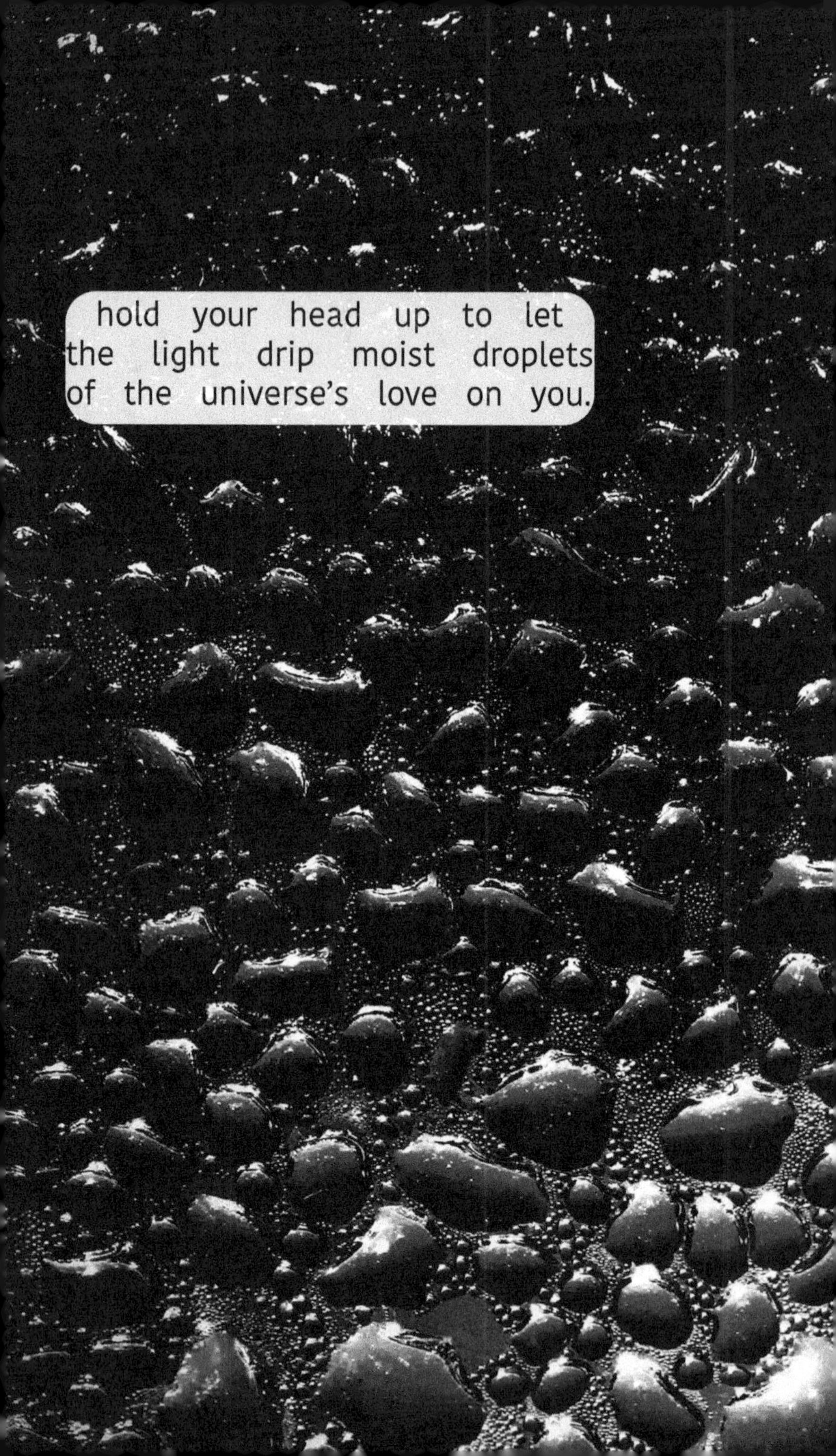

hold your head up to let
the light drip moist droplets
of the universe's love on you.

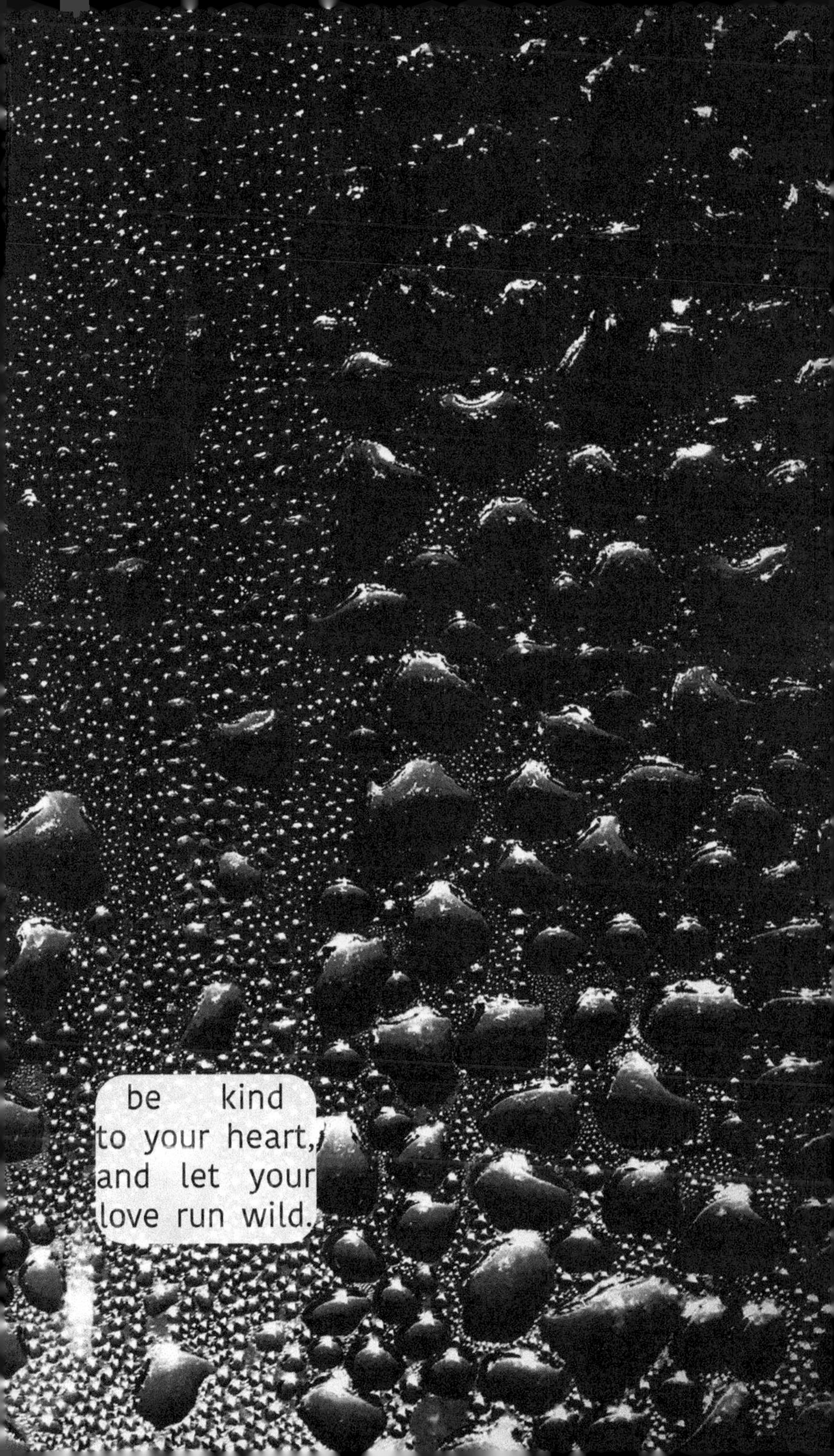

be   kind
to your heart,
and let your
love run wild.

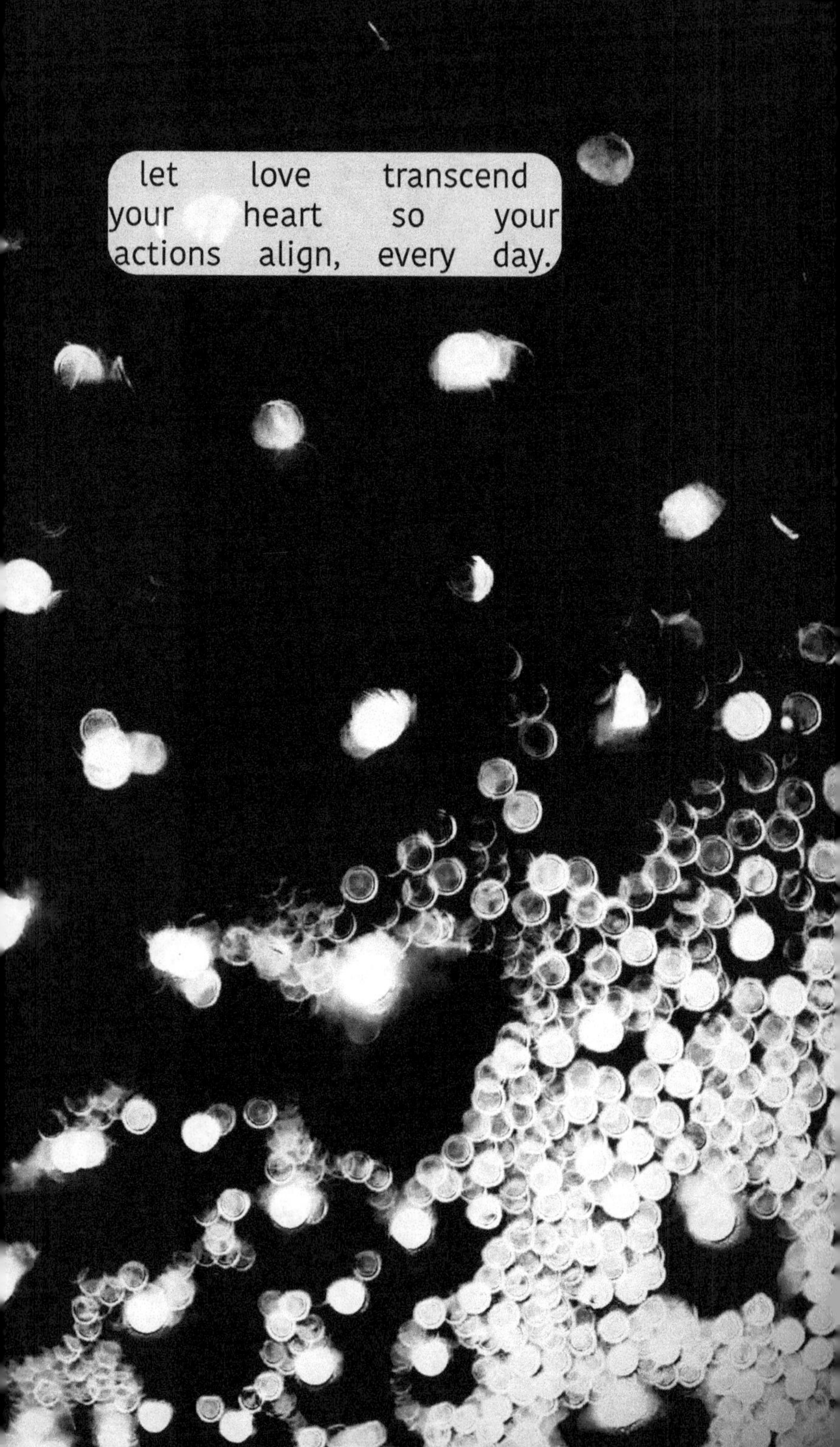

let   love   transcend
your   heart   so   your
actions   align,   every   day.

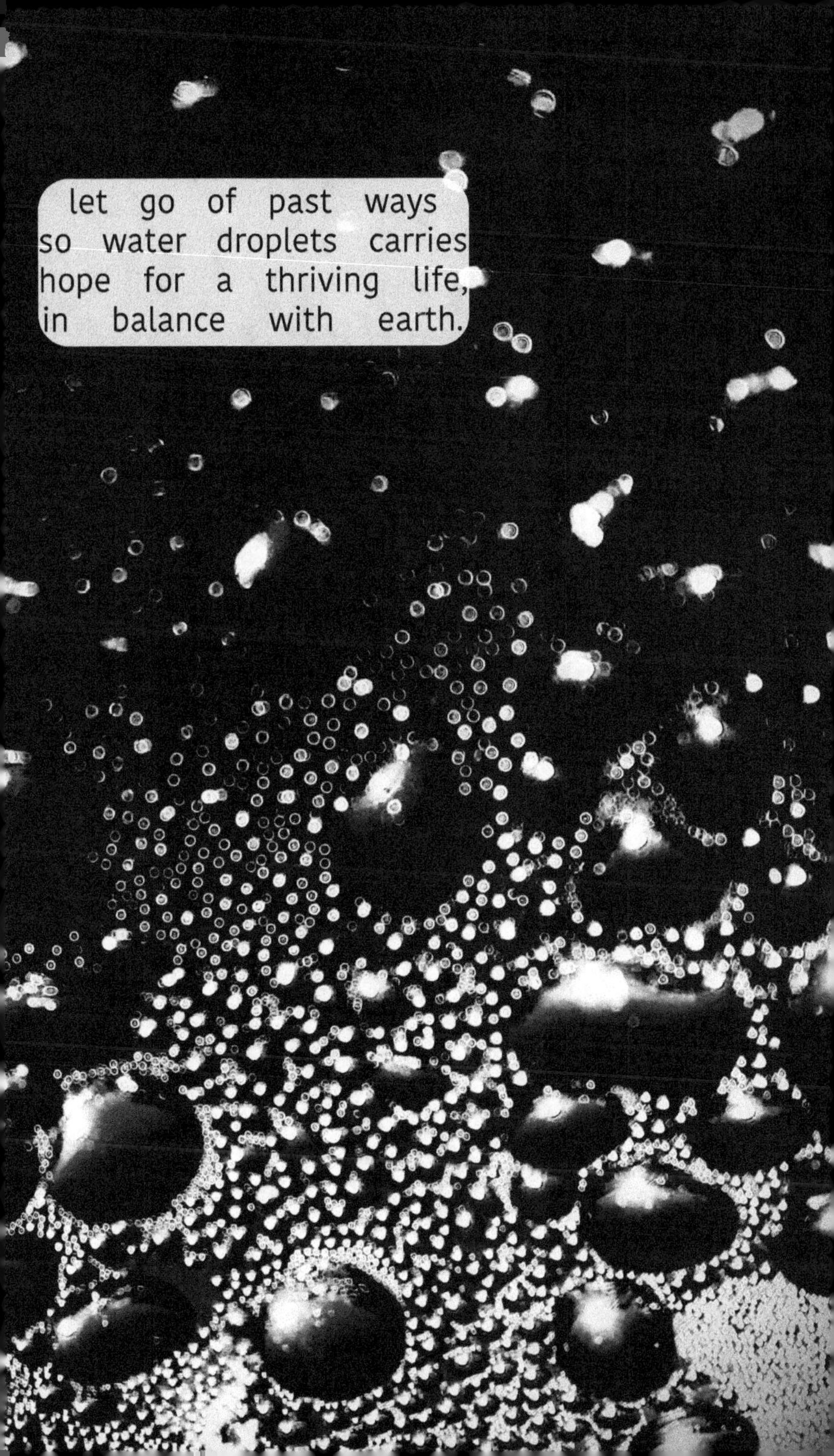

let go of past ways
so water droplets carries
hope for a thriving life,
in balance with earth.

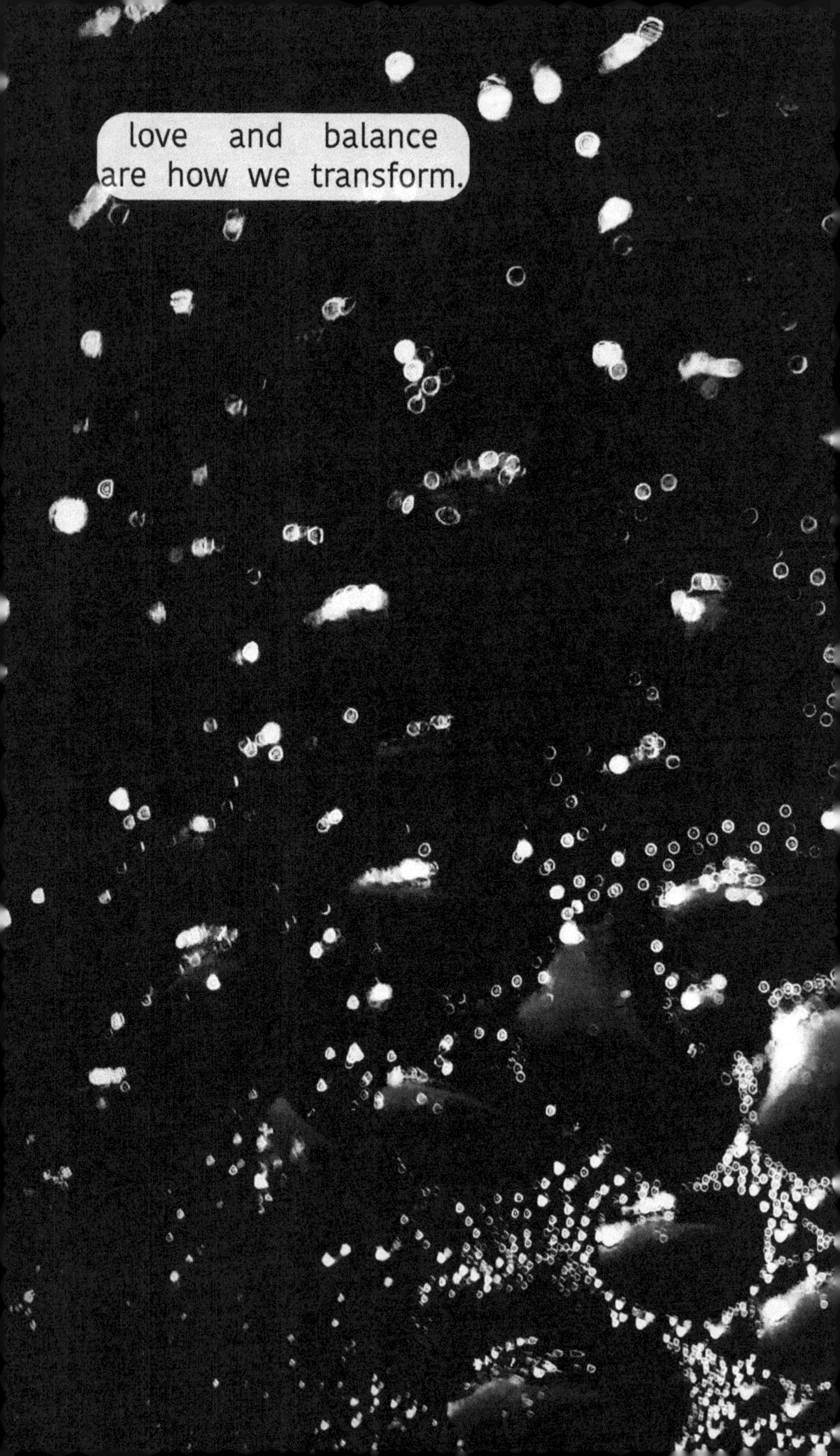
love   and   balance
are how we transform.

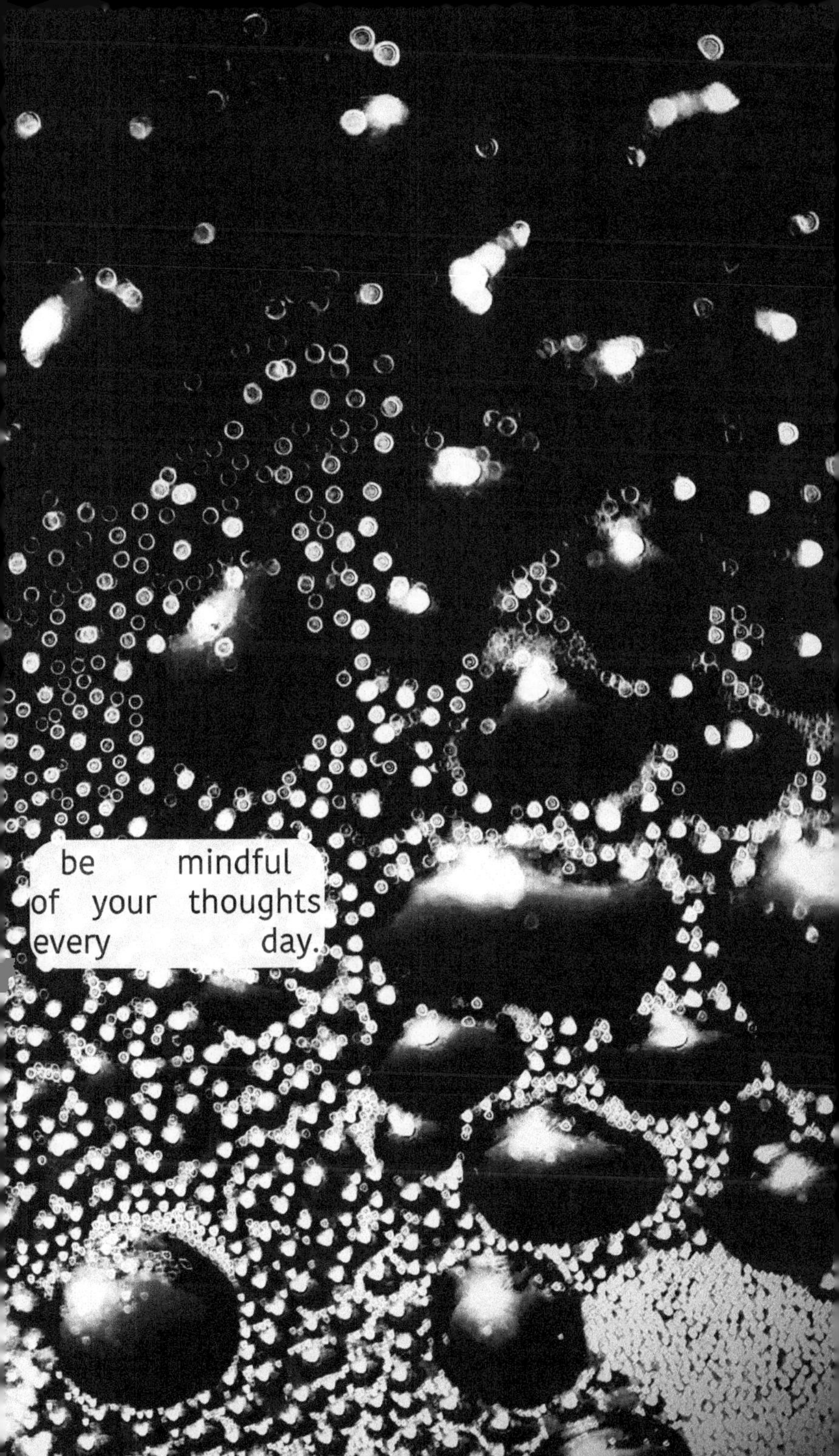

be   mindful
of   your   thoughts
every   day.

www.ingramcontent.com/pod-product-compliance
Lightning Source LLC
Chambersburg PA
CBHW061533050726
47593CB00002B/768